BRANGELINA

Books by the Same Author

Céline Dion: Behind the Fairytale

Who Killed Kurt Cobain?

Shut up and Smile: Supermodels, The Dark Side

Fire and Rain: The James Taylor Story

Best CEOs: How the Wild, Wild Web Was Won

Bad and Beautiful:
Inside the Dazzling and Deadly World of Supermodels

Miss Supermodel America

Love & Death: The Murder of Kurt Cobain

Hollywood Undercover:
Revealing the Sordid Secrets of Tinseltown

Guy Laliberté: The Fabulous Life
of the Creator of Cirque du Soleil

Unmasked: The Final Years of Michael Jackson

Ian Halperin

BRANGELINA

TRANSIT
New York • Montréal • Paris

Published by Transit Publishing Inc.

ISBN: 978-0-9812396-6-8

Editor: Timothy Niedermann
Copyeditor: Shannon Partridge
Proofreader: Nachammai Raman
Cover design: François Turgeon
Text design and composition: Nassim Bahloul
Photos insert design: Pierre Pommey

Cover and back cover pictures:
Valery Hache/AFP/Getty Images
Lester Cohen/WireImage
Francois Durand/Getty Images
Sean Gallup/Getty Images
P. Lapoirie/Maxppp/ZUMA/KEYSTONE Press

Transit Publishing Inc.
1996, blvd St-Joseph East
Montreal, QC
H2H 1E3

Tel: 1-514-273-0123
www.transitpublishing.com

Printed and Bound in U.S.A.

DEDICATION

To my family, for always being there.

To my daughter Clover-Sky,
for bringing me each day all the joy and
happiness in the world.

ACKNOWLEDGEMENTS

This book would not have been possible but for the help and encouragement of many others. My heartfelt gratitude to:

Pierre Turgeon, the amazing head of Transit Publishing, for his continuous support and for structuring the shape of the book. Thank you for being there every step of the way.

Jarred Weisfeld, certainly the best agent in the world and also the most devoted friend. My daughter advised me to keep Jarred on for life—done deal! You are there at every moment.

Francois Turgeon, the whimsical genius whose creativity and insight has inspired me to keep going.

Timothy Niedermann, my undying gratitude for being a first-class editor. Here's to you!

Max Wallace, for your insight, vision, and relentless hours of fact checking. Here's to continued friendship, health, and success.

Sean O'Brien, my business partner at ianundercover.com. You have always been a rock. Here's to much continued success for your design business.

The brave people who spoke on the record and those who spoke off the record because they are still affiliated with Brangelina.

The entire staff at Transit Publishing for your incredible support and friendship.

Thanks to (in completely random order):

Ruth Fishman, Alan Kaufman, Anthony Ziccardi, Ian Kleinert, Howard Stern, Judith Regan, Shloime Perel, Ron Deckelbaum, Alison Moyet, Randolph Freedman, Dylan Ratigan, Geraldo Rivera, Charles Small, *Paris Match*, the City of Oslo, Skavlan, Samantha Lockwood, Denise DuBarry, Michele Frenière, Robert Brouillette, Fran Weinstein, D. J. Petroro, Mancow Muller, Isabelle

Dubé, Stuart Nulman, Larry and Belinda Seidlin, Dax, Renee Bosh, Andrew Rollings, Dr. Tony Stanton, Michael Cohen, Jeffrey Feldman, Jesse Jackson, Elliot MacDonald, Jon Reisler, Fleeze Fleming, Mitch Melnick, Christopher Heard, George Thwaites, Paula Froelich, Page Six, Noah Levy (*In Touch*), Lloyd Fishler, Karin Thomsen (1969–2009), Vanesa Curutchet, Peter Daley, Nate Colbert, Miles Wilkerson, Jimmy Davidson, JetBlue, Sofitel L.A., The L.A. Public Library, Norah Lawlor, Samantha Harris, Kia Zalewski, Annette Witheridge, Kevin Stinson, Jack Stinson, Amy Stinson, Meredith and Matt, Liz Jote, the gang in Austin (Christine, Angie, and Nuno), Morgan Nicholls, Jillian Harris, Esmond Choueke, Jim Nelson, Paul Santana, OTR, Dany Bouchard, Varda, Noir Chocolat, David Gavrilchuk, Elisa Gross, Irwin Gross, Bill Reed, Julius Grey, Nathalie McLennan, Al Barry, Pumpkin Jones, Kate and Keane, Kris Kostov, Michael Peshev, Denny Jacobsen, Nancy Grace, Terrance Hutton, Laura and Amanda, Petro Karloski, Sean Gottlieb, Rudy Bing, Alain Sommet, Brigit Laferrière, Daschl Wallace, Steven Sherman, Aldon James, The National Arts Club, Dawn Olsen, Mike Hess, Tommy Mays, Jacob Cohen, Al Reed, Stanley Hart, Laurent Medelgi, Gerry Gorman, Jennifer Robinson, Bob Shuman, Bryan White, Cynthia Jackson, Robert Lee, Ella Donaldson, Justin St. Marie, Peggy Allison, Clarissa Young, Bonnie Fuller, Michael Thomas, Terrance Dean, Ceasar DiSantos, Allison Lewis, Mr. Keating, Jerome Sabu, Yitzhak Klein, Bob White, Ted Ridder, Paul Carvalho, J. P. Pawliw Fry, Joe Franklin, Carl Horowitz, Leonard Wexler, Harvey Levin, Britt Taylor, Wendy Peterson, Jean Anne Rose, Lynn Grady, Matthew Benjamin, and Etienne Champagne. If I've forgotten anyone, mucho thanks!!!!

TABLE OF CONTENTS

INTRODUCTION

Maybe it's because I'd seen *One Flew Over the Cuckoo's Nest* too many times, but when I set out to infiltrate the psychiatric hospital where Angelina Jolie was once committed, I couldn't help but be nervous.

In my career as an author and documentary filmmaker, I have specialized in undercover investigations. I have posed as a male model to expose the fashion industry, a gay actor to get the goods on Hollywood and Scientology, a hairdresser to meet Michael Jackson, a paparazzo to expose the behind-the-scenes reality of the movie industry, and I have assumed countless other guises. But those experiences merely required chutzpah; there was no real risk involved.

This time, I had recurring nightmares of being found out and ending up like Jack Nicholson's character, Randle P. McMurphy—a lobotomized vegetable. Still, it seemed the only way I could hope to gain any insight into the central question that kept popping up as I tried to make sense of Angelina Jolie's remarkable life and career: is she really crazy, as she once would have had us believe, or is it all an act?

Having followed her and Brad Pitt for a number of years, spoken to countless friends and colleagues, and watched her astonishing transformation almost before my eyes, I still couldn't make up my mind. One person who had known her for more than fifteen years insisted to me that she was still "crazy as a loon." Her father publicly echoed that assessment, referring to her "mental problems" on national television. Yet many others who knew her insisted that she had put all that behind her and that her metamorphosis into a philanthropic humanitarian who just happened to be a Hollywood idol—a virtual Saint Angelina—was both sincere and inspirational.

I knew all too well that in Hollywood nothing is as it appears. For almost a century, the town has perfected the art of illusion, both on and off the screen. Our perceptions about celebrities are often tightly controlled by a publicity machine that makes us believe only what it wants us to. Piercing that illusion to discover the truth about any star is difficult, even for a probing journalist. In the case of Jolie, it was proving next to impossible. In order to get a handle on what makes her tick, I decided to visit the place where she reached rock bottom a mere eight years earlier, when she self-destructed for reasons still unknown.

Posing as a suicidal psychiatric patient, I quietly slipped onto the ward where Jolie had spent the last seventy-two hours of what one friend aptly called the "cocoon" of her previous life before she emerged to become the glamorous movie star the world knows today, half of the iconic Hollywood supercouple known as "Brangelina."

In order to make sense of those three days, however, and the incredible career trajectory that followed—not to mention her storied relationship to Brad Pitt—it is essential to first understand the life and events that led Angelina Jolie to the Resnick Neuropsychiatric Hospital at UCLA in the spring of 2000.

DADDY'S GIRL

As any psychoanalyst or biographer worth their salt will tell you, the logical place to start in order to gain an understanding of the subject is at the beginning. But as both practitioners know all too well, this is easier said than done. The subject is often adept at laying strategically placed roadblocks to ensure that the truth remains inaccessible.

Just as the world knows two distinct versions of Angelina Jolie—the wild, disturbed bad girl and the doting mother and humanitarian—there are two different, deeply contradictory versions of her early life and childhood. Neither is completely true nor completely false, and each is equally important for distinguishing fact from myth. In both versions, however, Jolie's father is central. And so, to understand her, it is essential to understand him.

When Jon Voight stunned moviegoers with his iconic role as the gay hustler Joe Buck in the 1969 classic *Midnight Cowboy*, the media proclaimed him an overnight movie star. In fact, he had already been slogging it out in bit parts for almost a decade by the time he slipped on the cowboy hat and played sidekick to Dustin Hoffman's tubercular con artist, Ratso Rizzo.

Voight grew up in Yonkers, New York, the grandson of a Catholic Slovakian immigrant, George Voytka. To help support his family, Voight's father, Elmer, went to work as a caddy at an all-Jewish golf club when he was only eight years old. The members of the club took the young Elmer under their wing, however, and taught him not just about golf, but also how to speak proper English, how to use a knife and fork, and other important skills that would help him assimilate into American society. By the time he was eighteen, Elmer's golf skills were good enough for him to turn professional, and thereafter he earned a good living as a country-club golf pro, becoming something of a local celebrity. To cap his successful Americanization, he changed his name to Voight.

Years later, Jon Voight recalled his father: "He was just a delightful man, a wonderful man, full of fun. And he had very strong principles. He didn't tolerate dishonesty, didn't like liars, and didn't suffer fools gladly . . . People loved him."

Each of Elmer's sons went on to considerable success in his chosen field. James became a songwriter and wrote a number of hits under his pseudonym, Chip Taylor, including the classic rock song, "Wild Thing." Jon's older brother Barry became one of the world's leading volcanologists.

Jon Voight attended Catholic University in Washington, D.C., where he first caught the acting bug and appeared in a number of student productions. In 1959, a year before he graduated, he landed his first professional acting assignment in the off-Broadway production, *O Oysters Revue*. After one critic panned him, declaring that he could "neither talk nor walk," Voight seriously considered giving up acting. But he persevered and landed the role of the singing Nazi, Rolf, in *The Sound of Music* on Broadway in 1961, replacing the original cast member. It was in this production that he met Lauri Peters, an accomplished young actress who played Liesl and who, along with her stage siblings, received a Tony nomination for best supporting actor. Each night onstage, Voight and Peters performed the memorable love song "I am Sixteen" together, in which Rolf promises to take care of Liesl. Although Rolf's devotion to the Nazi party gets in the way of his budding romance with Liesl in the story onstage, offstage a real-life romance began to develop between the two, and in 1962 they were married.

Through the mid-1960s, Voight's acting career developed slowly. He played a number of small roles on TV shows such as *Gunsmoke* and *Coronet Blue*, along with bit parts in Hollywood westerns and B-movies. In 1966, he started to get more notice for his acting abilities when he spent a season with the California National Shakespeare Festival, and in 1967 he won a Theater World award for his role in the stage production of *That Summer, That Fall*, acting opposite a young Tyne Daly. Success had its price, though; his marriage to Peters ended that same year, apparently due to their conflicting acting schedules, which seldom allowed them to be in the same part of the country for any length of time.

In 1969, Voight's groundbreaking role in *Midnight Cowboy* vaulted him into the Hollywood elite. Shortly thereafter he met a stunningly beautiful young actress, the late Marcheline Bertrand, at a party in the Hollywood Hills. In 1971, they were married.

Bertrand was born in a suburb of Chicago, the daughter of a working-class French Canadian, Rolland Bertrand, and his wife, Lois June Gouwens.

Although Bertrand is often described as a French actress, Jolie tried to set the record straight in a 2001 interview with *Allure* magazine: "My mom is as far from French Parisian as you can get. She's part Iroquois Indian, from Chicago. She grew up in a bowling alley that my grandparents owned." It is unknown whether Bertrand actually had any Iroquois blood; the story seems to come from something Voight told Angelina when she was little about her French Canadian ancestry to make it seem more exotic. (It is well-known that there was a lot of intermarriage between the early French settlers in Canada and the native peoples.)

When Bertrand was fifteen, her family moved to Los Angeles. There, Bertrand got the acting bug and promptly enrolled at the Lee Strasberg's Actors Studio. It is often said that Bertrand gave up a promising acting career when, at the age of twenty-one, she married

Voight, but this is an exaggeration. Before she met her future husband, she had no professional experience to speak of, not that she hadn't made an impression on people. "She was an unusually good person in the best sense of the word," remembers Strasberg's widow, Anna, with whom Bertrand trained. "It's rare in your life when you meet somebody like her." In 1971, Voight used his connections to land his fiancée a small role on the TV show *Ironside*, but this and a number of subsequent minor movie roles made no impression, and her career stagnated.

In May 1973, less than two years after their marriage, Bertrand gave birth to a son, James Haven Voight. A baby daughter arrived two years later, in June 1975. They christened her Angelina Jolie Voight. Later it was explained that the children's middle names were specifically chosen to give them potential stage names in the event they decided to take up acting. Interviewing his daughter for the June 1997 issue of *Interview* magazine, Voight described for her his recollection of her birth:

> You don't remember it, but when you emerged from your mother's womb, I picked you up, held you in my hand, and looked at your face. You had your finger by the side of your cheek, and you looked very, very wise, like my old best friend. I started to tell you how your mom and I were so happy to have you here, and that we were going to take great care of you and watch for all those signs of who you were and how we could help you achieve all that wonderful potential God gave you. I made that pledge and everybody in the room started crying.

Sadly, less than a year after Angelina was born, Voight and Bertrand separated, amid reports of Voight's womanizing. A mutual friend, Larry Groen, provided some insight into the couple's relationship:

> Jon was absolutely smitten with Mar. She was drop-dead gorgeous, and heads would always turn when she entered the room, even in a town where beautiful women were everywhere. I wouldn't call their relationship tumultuous; they didn't fight. But she was at

home raising two small children and Jon was this movie star who everybody wanted a piece of. And I mean everybody. These were the days when swinging started to be in vogue, and there were orgies literally every night, especially in Malibu, where people threw wild parties at their beach houses. The temptations were everywhere and most people succumbed, not just Jon. Keep in mind that after *Midnight Cowboy*, he was very, very hot. Women threw themselves at the guy wherever he went. And not just women, men too. He had played this famous gay character, and people assumed that he was homosexual. Most actors were, or they went both ways. But not Jon, at least not that I could tell . . . He liked women a lot. I think somebody told Mar about a party where they saw Jon all over a woman, and that's what alerted her. As far as I remember, it wasn't one affair that broke up their marriage. Of course, everybody was cheating; everybody in Hollywood was getting married and divorcing. Very few marriages survived those crazy times. There was a lot of sex; a lot more than today, that's for sure.

Other accounts say that Voight was having an affair with another actress. He himself will not elaborate, explaining simply, "I was having difficulty with the marriage. I had an affair, and there was a divorce." Voight moved out and paid enough alimony and child support for Bertrand to live comfortably but not extravagantly. According to numerous allegations, Voight virtually abandoned his young family, causing his son and daughter to harbor years of resentment. "My father and I were never close," Angelina told *People* magazine in August 2003. Voight "seldom saw his daughter while she was growing up," wrote *Vanity Fair* in November, 2004 after interviewing Jolie. "My mom raised me," Angelina now tells interviewers. Likewise, James has frequently spoken in recent years of his bitterness towards his father for leaving them in the lurch. But the facts appear to speak otherwise.

Bertrand and Voight shared custody in a very amicable agreement and split their time with the children fairly.

According to Groen, "Jon doted on his kids. I don't remember a lot of animosity between Jon and Mar. They stayed friends, and they had the kids in common. They handled the breakup fairly healthily, I think. Angie and James were very close to their mom, no question about it, but they always had fun with Jon, and he took a real interest in their lives. They spent a lot of time with him."

Indeed, one of Jolie's kindergarten teachers related to Jolie's biographer Rhona Mercer that Voight was very present. "Her father was always picking up her and her brother," the teacher recalled. "He was always around. I don't know if they had a good relationship; all I know is that he did the fatherly thing. He came to sports day. He came to the school. They lived in Palisades, where all the big stars like Al Pacino lived."

And even Jolie herself, before her estrangement from her father in 2003, seemed sympathetic to his side of the marriage breakup, explaining, "My father is a perfect example of an artist who couldn't be married. He had the perfect family, but there's something about that that's very scary for him."

In an interview Voight gave to *People* magazine when Angelina was seven years old, he addressed his role as a divorced father. "The focus," he explained, "is always the kids. Whatever Marche and I go through, we consider how it affects them. We've each made mistakes. The kids are aware of the deep disruption that went on early in their lives. The guilt, anger, and confusion made their way into their subconscious, and I don't know what dues we'll pay later on. But they will have learned how to deal with adversity."

Shortly after the couple finally divorced, in 1978, Marcheline took up with UCLA filmmaking student and later documentary filmmaker Bill Day, who was fond of young James and Angelina. This prompted occasional jealousy on the part of Voight. "The kids are crazy about this guy," he acknowledged in an interview at the time. "There are male egos involved, and there is friction, the whole territorial thing. We don't necessarily sync, but we each give ground. He's crazy about Marche and really loves the kids." For her part, Marcheline always defended Voight's role as a father. "Nothing means more to Jon than the children," she told *People* magazine in 1993.

When Angelina was only six years old, Voight wrote and starred in a movie called *Looking to Get Out*, teaming up again with the brilliant director of *Coming Home*, Hal Ashbee. They couldn't recreate the magic of their first collaboration, however; most critics agreed the film was awful. But Voight did manage to arrange a small role for Angelina, her first big-screen appearance, as a cute little girl named Tosh, who appears in a long scene with her father. The acting wasn't memorable, but it was clear even at that age that the camera loved her.

The same year, Bertrand moved east to escape the brutal smog of Los Angeles, which had been wreaking havoc with her allergies. She settled with her children in a small community on the Hudson River north of New York City, Sneden's Landing. The separation was hard on Voight, who was used to seeing James and Angie several days a week. He told one interviewer at the time that he missed his children terribly. Before long, he was commuting east each month to spend time with the kids, staying at his mother's home in Scarsdale, about half an hour away.

Since their estrangement in 2003, Jolie has given a number of interviews downplaying her father's involvement in the lives of his children, often claiming "he wasn't there." But in 2001, she sounded very different: "I never remember a time when I needed my father and he wasn't there. But he's an artist, and it was the '70s, a strange time for everybody. To this day, I think my parents really love each other. It's a beautiful story. I saw them at Christmas; they came to our house." Jolie even addressed the occasional press report that claimed that Voight had been estranged from his family: "The press likes to use the family angle, because then they get to include this whole other aspect of my life, but they're always disappointed to hear I'm not trying to hide anything about some huge, sordid estrangement between us. The fact is, he's very much a part of my life, but I've always been pretty independent of him, too."

By most earlier accounts, including her own, Jolie's L.A. childhood was a happy one before she moved east. She loved to watch Disney movies with her brother and play with her pet lizard named Vladimir and her snake, called Harry Dean Stanton, after the actor. "I think a lot of people think I had a very different childhood than I had," she said years later. "I probably had a more normal childhood than most people would think."

To Voight's delight, when Angelina was twelve years old, Bertrand moved back to L.A. with her children. The details of Angelina's life in New York are murky, but it was clear that something about her had changed by the time she returned to the West Coast. Angelina Jolie had discovered her dark side.

BACK TO 90210

By the time Angelina moved back to Los Angeles with her mother and brother in 1986, she was no longer the fun-loving little girl people remembered. This may have been due to her frequent forays into Manhattan, accompanying her mother on auditions. In the city, Angelina had been exposed to a seamier, edgier world, one that she had never experienced in California or in tranquil upstate New York. And she liked it. She began to change herself to fit in with the sort of people that were increasingly attracting her. By the time they arrived back in L.A., she was in full rebellion mode.

"When we moved back from New York I had really gotten into leather," she later recalled. "I think I loved Michael Jackson or something. I used to wear the leather jackets with the zippers or collars with studs on them, and I used to ask if I could go to school wearing them." To complete her look, the eleven-year-old started dyeing her hair jet black.

The family moved to an apartment building in a middle-class section of Beverly Hills. Once they were settled, Bertrand immediately enrolled Angelina in the Lee Strasberg Theater Institute's Young Actors Program. The legendary Strasberg had passed away four years earlier, but his influential method acting technique lived on. The Method, a refinement of the earlier Stanislavski technique, teaches actors to recall emotions or reactions from their own lives and use them to create lifelike performances.

Among the actors who studied under Strasberg and who have credited the Method with their success are James Dean, Dustin Hoffman, Al Pacino, Paul Newman, and, most famously, Marilyn Monroe, who came to regard Strasberg and his wife as surrogate parents and to whom she left the bulk of her estate. Bertrand herself had studied there several years earlier, and for two years Angelina attended the institute regularly on weekends, but she wasn't entirely convinced it was for her: "They'd ask me to go back five years in my life and relive something, and at age six there isn't that much to work with."

Once again, Voight and Bertrand shared custody, with Angie and Jamie living at their father's house two nights a week and every other weekend. As before, there is no evidence that the custody arrangements were causing any particular emotional problems. By most accounts, Voight and Bertrand were agreeable with each other, with Angelina later describing them as "each other's best friend." Angelina was attending El Rodeo Elementary School, reputedly one of the best public schools in the nation, and she did very well there. James credited their mother's domestic routine. "There was very much that home feeling when we got back from school," he recalls. "Angie and I would walk in, and we could smell things cooking and baking in the kitchen. My mom was methodical in making sure we did our homework perfectly, and she would do outlines to help us. When we were younger, she used flash cards, or she'd be in the middle of cooking and pick up a carrot and teach us about the vegetable or the fruit so that it was visual as well."

For his part, Voight seemed thrilled that his daughter had caught the acting bug and did his best to encourage her new pursuit. "She'd come over to my house and we'd run through a play together, performing various parts," he told the London *Independent* in 2001. "I saw that she had real talent. She loved acting. So I did my best to encourage her, to coach her, and to share my best advice with her. For a while, we were doing a new play together every Sunday."

Unlike many actors of his caliber, Voight was selective in the films he chose and rarely acted just for the money. "I didn't want to do the pretty-boy roles they were always offering me," he explains. As a result, unlike many of his less acclaimed colleagues, he was not affluent. No beach house in Malibu. No swimming pool. In fact, Voight didn't even own a house. He too lived in an apartment.

Despite the claims of his son, James Haven, who has spent much of the past few years attempting to discredit his father, Voight was quite generous toward Bertrand and always paid his alimony. We know this because Angelina herself was publicly emphatic about her father's integrity right up until their 2003 estrangement. "He always took good care of us and our mother," Jolie declared to an interviewer in 2001. "He always met his obligations. He just didn't have a lot of money."

This period of Jolie's life continued uneventfully for almost two years. But then, at the age of thirteen, Angelina suddenly quit the Strasberg Institute and slipped into what she would later describe as "a very bad time."

This probably had been brewing for a long time. She describes turning ten years old as a time when her life "started not to be fun" anymore and when she developed a fascination with death. "My mother's father died when I was nine," she explains. "He was a wonderful, spirited man, but his funeral was horrible. Everyone was hysterical. I thought funerals should be a celebration of life rather than a room full of upset people. I'm not scared of death, which makes people think I'm dark; in fact, I'm positive."

She could never point to a specific trauma as the turning point in her personality, although she describes a day when she was playing a game with a friend. She wanted to get into the fantasy world such games demand, but she could no longer find her way there. Perhaps that's why she first decided to take up acting initially, to try to regain the comfort of the imaginary places of her childhood.

Now, though, having dropped out of acting, she talked about wanting to be a funeral director. She even started taking mail-order courses on embalming from the Funeral Services Institute. Before long, her preoccupation with death led Angelina to consider ending her own life, a state of mind that she has spoken about many times over the years. In one interview, she dismissed the idea that her thoughts of suicide were related to depression or sadness, however: "I always thought I was sane, but I didn't know if I'd be comfortable living in this world. As a child I contemplated suicide a lot—not because I was unhappy, but because I didn't feel useful. I had insomnia and was up all night, with a mind that wouldn't stop." And yet in a different interview, she says of her childhood, "I had a lot of sadness and distrust. I came very close to the end of my life a few times."

In a 2001 article, *Rolling Stone* magazine writer Chris Heath described Jolie showing him a notebook she had kept when she was fourteen:

> On the cover is some kind of sword. On the second page is a drawing of three daggers and the words DEATH: EXTINCTION OF LIFE. There are other drawings of weapons and a quote: ONLY THE STRONG SHALL SURVIVE. There are further definitions: PAIN: PHYSICAL OR MENTAL SUFFERING. AUTOPSY: EXAMINATION OF A CORPSE. She grabs the book back, seemingly embarrassed, but then relinquishes it. There is the word HELL and a picture of the devil, and there is a ripped-out page with only a middle strip of paper visible. The only word remaining is SUICIDE. "I can laugh at it now," she says.

At this point, probably the darkest period of her life, Jolie entered high school, and many chroniclers have attempted to link her well-documented psychological abyss to her particular school and its culture. This is doubtful, but it certainly was at Beverly Hills High School that Angie Voight took the first steps toward creating what has become the Angelina Jolie myth.

In 1989, like today, Beverly Hills High was frequented by many of the offspring of the Hollywood elite. The school boasts more than a few notable, and some ignoble, alumni, including Nicolas Cage, Richard Dreyfuss, Nora Ephron, and Monica Lewinsky. But its reputation—solidified in popular culture as the supposed setting for the TV show *Beverly Hills 90210*—is misleading. The student body is quite diverse. Today, forty-two percent of the Beverly Hills High student population was born outside of the United States, and many students come from modest means. Although the mix certainly has changed since the late 1980s when Angelina first enrolled, she was by no means the only middle-class student there.

Countless profiles over the years have claimed that Angelina was bullied by her classmates because, in a school full of rich kids, she didn't have fancy clothes or an expensive car. "These rich brats were merciless with Angelina Jolie, taunting her for her extreme thinness, her second-hand outfits, her glasses and her braces," declared one magazine profile.

But according to those who knew her during those years, nothing could be further from the truth. A former classmate who now works in the television industry says, "Angelina was never picked on because she wasn't a rich kid. Come on, her father was an Academy Award-winning actor. Everybody respected those kinds of things at Beverly, believe me. The fact is that our school was very typical of an American high school in those days. There were all the same cliques you would find anywhere else, sort of like *The Breakfast Club*. There were the jocks, the brains, the popular kids, the potheads, the misfits, and the outsiders, who deliberately went out of their way not to fit in. Angie was one of those. She didn't dress in second-hand clothes because she couldn't afford to shop on Rodeo Drive; she dressed like that because it was cool. That was the beginning of the whole grunge thing, and I'd say Angie was a combination of a Goth and a grunge girl. There were other kids like that as well; they had their own crowd just like all the others."

While the rich girls shopped at the Beverly Center, Angie hung out on the seedy Sunset Strip and shopped at the punk-rock stores on Melrose Boulevard. "I was always that punk in school," Jolie told *Vanity Fair* in 2003. "I didn't feel clean and, like, pretty . . . I always felt interesting or odd or dark or maybe, uh, you know, I could feel sexy . . . I'd be in my black boots and my ripped jeans and my old jacket, and I felt more comfortable like that. I wasn't gonna pretend to be the smart, clean, centered girl. I could understand the darker things, the more moody things, the more emotional things."

While most of her fans have seen photos of Angelina looking geeky in braces and thick-rimmed glasses, those were taken when she was still in elementary school. By the time she was attending Beverly Hills High, the familiar features the world knows today were already evident, and she usually wore contact lenses. In her school yearbook photo, Jolie is clearly a striking teenager. According to one of her classmates, Michael Klesic, who also went on to pursue an acting career, "All the guys knew that she was a hot chick. I mean, when she walked down the hall, heads would turn."

Klesic remembers that Angelina stood out from the other "hot" girls. "She was the one you didn't want to mess with," he recalls. "She was the tough pretty girl. She was very direct when she spoke to you. She could always tell if anybody was speaking to her with an ulterior motive or anything like that. She really stuck out like a sore thumb in terms of Beverly Hills girls. She wasn't one of them. She didn't dress like them. She wasn't interested in the same things that they were. She was her own human being and her own person, and she had her eyes on the stars. She wanted to get out of that school."

Angelina later described this period as her "awkward, mental-breakdown" adolescence. "I wore black fishnets and boots because I wanted to hide myself," she recalled. "I wanted to feel everything. But at the same time, I was doing plays and taking ballroom classes at Arthur

Murray. I'd wash off all the ink I had drawn on my arms, and take off my twenty-hole Doc Martens, and put on high heels and a dress and win tango competitions. My friends thought I was insane. But I thought it was fun."

Another classmate, Jean Robinson, recalled for Rhona Mercer the actress's now legendary obsession with cold metal. "She was deliberately different and didn't want anything to do with the rich kids. She had a serious thing with knives. All kinds of knives—pen knives, kitchen knives. She would just whip one out and start playing with it." Robinson remembers another side of Angelina that contributed to her unpopularity: "When she was fourteen at Beverly Hills High, she was stealing boys who were seventeen. Once they were panting after her, she would walk away. It was all about the chase." But it was not only about boys. "The same happened with girls. Angie could seduce you into thinking she was your best friend and then not speak to you again," said Robinson. "That kind of cruelty is common, but Angelina was devastatingly good at it."

One boy she didn't walk away from was a sixteen-year-old punk rocker she started dating when she was only fourteen. Within a month, the boy had moved in with her, with her mother's blessing. Evidently, Bertrand thought the best way to keep tabs on her wild daughter was to keep her and her boyfriend under the same roof.

Jolie claims to have been highly sexual from a young age, recalling, "I was very sexual in kindergarten. I was a member of a group called the Kissy Girls. I created a game where I would kiss the boys and give them cooties. Then we would make out and we would take our clothes off. I got in a lot of trouble!" Despite the early start, she claims that the punk-rock boyfriend was her first sexual conquest.

"I lost my virginity when I was fourteen," she told the *Daily Mirror*. "He was my first boyfriend at the time. I wanted to be promiscuous and was starting to be sexual . . . I got lucky. We were in my bedroom, in my environment, where I was most comfortable, and I wasn't in danger."

She has frequently rationalized the unusual living arrangement. "He lived in our house with my mom and my brother, so it wasn't like we were on our own," she told the Melbourne, Australia, *Herald Sun* in 2005. "And I could always talk to mom if there were any problems. She was more connected and more aware of what was going on than most mothers. She knew I was at that age where I was going to be looking around. Either it was going to be in weird situations or it was going to be in my house, in my room."

In her simple description of the relationship, it appears that Angelina possessed a remarkable maturity for one so young. Indeed, logic might prompt one to ask why more mothers don't invite their daughters' boyfriends to live under the same roof. But those who knew her during this period knew that her love life was not as simple or idyllic as she made it out to be. They could see the truth for themselves in the scars on her skin.

DRAWING BLOOD

"Some people go shopping. I cut myself."

In the late 1990s, when a newly famous Angelina Jolie started discussing her teenage penchant for self-mutilation, she made it seem like a harmless manifestation of adolescent angst. But those around her at that time were deeply worried.

People started noticing the scars around the time she took up with her live-in boyfriend. It seemed this was no coincidence. "I started having sex, and sex didn't feel like enough; my emotions didn't feel like enough," she recalls. "My emotions kept wanting to break out. In a moment of wanting something honest, I grabbed a knife and cut my boyfriend. And he cut me. He was a really good person, a sweet guy—not threatening, not scary. We had this exchange of something, and we were covered in blood. My heart was racing; it was something dangerous. Life suddenly felt more honest than whatever this 'sex' was supposed to be. It felt so primitive and so honest, but then I had to deal with not telling my mother, hiding things, wearing gauze bandages to school."

In another interview, she rationalizes her self-mutilation by comparing it to sexual deviance, which she insists was not part of her schtick. "There were moments when I just wanted physically to have something, whether it be a knife or a whip. You want to be drained of everything; you want somehow to have everything go quiet. Other people do sexual things or try to make themselves perfect—that's another kind of sickness."

In their landmark 1991 study, "Self-Injurious Behavior," published in the *American Journal of Psychiatry*, Dr. Ronald M. Winchel and the late Dr. Michael E. Stanley of Columbia University's College of Physicians and Surgeons define *self-injury* as "the commission of deliberate harm to one's own body. The injury is done to oneself, without the aid of another person, and the injury is severe enough for tissue damage (such as scarring) to result. Acts that are committed with conscious suicidal intent or are associated with sexual arousal are excluded."

This alarming trend among adolescent girls first gained attention in the mental-health sector in the early 1960s, though the practice is known to date back to at least a century before. The term *self-mutilation* first occurred in a 1913 study by L. Eugene Emerson, Ph.D., where he described self-cutting as a symbolic substitution for masturbation. The term cropped up again in 1938 when Dr. Karl Menninger, in his book *Man Against Himself*, concluded for the first time that self-mutilation was not necessarily a form of suicidal behavior but rather an "attenuated death wish." In his book, he coined the term *partial suicide* to describe the phenomenon.

According to the Cornell University Research Program on Self-Injurious Behavior in Adolescents and Young Adults, "There are important distinctions between those attempting suicide and those who practice self-injury in order to cope with overwhelming negative feelings. Most studies find that self-injury is often undertaken as a means of avoiding suicide." The institute notes that self-injury can be performed on any part of the body, but most often occurs on the hands, wrists, stomach and thighs. The severity of the act, it concludes, can vary from superficial wounds to those resulting in lasting disfigurement.

Most studies conclude that females make up about two-thirds of adolescent self-injurers, though it is possible that women are simply more willing to admit their self-injuries than men. The Cornell self-injury program's literature cites in a recent study that between thirteen and seventeen percent of American high-school students engage in self-injury at least once. The Cornell research also states that "early onset self-injury is common around the age of seven, although it can begin earlier. Most often, however, self-injury behaviors begin in middle adolescence, between the ages of twelve and fifteen, and can last for weeks, months, or years. For many, self-injury is cyclical rather than linear, meaning that it is used for periods of time, stopped, and then resumed. It would be erroneous, however, to assume that self-injury is a fleeting adolescent phenomenon." If Angelina began self-injuring at the age of thirteen, this puts her in the average age range of adolescent self-injurers.

In his book, *Psychological Self-Help*, Dr. Clayton Tucker-Ladd, former director of the Counseling and Testing Center at Southern Illinois University, summarized some of the myriad explanations he had come across while treating adolescent self-injurers:

Young people are sometimes emotionally abused and told they are bad, sinful, selfish, hurtful, hateful, uncaring, crazy, or weird. They may be blamed for their parents' troubles or divorce, etc. It isn't surprising they may end up feeling guilty, shame, self-hatred, and wanting to hurt or punish themselves.

Some have grown up in physically and sexually abusive families (beatings, threats & torture) and were called useless, stupid, ugly, slut, and a total failure; many were bullied by peers; some were raped. Some responded with resentment, intense anger, and repressed rage; others adopted the negative evaluations and felt worthlessness, felt no one could ever care for them, and felt like a piece of trash. Some responded to being hated with a defiant attitude, e.g., "You can't make me change" or "I deserve to be abused but I can hurt myself more than you can." Some wanted get back at the abusive person by hurting themselves via self-mutilation, i.e., showing visual signs of their feelings. Some physically responded to pain, punishment, and self-punishment by actually feeling better, something like having an adrenalin rush or taking drugs; others found that burning or cutting themselves numbs them to pain.

Others were feeling depressed, helpless and hopeless or were without feelings, almost like being dead. Some responded to self-injury while feeling dead with "The self-abuse showed me that I could feel and was alive." Others felt alone, uncared for, scared, sad, not just neglected but utterly worthless, rejected by family and friends, placed in foster care, dumped by boy/girlfriend, etc., so, it felt better to hurt themselves and, in that way, escape the hurt from others. Many were well aware they had seriously disabling psychological problems and felt weird, unable to cope, scared, helpless, and inferior. Still others felt out of control, couldn't do anything right, but were reassured by the courage they had when self-cutting, surprised at what injuries they could force themselves to inflict.

Although in recent years Angelina Jolie has become the poster child for self-injury, she is by no means the first celebrity who has admitted to the practice. Other high-profile practitioners are actress Christina Ricci, Courtney Love, and singer-songwriter Fiona Apple, who admitted to *Rolling Stone* that she cut herself for years. Apple, as her fans know, was raped outside her mother's apartment building when she was twelve years old, an incident that has haunted her ever since.

Like Angelina, Apple has tended to downplay the significance of her self-injuries. "I have a little bit of a problem with that [self-injury]," she said in one interview. "It's a common thing." Asked by the interviewer if it made her feel better, she responded, "It just makes you *feel*." She is quick to point out, however, that self-injuring doesn't mean she is crazy. "The most annoying thing for me to hear about myself is that I'm trying to make people have a pity party for me," she told *Rolling Stone*.

"Everything that I've gone through has been dramatized by the people who've written about it, not by me. I'm just saying, 'This happened to me, this happened to a lot of people.' Why should I hide shit? Why does that give people a bad opinion of me? It's a reality. A lot of people do it."

Probably the most famous self-injurer of all was Princess Diana, who talked about it and other disorders in a 1995 interview with the BBC. She revealed that she had frequently cut her arms and legs over the years. "You have so much pain inside yourself that you try and hurt yourself on the outside because you want help," she explained at the time. According to Andrew Morton's definitive biography, *Diana: Her True Story*, the troubled princess—who also acknowledged a struggle with bulimia—had often thrown herself into a glass cabinet at Kensington Palace and cut herself with the serrated edge of a lemon slicer. Once, during a heated argument with Prince Charles, she reportedly picked up a pen knife and cut her chest and thighs. Another time, during a fight with Charles on an airplane, Diana locked herself in the bathroom, cut her arms, and smeared the blood over the cabin walls and seats.

The actress Christina Ricci has also publicly discussed her history of self-injury. In a 1988 interview with *US Weekly* magazine, Ricci showed the interviewer a small, smile-shaped scar on her hand. "I was trying to impress Gaby [Hoffmann, her best friend]. So I heated up a lighter and pressed it on my hand." Revealing a number of other burn scars on her hands and arms, she explained, "I wanted to see if I can handle pain. It's sort of an experiment to see if I can handle pain." In a different interview, she revealed that she sometimes puts cigarettes out on her arms. Asked whether it hurts, she replied, "No. You get this endorphin rush. You can actually faint from pain. It takes a second, a little sting, and then it's like you really don't feel anything. It's calming actually." In *Rolling Stone* magazine she went further. "It's like having a drink. But it's quicker," she told them. "You know how your brain shuts down from pain? The pain would be so bad, it would force my body to slow down, and I wouldn't be as anxious. It made me calm."

Perhaps the most surprising celebrity self-injurer, however, is Johnny Depp, who has scars up and down his arms from the days when he used to cut himself. "It was really just whatever; good times, bad times, it didn't matter," he told *Talk* magazine about his former habit. "There was no ceremony. It wasn't like 'Okay, this just happened, I have to go hack a piece of my flesh off.' " In another interview in 1993 he explained the still-visible scars: "My body is a journal in a way. It's like what sailors used to do, where every tattoo meant something, a specific time in your life when you make a mark on yourself, whether you do it yourself with a knife or with a professional tattoo artist."

Over the years, the mental-health profession has struggled to figure out how to classify and treat self-injury, especially among adolescents. The most frequent diagnosis appears to be borderline personality disorder (BPD), though critics insist that such a label is a rush to judgment. One of the foremost researchers into the disorder is Marsha Linehan, director of the Behavioral Research and Therapy Clinics at the University of Washington. She believes that, while self-injury often fits into this category, diagnosing a personality disorder requires an understanding of a person's long-term pattern of functioning, which often gets ignored. "That this does not happen," she writes, "is evident in the increasing numbers of teenagers being diagnosed as borderline . . . One wonders what justification is used for giving a fourteen-year-old a negative psychiatric label that will stay with her all of her life?

In the case of Angelina Jolie, the official diagnosis was considerably more serious. Sitting in her Beverly Hills High School file to this day is a troubling description, delivered by a psychotherapist who had been treating her for some time: "Angelina Voight is unrestrained, inclined to antisocial psychopathy." In other words, while still in her teens, Angelina was labeled a psychopath.

Jolie has tried to downplay her mental-health issues as well as her mandatory thrice-weekly sessions with the school therapist. "They enrolled in there everybody whose parents were divorced," she recalls. "Our psychotherapist used to say that it was our [parental] 'units' who were guilty of everything. It seemed to her that we, poor children, would never be able to adapt to life."

But according to one of Angelina's former classmates, who now works in the television industry, her explanation doesn't ring true. "You've got to be kidding me," he says. "This was Beverly Hills High. Most of the kids in the school came from so-called broken homes. Everybody's parents were divorced, mine included. If they made us all see a school therapist, it would have been like an assembly line a mile long. I have no idea what Angie did to be sent to therapy. I don't even think I knew at the time that she was going, though it was a given that lots of kids saw some sort of therapist privately. I never did personally, except for some family therapy when I was younger, but it was kind of in vogue in those days."

In a 2000 interview, Angelina appears to contradict the explanation that she gave earlier about being forced to attend therapy. She also emphatically denied that her problems had anything to do with her parents' divorce. "I was in school, and you could get extra credit for going to a therapist," Jolie told *Marie Claire* magazine. "It was just a part of life studies, psychology. So I went. And I realized how dangerous these people could be. This person kept talking about my feelings for my father. I'd say, "No, I'm not angry. I understand. I think my parents are both wonderful individuals." And she just couldn't believe it wasn't a problem for me. I can remember coming in one day and saying I had a dream. I totally lied. I said I dreamt that I stabbed my father with a fork, and she said, 'Aha, I see." And I thought, 'You fucking asshole." My therapy is my films; my therapist is everybody who goes to see a movie and tells me whether I'm completely off."

Short of locating the therapist that came up with the original diagnosis, it's difficult to determine what it was based on.

According to experts, it is highly unusual for a fourteen-year-old to be diagnosed with an antisocial psychopathic disorder, since most of the literature suggests reserving such a diagnosis until at least the age of eighteen. In his 2006 book, *The Psychopathy of Everyday Life*, Dr. Martin Kantor makes a clear distinction between the kind of disorder that Angelina was diagnosed with and the kind of severe psychopathic behavior of serial killers and other extreme examples. "One of the biggest problems in understanding psychopathy," he writes, "is the literature's tendency to lump serious but rare psychopaths like John Wayne Gacy and Ted Bundy with the less serious but common psychopaths, the many in our midst who suffer from a milder and less obtrusive form . . . [clinical psychologist and author] Martha Stout calls these less serious, more common psychopaths 'the sociopaths next door.' "

Most experts agree that one of the defining characteristics of psychopathy is a lack of empathy. Given Angelina Jolie's present day status as a philanthropist and humanitarian, it is hard to believe that she was ever given this diagnosis in the first place. Could it have been the rash assessment of a lazy therapist? Or did the rebellious teenage Angelina deliberately act crazy during her sessions to get a rise out of the shrink?

"Growing up, I actually wished I was insane," she has said. "I remember being very upset that I wasn't. I think there's a romance to going insane. I wanted my mind to take me away, but it couldn't tell me where to go." It's possible that it was all an act, but at the time there was clearly plenty of reason for those around her to suspect that there was something desperately wrong.

While she has described the period she spent with her live-in boyfriend as "very sweet, almost like a marriage," her penchant for knives and self-mutilation was intensifying every day. It soon became an integral part of their sexual relationship. "[Normal sex] didn't seem primal enough, nor satisfy me," she later explained. S & M became her chosen kink, but even that wasn't enough for her: "S & M sex can be misinterpreted as violence," she explained to *Vanity Fair* in 2004. "It's really about trust. I like to push boundaries, both emotional and sexual, with another person. That's when I've felt the sexiest. I've been in both submissive and dominant roles because I want more. I was always the top until I read somewhere that the bottom controls the top so I thought, 'Wait a minute, that's right. I'm doing all the work!' I've never been tied up though. I have a feeling the person that does it will be The One. I think that's what I'd like."

During one of their sessions, things went a little too far and sixteen-year-old Angelina ended up slashing her neck, cutting an X into her arm, and slicing her stomach. When the blood flowed longer than usual, she was rushed to a hospital by ambulance and given a life-saving transfusion. "I nearly cut my jugular vein," she recalled years later.

Tiring of the constant drama and afraid for her daughter, Bertrand eventually decided to end the experiment and ordered the boyfriend to move out. Infuriated by her mother's sudden penchant for authority and rules, Angelina decided she could no longer live under Bertrand's roof and moved into a nearby apartment, financed by her father. She also broke up with the boyfriend. "He cried a lot," she later recalled about the break-up. "And it was just a load of high drama that I could do without."

There may have been another reason Jolie moved out of the house and broke up with her boyfriend, however. In May 2009, unsourced media reports claimed that, as a precocious sixteen-year-old, Jolie had been caught sleeping with her mother's boyfriend. When her mother found out, so the story goes, she ended her affair with the man, but eventually forgave her precocious daughter.

The incident in question would have happened in 1991, which is indeed the year that Bertrand ended an eleven-year relationship with her live-in filmmaker boyfriend. It also coincides with the time that

Angelina, still a minor, suddenly moved out of her mother's house and broke up with her own boyfriend, who had been living with Jolie under her mother's roof since she was fourteen.

Could her psychotherapy sessions, and subsequent diagnosis as an antisocial psychopath, be related to this affair? In California at the time, the age of consent laws considered sex with a minor under sixteen to be a felony or misdemeanor. Thus if she was sixteen or over at the time of the alleged affair, she would not have fallen into this category, and the sexual relationship would not have been considered a crime. Yet such an action could have easily been diagnosed by a therapist as antisocial behavior, to say the least.

Still, it is clear that Jolie was extremely close to her mother until Bertrand's death in 2007. It is difficult to imagine that Bertrand would have so easily forgiven such an unconscionable act.

The end of the relationship, according to Angelina, also coincided with the end of her self-injuring. "By the time I was sixteen, I had gotten it out of my system," she says, implying that her unstable adolescent behavior was just a phase. In fact, the worst was yet to come.

BRAD PITT

When Angelina was sixteen years old, she and her mother traipsed one day to the Beverly Center from their nearby apartment and took in the new movie, *Thelma and Louise*. Marcheline Bertrand enjoyed the film for its liberating theme of female independence, as the two main characters go on a wild road trip to escape their dreary lives. Angelina, on the other hand, was struck by the handsome young cowboy, J. D., a charismatic young con artist who gives Thelma a night she will never forget. Little did Angelina know that fifteen years later, her name and that cowboy's would be merged to form one of the most powerful brands in Hollywood history.

It is hard to believe, comparing their early years, that Brad Pitt and Angelina Jolie were destined to be together one day. Their backgrounds couldn't be more different. Pitt was born in Shawnee, Oklahoma, in December 1963. Shortly after his birth, his parents moved to Springfield, Missouri, a pleasant city in the southern part of that state, which is known as the "gateway to the Ozarks." Living in Springfield at that time was somewhat like hiding in a Norman Rockwell painting. It was an oasis of traditional American values amid the turbulence that shook America in the 1960s. "I came from a very white-bread Christian community," he has said.

His parents were conservative Southern Baptists; his mother was a high-school counselor, and his father managed a small trucking company. But that didn't mean they were rednecks or in any way stereotypical Southerners. Frank Carver, who lived in Springfield until his retirement, knew the Pitt family well. "There was a lot of racism, a lot of backwards thinking in those days," he recalled. "You're talking about the South just before the civil-rights movement took hold—although some people will tell you it's the Midwest—and there were a lot of ignorant attitudes. But you could say that Brad's parents were a little more sophisticated than some. They were Baptists, but to them that meant having a traditional outlook, not some fire-and-brimstone way of looking at the world. They were probably Harry Truman Democrats. Truman was from Missouri and left his mark there. So they would have supported civil rights but probably disapproved of the radical stuff. They were God-fearing and church-going, but they weren't exactly fundamentalists in today's sense of the term. They were this tight knit, solid, middle-class American family."

"Brad looks like his father, and he has the personality of his mother," recalled Chris Schudy, one of Pitt's early friends. "His mother is so down-to-earth, just a super woman. His dad is a great guy but more reserved. *A River Runs Through It* [the 1992 Oscar-winning film Pitt starred in] is almost a mirror image of Brad's family."

The family included two younger children, Doug and Julie, and all the siblings had a close bond growing up. "I always looked up to both of my brothers," Julie later recalled. "I just thought they were the greatest things that ever happened. Doug and Brad really play off each other. We just had such a close family, and that gave us confidence. I think that's what allowed Brad to try to be an actor. Sometimes I can't believe that this guy from Springfield made it, but Brad has always succeeded in what he's done, and he's always had a way with people." "The first time my mom met him, she called him a little Roman god," echoed Schudy.

Pitt's brother Doug, who still lives not far from where they grew up in Springfield, is quick to avoid placing Brad on that kind of pedestal. "He's a regular Joe," he said, noting that his brother always had an independent streak growing up. "If the rush was for everyone to go out and buy Harleys, Brad wouldn't buy one."

Pitt still refers to his parents as "the biggest guides in my life." Like his future partner, he has always credited his mother—the first person to ever think he was talented—for his later success. "She just thought it from day one," he said. His mother would drag the children to the South Haven Baptist Church every Sunday, where Brad often felt stifled by the piety. In retrospect, he appreciates the weekly routine. "It kept my mind on bigger things," he later explained, recalling that he often felt like he wanted to let out a whoop or a fart in church and then "stand up and yell, 'It was me! Right here!' The preacher would pick someone to read the final prayer, and I would go into a sweat, afraid he would pick me. I would sit there and say, 'Please, God, not me.' That was my final prayer."

For a time, he was even a choirboy, singing Baptist hymns every week. "You couldn't keep from watching Brad because his face was so expressive," said Connie Bilyeu, the piano accompanist at the church, who was later his high-school drama coach. "He would move his little mouth so big with all the words that he attracted everyone's attention."

But his first foray into show business may not have entirely met with the approval of his Christian mother. According to his Springfield friend Pam Senter, who has known Pitt since he was five, his first troupe was somewhat unconventional. "Brad and I went on church trips together, and he was always fun to be with—constantly entertaining," she told his biographer, Brian Robb. "He and his friends sang at assembly. They called themselves the Brief Boys. It was ridiculous. They wore their underwear and sang Beach Boys songs with made-up lyrics. I think it was Brad's idea—he showed off his body anytime he could. He never talked about wanting to be an actor, but now that I look back on it, he was an entertainer all along."

Pitt attended Springfield's Kickapoo High School in the mid-1970s. At the time, only four out of the 1,800 students were black. Since that time, the school—whose team slogan is "Fear the Poo!"—

has become much more diverse and now includes a sizable number of Asian students as well.

Unlike Jolie, whose own high-school years marked a dark and unhappy period, Pitt appears to have thrived. "Brad was a super kid," assistant principal Sandra Grey Wagner told *People* magazine in 1995. "He was into everything," said Kate Chell, who attended Kickapoo at the same time as Pitt. "I guess Big Man On Campus usually refers to college, but if there was a high-school equivalent, that was Brad. He organized the dances, he did school plays, he sang, he did sports. People loved him. He wasn't stuck up on himself; he just had this leadership aura where people were drawn to him. You could tell he was going to do something big, but I don't think people thought he would be some big Hollywood star. The girls all had a big crush on him. I know I did. He had a steady girlfriend for a while, but I think he had a lot of girls. He liked blondes."

Unlike Jolie, it was clear from an early age that Pitt was decidedly heterosexual. Indeed, Pitt once recalled his teenage reputation in an interview. "Loved girls, was always completely intrigued, taken over, would do anything for 'em," he said. Chell, who remembers girls fighting over Pitt, called him the "cock of the walk." Pitt admitted he got into occasional brawls: "I had the usual sort of fights over girls. From memory, I won one—probably because I took a cheap shot like grabbing the guy's nuts, or something—and lost one. The only serious damage was to my ego."

Pitt has always tended to be discreet about his sex life and has never revealed how old he was when he lost his virginity, although he did share with *Premiere* magazine the details of the first time he saw a naked woman. "Somewhere in early elementary school," he says, "we found a house that was being built, and we found a stack of old *Playboys* at the site. Well, I was very impressed. I was just so overwhelmed."

It wasn't long after that when he got the birds-and-the-bees lecture. "Two little kids up the street kept using the word 'fuck,' " he recalled, "and I asked my mom what it was, and that's how we got into that whole sex talk. She told me, 'We don't use this word; this word is slang. But we do use the phrase "sexual intercourse," and here it is.' With the diagrams. I remember vividly, at that time, being horrified."

By seventh grade, he says he was hosting make-out parties in his basement, fitted out in true seventies style with a number of comfortable beanbag chairs. "The girls usually overdid it with flavored lip gloss," he said. "But we didn't know it at the time. We thought it was fine. My mom always made a lot of noise before opening the door to the basement. She'd call down, 'Brad? Can I come down and get something out of the freezer?' Of course, you had to wonder why Mom needed a frozen steak at ten o'clock at night."

Pam Senter also recalled girls falling all over the young Pitt. "There were plenty of them," she remembered. "He had a real charm and a way with women. I made sure not to fall in love with Brad—I knew he'd break my heart. That's just the way he is; he can't help himself."

His friends recalled that he loved going to films, especially the classics. But it was *Saturday Night Fever* that had the most lasting impact. "Not the dancing or the clothes," he later explained, "but seeing these other cultures and these guys with their accents and the way they handled themselves and talked. It blew my mind, and it got me on this quest for travel and other cultures."

As much fun as he was having in high school, Pitt was itching to get out and see the world. After he graduated from high school, he enrolled at the University of Missouri at Columbia, a three-hour drive from Springfield. "It was incredible just to get away from home," he recalled, "living with a bunch of guys. That school kind of revolves around a keg. We had this idea of *Animal House,* and there was definitely that aspect. It was a highlight, without a doubt. Then, like everything, you grow out of it."

At the University of Missouri, he was no less popular with the girls. "In our first year of college we put on a charity strip show," Pitt's friend Greg Pontius told Brian Robb. "Hundreds of girls paid to watch Brad— he was the hottest guy in the county. We didn't strip completely naked, but the girls got their money's worth."

Majoring in journalism, Pitt began to acquire a wider world view and started questioning everything, especially his parents' deep-seated religious beliefs. "I remember one of the most pivotal moments I've had was when I finally couldn't buy the religion I grew up with. That was a big deal. It was a relief, in a way, that I didn't have to believe that anymore, but then I felt alone. It was this thing I was dependent on," recalled Pitt, who today describes himself as "twenty percent atheist and eighty percent agnostic."

Despite his major, Pitt was determined to go into advertising or marketing until, in his senior year, he suddenly realized that he wasn't cut out for a nine-to-five job for the rest of his life. In the spring of 1986, just two credits short of graduation, he decided to chuck it all and head to California. Lying to his family that he was going to attend art school, he had instead decided to try his luck as an actor. With $325 in his pocket, he drove his beat-up old Datsun, which he had nicknamed "Runaround Sue," to L.A. without much of a plan or even much of an acting résumé.

"I always knew I'd leave Missouri," he later said. "But it's like that Tom Waits song: 'I never saw the morning until I stayed up all night/I never saw my hometown until I stayed away too long.' *I love* my hometown. I just wanted to see more. You'd come across a book or something on TV, and you'd see all these other worlds. It blew me away."

"He hadn't done a whole hell of a lot of acting," recalled his old friend Chell. "I don't think he ever had the lead in a school play even, but if you saw the way people reacted to him, you'd know why he would think he was going to make it. He was a pretty boy and he knew it. If he didn't make it as an actor, he would have made money as a model, he was that good looking. That goes a long way in this world."

His first professional job when he got to L.A. was promoting a Mexican food chain called El Pollo Loco, which paid him a whopping $9.00 an hour to dance around in front of the restaurant on Sunset and Labrea dressed as a giant chicken. "That's a lot of money when you're used to making $3.50 for bus-boy jobs," he said. He shrugged off the daily insults and jibes from rowdy customers: "I didn't care. They weren't yelling at me; they were yelling at the damn chicken."

Dressing as a chicken was only slightly less demeaning than his next job, driving strippers to their appointments for a strip-o-gram company. "That was a good job. There were some interesting rides home," he recalled, describing the nightly routine. "I'd drive them there in my car. We'd have a private room. They'd come out, and I'd introduce them and play the music. Most of them wanted Prince, whatever the 'fuck me' songs were, and they'd take their clothes off and throw them my way, and I'd catch them so guys wouldn't steal them."

After going to hundreds of auditions, he started to land some jobs as an extra, including standing in a doorway in *Less than Zero* and playing an airport cop in the Kevin Costner thriller *No Way Out*. And then, at twenty-four, he finally landed his first speaking parts, including an episode of the soap opera *Another World* and a four-episode stint on *Dallas*. He was on screen "probably for a total of four minutes," he recalled of his *Dallas* role. "I was some reject boyfriend. An idiot."

His on-air girlfriend in those episodes, Shalane McCall, soon became his first Hollywood romance, even though their fling only lasted six weeks. His manager, Phil Lobel, later claimed that this was the beginning of a long pattern. "He fell in love very easily," Lobel told *People* magazine, recalling that he would often loan Pitt money to help finance some of the lavish gifts Pitt liked to bestow on his many girlfriends. "I've never seen Brad try and get a girl to go home with him. They come to him," a friend told the magazine. "He's actually kind of shy."

Following his *Dallas* stint, Pitt spent four years kicking around Hollywood making guest appearances on various TV shows and taking bit parts in movies. He later described this work as "butt-awful." Still, he was beginning to attract some attention. "Brad walking into a room was more exciting than most actors doing a scene," said producer Patrick Hasburgh, who cast him in an episode of *21 Jump Street* in 1988. Two years later, Pitt landed his own series on Fox, *Glory Days*, a *90210*-style drama that was cancelled only six episodes into its run. "It was terrible," he said of the short-lived series. "Man, I'd rather do nothin'."

The role that finally put him on the map for good almost went to Alec Baldwin's younger brother, William, who was Ridley Scott's first choice to play the charismatic drifter, J. D., in his new road movie, *Thelma and Louise.* But when Baldwin opted to appear in Ron Howard's *Backdraft* instead, Pitt got the call. His role was a small one, but critics later said he nearly stole the film. He plays a hitchhiker who steals Louise's few thousand dollars in life savings after he charms Thelma into bed and gives her the first sexual satisfaction of her life. Pitt would later describe that career-making scene as the "$6,000 orgasm." A crew member on the film later related to *People* magazine Pitt's "skittishness" about filming the sex scene with Geena Davis, who played Thelma: "He was absolutely charming, very shy, and nervous. His biggest concern was that his mother wouldn't approve."

Today, Pitt speaks eloquently before congressional committees and international delegations with seemingly little effort, but in those days, it seemed that the only two words in his vocabulary were "cool" and "boring." Asked by one publication what he thought about working with Ridley Scott, who also directed *Alien*, Pitt responded, "What do you think? It's pretty cool. Ridley was really cool. I was really impressed . . . You know, we talked in big detail about the scenes, which is really cool.

What is really cool is to be part of something where all the elements come together."

As Jolie would be nine years later, after her role in *Girl, Interrupted*, Pitt was repeatedly compared to James Dean after *Thelma and Louise*. "That James Dean stuff is pretty boring," he scoffed. "He bores me and what he has become bores me and young actors trying to be like him bore me. It goes way beyond this film. It's a personal thing, I guess." Like it or not, though, the James Dean comparisons signaled that he had already been anointed the next big thing.

IN A DARK PLACE

To hear Jolie's version today, her first attempts to make it as a teenage model failed miserably because she was too short, too thin, too fat, and too scarred. But again, the facts tell a different story.

In 1991, Sean McCall was an up-and-coming fashion photographer when he got an assignment to photograph a high-end swimsuit line for La Perla. He needed a new model for their latest high-profile national campaign. Ordinarily, the company opted for a supermodel or a recognizable face, but this time they wanted something different. "La Perla didn't want the stardom of the gal to overshadow the line itself," McCall remembers. "So they were looking for a brand-new face."

McCall's makeup artist had just worked with a teenage girl whose agency had sent her in to shoot her first theatrical head shots, compulsory for an aspiring actor looking to break into show business. "She told me that she had just seen this girl who was perfect for what I was doing," he explains. "She knew I was looking for somebody a little enticing and different. She told me the girl happened to be the daughter of the actor Jon Voight, which didn't impress me that much, but I decided to give her a look. I contacted her through her mother and arranged for her to come in and test."

The next day, a sixteen-year-old Angelina Voight came to McCall's condo in Santa Monica, and he knew instantly that he had found his face. "I immediately thought that she had one of the most unique looks that I ever saw," he recalls. "I didn't even have to test her. I wanted to do a full-blown editorial shoot."

Many assume that Jolie's distinctive look results from cosmetic procedures. Innumerable articles must have been written speculating whether she has had collagen injections to give her those trademark full, sensuous lips, for instance. Yet if one examines the photos that McCall took that day, it is instantly obvious that Jolie's look has changed very little since the age of sixteen. If she is known today as the sexiest woman in the world, she didn't earn the title through artificial means. "I'm a professional; I know when people have had work done, when they've altered their looks," says McCall. "Believe me, the Angelina I saw then is the same Angelina the world knows today. I've heard that she had her nose thinned since then, but very little else has changed."

What struck him most that day, he recalls, is how much they had in common. "She was very nice and obviously highly intelligent," he says. "I think we struck up a conversation about fencing. I had just come from a fencing lesson, and when she heard that, she started talking about swords. She told me she collected knives and swords. I also had all kinds of them, some dating back to the Civil War. She asked me where she could get a sword rack. Then it turns out we knew somebody in common, Jean-Pierre Hallet."

Hallet was a legendary figure who had devoted his life to saving the pygmy tribe in the Ituri region of Zaire from physical and cultural extinction. As an anthropologist, he had lived among the pygmies and even introduced a new plant for them to cultivate, helping to save them from starvation after deforestation wiped out most of their traditional food sources. He strongly believed the pygmies to be the most ancient people on earth, likely the ancestors of all humanity, and that they had originated many of the ethical and religious concepts that were later adopted by much of the rest of the world. By 1991, Hallet ran one of the world's largest shops specializing in Central African artifacts, located on the Third Street Promenade in Santa Monica. Angelina bought a Masai sword from him there, and they struck up a friendship. She was fascinated with his stories about the African people. "I'm fairly certain that her affinity with Africa, which is well known today, dates back from her association with Jean-Pierre Hallet. I also knew him well from buying swords from him," says McCall.

In the end, the photographer never used Angelina for his La Perla shoot because her agent called up and said Angelina wanted to focus on her film career instead. "I was very disappointed," he recalls. "I thought she would have been big. But as it turns out, the girl I chose instead, Caprice Bourret, went on to a huge modeling career and even became the first Wonderbra model . . . Maybe Angelina's people were smart to pull her out. The world would have known her face but would have been deprived of her acting talent."

This seems to have marked a turning point. Although the La Perla shoot would have been her first national campaign, Angelina had modeled successfully since the age of thirteen and had even traveled to London and France for numerous assignments when she was younger, represented by her mother's best friend, the model agent Jade Dixon (now known as Jade Clark-Dixon). "Angie was an angel, as was her mother," Dixon says. "She was my first client and she was very poised, very pretty even then. I eventually steered her to acting when I saw her giant talent. It was obvious from an early age."

Thus encouraged, at sixteen, with her obsession with death, her need to cut herself, and her first sexual experiences all behind her, Angelina now set her sights on an acting career. Although Jolie now attributes her decision more to her mother's influence rather than her father's, Jon Voight in fact played a major part in encouraging her interest.

"Looking back, there was evidence at an early age that she would be an actor," recalls Jon Voight. "She would take anything and make an event out of it. She was always very busy and creative and dramatic." When she had play dates with her ten-year-old friends, her father went so far as to set up scenes for them. "I wanted to show the kids things about acting," he explains. "I'd say, 'I'm going to give you the lines; how are you going to say them?'"

For her part, Angelina explains that her earliest acting ambitions dated back to when she was a young child. "I remember Jamie pointing the home-video camera at me and saying 'Come on, Angie, give us a show!' Neither [Dad] nor Mom ever said, 'Be quiet! Stop talking.' I remember [Dad] looking me in the eye and asking, 'What are you thinking? What are your feelings?' I don't know exactly what I wanted then, but I knew I could know. I loved some kind of expression. I wanted so much to try to explain things to somebody. I'm very good at trying to explore different emotions and listening to people and feeling things. That is an actor, I think. So that's what I had to do."

After Angelina emerged from her obsession with death, her father helped her build on the skills that she had picked up at the Strasberg Institute years before. He gave her weekly acting lessons at the home he rented in the San Fernando Valley where they read or acted out a different play every Sunday.

Voight later described being "moved to tears" when she read from the Arthur Miller play that had given him his first big break three decades earlier. "It was in stages, different stages. There was a point where we read *A View from the Bridge*, which I did as well as anything I've ever done in my life. There's a scene where this Italian boy comes in and meets this young girl Catherine, and they fall in love. I've played with many Catherines. One Sunday Angie read it, and the first time she read Catherine, it was a performance. She was studying acting and sixteen, and it was, I'm telling you, as good as anybody had ever played the part. The accent, the emotion was there, and absolutely perfect. I was overwhelmed. It was very touching to me. That was the first time I knew.

"The next week, I had a friend of mine, Tom Bauer, a wonderful actor, come over and we read it again. And same thing, a great performance. Tom's going, 'This is great!' Tom was running the Met Theater in Los

Angeles. So she went down with Tom and auditioned for Saturday workshops, which were monitored by Ed Harris, Holly Hunter, and Amy Madigan, who are [now] like godfather and godmothers to her. And one day, Tom came back from class and said, 'Jon, she's really special.' "

Bertrand encouraged her daughter to re-enroll at the Strasberg Institute to hone her talent. For her first production there, the comedy *Room Service*, she made an unusual choice of roles. "I thought, which character do I want to audition for?" Angelina explains. "The big, fat, forty-year-old German man, that's the part for me." She put her own take on the character, however, turning the part of an overbearing hotel manager into "Frau Wagner," a German dominatrix.

Voight later recalled the surprise of seeing his daughter in the production. "I was a little shocked seeing her walk around as Frau Wagner. But the shock came from the realization that, 'Oh my God, she's just like me.' She'll take these crazy parts and be thrilled that she can make people chuckle or whatever."

Meanwhile, her brother Jamie had enrolled at University of Southern California's School of Cinema-Television (renamed the School of Cinematic Arts in 2006) and was living with his father at his house in the Valley. During this period, he made five short films, all starring his sister and all financed by his father, who at the time was still very close to his son. One of them even earned a George Lucas Award, whose winners were personally selected by the *Star Wars* director, one of the school's most prominent alumni and generous benefactors.

Around this time, Angelina decided to drop the name Voight and started billing herself by her middle name, Jolie. As she later explained, "I love my father, but I'm not him." Despite this, and despite Bertrand's subsequent claim that at most auditions nobody knew her daughter's bloodlines, many of her early casting directors have acknowledged that she was introduced to them as the daughter of Jon Voight, a fact that couldn't help but open doors in Hollywood.

Still, it was slow going at first. Her first break, if it can be called that, came when director Michael Schroeder offered the seventeen-year-old Angelina a screen test and then a lead role in his science-fiction film *Cyborg 2: Glass Shadow.* This was the sequel to Albert Pyun's 1989 hit, *Cyborg,* which launched Jean-Claude van Damme to fame. Neither Pyun nor Van Damme signed on to the sequel, however, which perhaps destined it to failure from the start.

The script for *Cyborg 2* had the world divided between two giant computer companies, Pinwheel Robotics in America and Kobayashi in Japan, both of which engage in violent corporate espionage. Angelina plays the part of Casella "Cash" Reese, an android who has been injected with an explosive liquid that can be detonated by remote control. Her masters at Pinwheel Corporation plan to use her to destroy their rivals at Kobayashi and take over the world. Cash figures out what's happening when she is tipped off by her martial-arts instructor and a mysterious stranger, played by Jack Palance, who has invaded the Pinwheel computer network. Cash saves the day at the end, giving Jolie her first taste of being an action hero, and foreshadowing her success as Lara Croft years later.

Just before the film was released, Jon Voight was acting in a theatrical production of Chekhov's *The Seagull* in New York. He gave a TV interview in which he comes off as a proud papa, discussing both his children's foray into show business. "My son Jamie is nineteen, and my daughter Angelina is seventeen," he told CNN, "and Marche and I have done our very best to be the supportive parents that we have learned to be and labored to be. And now these two children are both going to be in my world, in the world of film and theater. Angie, my daughter Angelina, has just done a little film. She is so proud that I am on stage. Jamie has been writing. He doesn't show me everything. He has only shown me three little pieces, one about a five minute piece, then a half-an-hour piece, then a two-hour movie script. But he says to me quietly, 'you know, Dad, I've written eighty works.'"

When *Cyborg 2* was finally released in 1993, the critics were harsh, with one newspaper slamming it for "hammy acting and a mumbo-jumbo plot that prompts unintentional laughter." It went straight to video obscurity and emerged only after Jolie achieved fame, probably because she had a topless scene in it.

Hollywood has always banked on its ability to anticipate coming trends, especially because the average film takes years to make, from conception to release. When the idea for *Hackers* was first floated, many people still didn't own a computer and most had never even heard of the Internet. But by the time the script was finally commissioned, Nirvana had brought punk music into the mainstream, and computers were suddenly hot. What better way to combine these two trends than to produce a "cyberpunk thriller"? The concept must have looked good on paper because its producers had high hopes that the film would score big with critics and moviegoers as the first Internet-era blockbuster. They hired British director Iain Softley; he had won praise for his film *Backbeat*, which captured the Beatles' early years while avoiding the clichés that so often plague such efforts. The producers felt his brand of distinctive originality was just what *Hackers* needed.

The script, set in New York, depicted a subculture of edgy high-school hackers and their inadvertent involvement in a corporate extortion conspiracy. It follows a Seattle youth, Dade Murphy, who, as an eleven-year-old child tech prodigy, was convicted of crashing more than a thousand computer systems in one day and causing a massive drop in the Dow Jones Average. Upon his conviction he was banned from owning or operating computers until his eighteenth birthday. When he turns eighteen, Dade takes up hacking again, at first simply causing mischief, such as tapping into a local TV station and changing the program it was broadcasting to an episode of *The Outer Limits*. After he enrolls in a new high school, he meets a beautiful girl named Kate Libby, whose own hacking skills rival his. Most of the film centers on a hacking duel between Dade and Kate, which eventually turns into a complicated tale about international corporate espionage and potential worldwide environmental disaster. The role of Kate was pivotal, and Softley was aware that the success of the film required just the right actress, especially because it was a film likely to appeal to a young male demographic. The director cast his net far and wide, auditioning, among others, Hilary Swank, Liv Tyler, and Heather Graham. None of them seemed to fit the bill. Then he was told that the daughter of Jon Voight had arrived to audition.

When she walked in, he later recalled, Angelina had long hair and was wearing glasses, perhaps believing that a computer hacker should look like a nerd. What she didn't know was that Kate Libby's alias was "Acid Burn" and that the character was a punk-rock cyber-rebel, the embodiment of teenage defiance. "I explained that she would have tattoos and piercings, and we would have to cut her hair," he remembers. "Angelina said straight away that she would have her head shaved. That was what she was like—she threw herself into it completely."

She got the part. It was her "compelling quality" that the director recognized immediately. "That thing that makes you interested in them for who they are, apart from their acting," he says. "Johnny Depp has it, and Angelina has it, too. When you have a distinctive presence like hers, it will always be a very potent ingredient. People like Angelina tend to select themselves. She just had this inner self-confidence in a very understated way. She was focused, daring, bold, and brave."

Similarly, Softley chose for the role of Dade an unknown named Jonny Lee Miller, whose previous experience had been confined to bit roles in British detective shows and soap operas, including a stint in the gritty cockney soap, *Eastenders*. Miller, however, came from a long family tradition of British actors. His grandfather, Bernard Miller, was best known for playing the role of M in the early James Bond movies.

Although Angelina eventually got together with Miller, it was not love at first sight. She confided to a makeup artist named Kelly that she assumed the soft-spoken Miller was gay when she found out that he had been part of a musical-theater company in London; she assumed that virtually all males in musical theater were "into other men."

Yet Angelina has implied to the press that their romance actually blossomed on set. "We met while filming *Hackers*, and I always fall in love while I'm working on a film," she told the British newspaper *Daily Express*. "It's such an intense thing, being absorbed into the world of a movie. It's like discovering you have a fatal illness, with only a short time to live. So you live and love twice as deep. Then you slip back out of it like a snakeskin, and you are cold and alone."

"To tell the truth," the makeup artist Kelly now says, "they were not a couple when we were shooting *Hackers*, and Angelina seemed to assume he was gay all the way through. They spent a lot of time together, so who knew what went on in their trailer, but I'm fairly sure that they didn't hook up until much later on." Indeed, Miller confided that he "chased Angelina all over North America until she succumbed. It took a while—a good few thousand miles."

After *Hackers* wrapped, Angelina took a part in an independent film, a gritty, low-budget crime drama called *Without Evidence*. The plot was based on the true story of the 1989 murder of the head of Oregon's prison system, Michael Francke, who was alleged to have been the victim of a political conspiracy. Angelina played a low-life drug addict in a little-seen performance that nonetheless offered an early glimpse of her true acting talent. Although the film never got a distribution deal, those who saw it were astonished by her performance. *Variety* later described her acting as "heartbreakingly touching."

Playing the part of a young drug addict, however, may not have been much of a stretch for Angelina during that period. According to those who knew the nineteen-year-old, she was strung out much of the time.

"Ace," a drug dealer in Venice Beach, California, claims to have been Angelina's regular supplier whenever she was in town. "She'd call me up, and we'd meet on the Santa Monica pier, and I'd give her whatever she needed," he says. "I forget exactly what she bought, but she was into all kinds of shit in those days. Sometimes she'd call me, and she'd be incoherent. I didn't sell smack—too risky—so I don't know if she ever shot up."

Angelina later claimed that heroin was in fact one of her drugs of choice, though she never publicly revealed many of the details of her drug addiction. Last year, the British newspaper *The Sun* published images of Angelina from a video taken in a drug den sometime in the 1990s, in which a woman beside her is doing heroin. Jolie, looking disheveled and smoking a cigarette, announces to the camera, "I've done coke, heroin, ecstasy, LSD, everything. I hate heroin because I've been fascinated with it. I'm not immune, but I won't do it now, at all." Tabloids also reported that a man was shopping around another video, at a price of $70,000, which purported to show Angelina sniffing lines of heroin from a plate and sucking up smoke through a tube as the drug cooks on tinfoil.

When *Hackers* was finally released in September 1995, the reaction was decidedly mixed. Although distinguished as Angelina's major film debut, it is generally considered something of a box-office flop. It got many facts about computer culture wrong, which drew online attacks from nerds and technology buffs. The *Miami Herald* described the film as "flashy but unfulfilling" and elaborated, "In the end, *Hackers* fails as a thriller. It's hard to get excited watching people pound on keyboards, and despite Softley's creative efforts to visually represent activities that are by nature invisible, the movie never really grips you." The *San Francisco Chronicle* called it a "shamelessly lousy movie" while the *New York Daily News* complained that the movie "gets lost in cyberspace."

At the same time, however, some of America's most influential critics were impressed, especially by the performances of Miller and Jolie. "The movie is well directed, written, and acted, and while it is no doubt true that in real life no hacker could do what the characters in this movie do, it is no doubt equally true that what hackers can do would not make a very entertaining movie . . . Jolie, the daughter of Jon Voight, and Miller, a British newcomer, bring a particular quality to their performances that is convincing and engaging," wrote Roger Ebert of the *Chicago Sun Times*.

Janet Maslin, film critic for the *New York Times*, was drawn to Angelina's performance as Kate. "Kate (Angelina Jolie) stands out. That's because she scowls even more sourly than Dade and is that rare female hacker who sits intently at her keyboard in a see-through top. Despite her sullen posturing, which is all this role requires, Ms. Jolie has the sweetly cherubic looks of her father, Jon Voight."

Voight himself was certainly impressed by his daughter's performance, telling an interviewer, "I hope she becomes a major star so she can look after me in my dotage. Of all my accomplishments, I am most proud of being Angelina's father."

Hollywood was starting to take notice of a fresh, new talent.

JONNY and JENNY

The first hints of a serious relationship appeared while Jolie and Miller were promoting *Hackers* together in the U.K., in early 1996. Miller offered the cryptic clue to a British reporter that he was "involved with an American girl who lives in L.A." Then Jolie made an appearance with a small gold band on her wedding finger. Eventually, during an interview with *Empire* magazine that spring, Jolie slipped her betrothal into the conversation. "We got married two weeks ago," she announced, "and no, we didn't have a big white wedding. We had a small black wedding." The *Empire* reporter noted that the announcement was made as "casually as one might request an extra sugar in their coffee."

The two had eloped on the spur of the moment on March 28, with only Jolie's mother, Marcheline Bertrand, and Miller's best friend, the still-unknown Jude Law, present to act as witnesses at the small civil ceremony.

When Jolie gave the wedding details to the press, it was the first time most people had heard of her. She certainly left a strong first impression: Miller wore black leather, she revealed, while the bride sported black rubber pants and a white shirt with the groom's name written across the back in her own blood. Asked about this dramatic flourish, she answered: "It's your husband. You're about to marry him. You can sacrifice a little to make it really special. I consider it poetic. Some people write poetry, others give themselves a little cut." She herself drew the blood "very carefully," she explained to the *New York Times*, "with a clean surgical needle."

Miller was quick to reassure his fans that he hadn't gone half mad. "It wasn't as gruesome as it sounds," he explained. "I think they imagine some kind of Satanic ceremony. It wasn't like that." Angelina was equally nonchalant about it. "It was no more shocking than promising your life to someone," she later explained.

Because they eloped, Miller had not yet met Jolie's father and was nervous about their first encounter. "It was a pretty weird experience, saying, 'Hello, I'm your son-in-law,' to Jon Voight. But Jon's a nice man, and we all breathe the same air."

Although *Hackers* was quickly forgotten, Miller was beginning to attract worldwide acclaim for the film he completed shortly afterwards, *Trainspotting*, which was released prior to *Hackers* in Europe. *Trainspotting* follows a group of working-class Edinburgh heroin addicts through their adolescence. Miller was proclaimed a rising star for his role as "Sick Boy," a punk obsessed with Sean Connery.

Jolie would have to wait a while for this kind of pronouncement on her own work. She complained during the European junket for *Hackers*, almost a year after its American release, that people cared more about her father and husband than about her. "It was weird to immediately be married, and then you kind of lose your identity," she lamented. "You're suddenly somebody's wife. And you're like, 'Oh, I'm half of a couple now. I've lost me.' We went on some morning show, and they threw rice on us and gave us toasters. I was thinking, 'I need to get myself back.' "

Indeed, to observers it looked like she was already having second thoughts about the marriage by the time they returned from Europe and Miller moved into her small L.A. apartment. She started to ban the subject of her nuptials in interviews, almost foreshadowing an eventual breakup: "The way we both feel about life is to live in the moment and not think of the future. Even if we divorce, I would have been married to somebody I really loved and known what it was to be a wife for a few years. Marriage is no bigger deal than signing a piece of paper that commits you to someone forever."

For his part, Miller seemed a little more open to the possibility of a long-term commitment. "When you love somebody, you want to be with them," he said. "We are a couple who are into extremes, and the extreme is to get married. Having this eye-opening and honest relationship really opens doors within yourself."

It was soon apparent that apart from acting, what the young couple really had in common was a proclivity for wild sex. In an interview with *Allure* magazine, Jolie hints that her bedroom saw plenty of action. "The English, they might be repressed, but they're good in bed," she said with a twinkle. "I've always been at my most impulsive when Englishmen are around. They get to me. When I was fourteen, I visited London for the first time, and that's when I discovered my problem. Englishmen appear to be so reserved, but underneath they are expressive, perverse, and wild." There were also hints that Miller was all too willing to indulge Jolie's fetishes, ones that had arisen out of her bizarre exploits with her sixteen-year-old punk boyfriend.

She continued to add to her already massive collection of swords, battle-axes, and knives, and it was clear that they were not just for show. "You're young, you're crazy, you're in bed, and you've got knives. So shit happens," she told one interviewer who asked about the role her collection played in her sex life.

She was not shy about publicly discussing her penchant for S & M to more than one interviewer. "I have always felt really naughty," she told the *Scotland on Sunday* newspaper. "I got involved in an S & M lifestyle and there were some people a lot further down that road than me. I had to be careful, because I am an actress. If I dominated for a few weeks, one person might recognize me. It fascinates me, though. I always felt that if someone approached me to try something, then I would be the last person to walk away. I'd have a go."

She also revealed that, unlike a typical sadomasochist, she didn't have a preference when choosing between master and slave. "I used to think dominating was the thing to do," she explained. "But then I realized that the person who was dominating was really the slave, because they did all the hard work. They are exhausted, while the other person was lying there enjoying it. I thought, 'I'm not getting anything for me.' So I changed to thinking on the lines of being both master and slave."

It's hard to know exactly how kinky the sex got between them, but Miller later provided a hint. He claimed that he frequently sucked Jolie's blood, saying, "She digs that kind of thing."

Jolie has frequently credited Miller with getting her to curb her excessive drug use. During their marriage she talked publicly for the first time about the negative aspects of her long-time habit. "I have done just about every drug possible. Cocaine, heroin, ecstasy, LSD," she told a Scottish paper. "The worst effect, oddly enough, was from pot, which made me feel out of control, and I became silly and giggly. I liked LSD for a while, until I went to Disneyland [high] and started thinking about Mickey Mouse being a short, middle-aged man in a costume who hates his life. My brain went the other way and I started thinking: 'Look at these fake flowers, the kids are on leashes, the parents hate being here.' Those drugs can be dangerous. I know friends who are no longer happy or interesting, living for junk all the time and using people."

Shortly after *Hackers* had finished filming, Jolie landed a role in the low-budget comedy *Mojave Moon*. It is a road movie in which she plays Ellie, a girl looking for a ride out of the city and into the Mojave desert where her mother lives. An older man, played by Danny Aiello, gives her a lift, and from there a series of bizarre events unfolds. The film was released in early 1996 but was effectively dead on arrival; it appeared that Jolie had another flop under her belt. Nevertheless, critics again singled out her performance among the mediocrity. "Jolie, an actress whom the camera truly adores, reveals a comic flair and the kind of blatant sexuality that makes it entirely credible that Aiello's character would drop everything just for the chance of being with her," wrote the *Hollywood Reporter*.

Jolie was on the cusp of stardom, and her mother, who had long since given up her own career ambitions, was determined to do whatever was necessary to get her there, with a little help from her ex-husband. Claire Keynes was a close friend of Marcheline Bertrand's and recalls those days when the town was starting to buzz about Angelina Jolie:

> I think Angie had her own agent already, but Marche was acting as her manager. She was reading scripts, taking meetings and trying to sort of plot out her daughter's road to the top. She was still close to her ex, and she enlisted him in all the decisions, constantly asking for advice and asking him to call in favors. You have to remember that Jonny was like a god in Hollywood circles. He wasn't what you would call a superstar, because he did so few movies, and he could no longer carry a film, but he was revered, literally worshipped by the whole town. It's hard to describe. You can't really say he was in the same league as a Brando, that was a whole different stratosphere, but everybody respected him for his brilliance as an actor and, I think, for the fact that he never sold out. People were in awe of him—actors, producers, writers, journalists . . . He was also very well liked.
>
> Nobody knew more than Marche that Jon held the key to his daughter's ambitions. You had Angie changing her name and wanting to get out from her father's shadow, but then you had her mother, who got her father to make the phone calls that opened the doors for her. Jonny was all too happy to oblige. He doted on both the kids; he would have done anything to make them happy. If Angie wanted to be a movie star, he'd do everything he could to make it happen, though he always said she would have made it with or without his help. He thought she was a terrific actress, just a little rough around the edges.

Around this time, in fact, Jolie explained to a reporter why she was using the name Jolie instead of Voight, a change she would legally make in 2002. "I'm not my dad, and I think people might have expected me to be him. I might never have known if I was being treated a certain way because it was me or because as soon as they were introduced to me they connected me with my dad." Whether she used the name Jolie or Voight, her dad made sure people knew her family tree.

One of the scripts that had come across Bertrand's desk was for a film called *Foxfire*. She didn't know if it was right for her daughter so, as usual, she consulted with her ex-husband. He immediately gave it the green light. The script was based on a novel by Joyce Carol Oates, who happened to be one of his favorite authors. He made a few phone calls and got Jolie an audition, though it would be a mistake to say that it was her lineage that won her the role.

Foxfire executive producer Paige Simpson describes the progeny of Hollywood's famous parents as "members of the Lucky Sperm Club." At first she thought Jolie was just another of those. "She was introduced to me as Jon Voight's daughter," Simpson recalls. "But she comes in, and you can't not look at her."

Jolie seemed tailor-made for film's central character, Legs Sadovsky, a drifter who bonds with a group of high school girls and inspires them to assert themselves as women. The film, directed by first-timer Annette Haywood-Carter, updates the Oates novel from 1950s upstate New York to 1990s Oregon. Jolie plays Legs as a charismatic, butch, James Dean-esque character complete with motorcycle boots and black jacket. In fact the film was compared by more than one critic to *Rebel Without a Cause*, though mostly unfavorably.

In *Foxfire*, four high school girls who barely know one another are galvanized into a gang by the sudden arrival at school of the mysterious Legs. Her motto is "Don't take any shit," and she convinces the girls to confront a teacher who is sexually harassing them. In their confrontation with the teacher, one of the girls, Rita, slams him against a lab bench and tells him, "If you ever put your hands on me again, I'm gonna snip your little nuts off with my toenail clippers." The incident results in a three-week suspension for the girls. When they sneak back to school to retrieve an art portfolio, they accidentally start a raging fire. Later, in a memorable scene that received considerable attention, Legs and the other girls bare their breasts so Legs can give each of them a flame tattoo to commemorate their torching of the school.

More than one critic wondered whether the nudity of this scene was exploitative rather than feminist. As if to confirm such suspicions, the rest of the film devolves into a confusing denouement involving violence and car chases that effectively smother the feminist themes of the first half.

It seems clear throughout that Legs is a lesbian, and the director even shot a passionate kiss between her character and another, which got left on the editing room floor at the insistence of the studio. Yet, in publicity for the film, Jolie presents a different take, perhaps for box-office expediency. "I saw Legs as being androgynous, but sexual in a very animal sort of way: free, fascinating, intriguing and touchy," she explained about her role. "The connection isn't directly about sex. I could see her being around it or watching it, but she is very much by herself."

Whether or not there was a lesbian vibe on screen, there was clearly one on the set. Jolie, still only twenty, began an intense relationship with her twenty-seven-year-old Japanese American co-star, Jenny Shimizu. "I fell in love with her the first second I saw her. I wanted to kiss and touch her," Jolie revealed. "I noticed her sweater and the way her pants fit, and I thought, 'My God!' I was getting incredibly strong sexual feelings. I realized I was looking at her in a way I look at men. It never crossed my mind that one day I was going to experiment with a woman. I just happened to fall for a girl."

Shimizu was known better at the time as a model than as an actress, having walked the runways for Calvin Klein and Versace, among others. She told the *Sun* some of the details of their affair:

During breaks in filming *Foxfire*, I got to sit down with this person [Angelina] and spend two weeks with them, meeting them and talking with them before anything got sexual. I actually felt like I was caring about someone much more than just simply having sex. And I didn't feel there was a straight girl that I was just bedding and she was going to freak out the next morning. We had established such a nice relationship that I felt this girl would have me back, no matter what. I knew this person would be loyal and wonderful to me. Our relationship only got closer the minute that we had finished being together. I felt intense emotions, and I felt intense emotions from her. From that minute on we hung out together . . . After the second week of filming, we kissed. She is beautiful. Her mouth is amazing. I've never kissed anyone with a bigger mouth than Angelina. It's like two water beds—it's like this big, kind of warm, mushy, beautiful thing. She's a gorgeous woman.

According to Shimizu, the two continued to date long after filming ended. "We used to visit strip clubs and there was this tension," she adds as she describes their regular liaisons. She claims their relationship lasted for years.

Still, there was nothing unusual about homosexuality on a Hollywood set or a gay liaison between two actors. It is a tradition as old as Hollywood itself. Venerated actresses from Greta Garbo to Marlene Dietrich to Ethel Waters are all well known to have had lesbian lovers. Another equally old tradition, however, is the necessity to cover up such relationships for fear that public exposure would end a career. Jolie would later smash this tradition with surprising results, but for now, both actors kept their affair quiet.

When *Foxfire* finished shooting, it was clear to Jolie that it wasn't going to make her a movie star. She later admitted that she didn't think the film would even be released; she believed distributors would have trouble with its "demographic niche or message," which she thought might be perceived as being anti-male.

Foxfire was eventually released in August 1996. But fortune had it that the film opened two days after the cruder but more powerful *Girls Town*, which shared many of the same plot elements. The inevitable comparisons were deadly. "Where *Girls Town* captures the hysterical pitch and hyperkinetic rhythm of actual teenage conversation," wrote one reviewer, "the voices in *Foxfire* are generic teenage suburban, without accent or personal inflection. We are in Anywhere, U.S.A., which is really the same place as nowhere on earth." Another reviewer called *Foxfire* a "vacant teen exploitation flick" while the *Atlanta Journal-Constitution* suggested, "Probably the kindest thing to do with the new movie *Foxfire* would be to burn all existing prints, thereby saving everyone concerned further embarrassment."

Yet once again, Jolie's performance and unique look were notable to critics, and she was repeatedly singled out for praise. The *Hartford Courant* wrote, "Jolie, a sexy, androgynous cross between James Dean and Isabella Rossellini, makes a striking visual impression (her acting isn't too bad either) in *Foxfire*, a *Thelma and Louise/Rebel Without a Cause* for the adolescent female set." The *New York Times* described her as a "face that is beautiful enough to stop traffic." The *Los Angeles Times* thought the role of Legs was "pure hogwash" but acknowledged that Jolie "has the presence to overcome the stereotype." But it was the *Kansas City Star*'s review that proved most prophetic. "If *Foxfire* is remembered for anything, it will be as one of the earliest screen appearances of Angelina Jolie, the daughter of Oscar-winner Jon Voight, who has a face the camera loves and seems a likely candidate for full-fledged stardom."

Although TV is usually considered a step backward when pursuing a movie career, Marcheline Bertrand was intrigued by a script for a TNT Network television miniseries about the segregationist Alabama governor, George Wallace. Her interest was sparked because the movie was to be directed by the legendary and brilliant John Frankenheimer, who had made such iconic films as *The Birdman of Alcatraz* and *The Manchurian Candidate*. Jon Voight, too, was a huge fan of Frankenheimer's work and immediately signaled his approval. Soon, Jolie was cast as Wallace's second wife, Cornelia. She also accepted another better-than-average TV project, a CBS miniseries called *True Women*, which saw her playing a Texas pioneer alongside Annabeth Gish and Dana Delany.

By the time the *George Wallace* miniseries aired, in August, 1997, the failure of *Foxfire* had taken its toll on Jolie's psyche. "There was a time when I was really going to give up acting—right after *Foxfire*," she confides. "I was trying to find characters with a certain strength and things going on, but I was always disappointed. *Wallace* was the first thing I did where I felt their ideas were better than mine."

Finally, Jolie's talents were being showcased in worthy projects. Millions of viewers tuned in to watch her bring life to Cornelia Wallace, who stood by her husband after he was rendered paraplegic by an assassin's bullet during the 1972 presidential campaign but was ruthlessly discarded just a few years later. Unlike in her other vehicles, here Jolie was now surrounded by talent, fine writing, and a brilliant director. It wasn't as easy for her to stand out, especially beside the towering performance of Gary Sinise as the racist governor.

She nevertheless was noticed. The *New York Daily News* was the first newspaper to comment on her work in the miniseries: "Hardly recognizable as the punk computer geek in *Hackers*, Jolie (Jon Voight's daughter) presents a performance that should have casting directors clamoring to hire her for bigger and even more challenging roles."

The *Boston Globe* called her performance "uneven," but in general the reviews were glowing. Her performance as Cornelia Wallace earned her 1998 Emmy and Golden Globe nominations for best supporting actress, the latter chosen by the influential Hollywood Foreign Press Association. Interestingly, her father was also nominated for a Golden Globe that year for his role in John Grisham's thriller, *The Rainmaker*.

She lost out on the Emmy, but at the Golden Globe ceremony, up against her own *George Wallace* co-star Mare Winningham, who played Wallace's first wife, it was Jolie's name that was called out when the envelope was opened. With tears in her eyes, she went up to claim her first major award:

> Oh, God, I'd like to thank everybody involved with *George Wallace*. I was so privileged to be part of that film. Gary, you're just brilliant and so brave and so amazing. And John Frankenheimer, I wish you were here. I know you are feared by many. At first I was terrified of you, but I just can't say enough about you, and Clarence, and everybody involved, and TNT. Geyer Kosinski. Thank you. Emily, Hi. Thank you the Hollywood Foreign Press. And most of all, my family. Mom stop crying, stop screaming [laughter], it's OK. Jamie, my brother, my best friend, I couldn't do anything without you. I love you so much. Dad, where are you? [the camera showed Jon Voight in the audience] Hi. I love you. Thank you so much. Thank you.

With that, and to tremendous applause, she raised the trophy high in the air. It would not be her last.

JUST LIKE GIA?

Word gets around quickly in Hollywood. It is entirely possible that HBO producers knew about Jolie's affair with Jenny Shimizu in 1997 when they targeted her to play the title role in their television movie *Gia*, the tragic story of Gia Carangi, the lesbian supermodel. Carangi had died of AIDS in 1986 at the age of twenty-six, less than seven years after landing her first magazine cover.

Jolie, of course, had herself been a model for a time, so the choice of her to play Gia seemed apt. But the parallels between Carangi and Jolie didn't end with modeling and sexuality: both were heavily involved with drugs. Carangi's life and career were destroyed by her heroin habit after she became infected with AIDS from sharing needles with other addicts. The timeline of Jolie's addiction is murky, but the offer to play Gia came during her first marriage, to Jonny Lee Miller. She has credited him with helping her "see the light" about drugs, so it is likely that her own struggles with heroin were fresh in her mind at the time.

Later, Jolie would talk candidly of her own substance abuse. "I have done just about every drug possible," she revealed. "Cocaine, ecstasy, LSD, and, my favorite, heroin." She even confided, on another occasion, that heroin "meant a lot" to her.

Perhaps the role hit a little too close to home for her, since she at first rejected the offer out of hand. After reading the script's horrifying scenes of drug abuse and self-destructive behavior, written by *Bright Lights, Big City* author Jay McInerney, she decided she didn't want to do the part. "It was such a heavy story," she explained. "And it deals with so many issues. If done wrong, it could have been very bad and not said the right things; it could have been very exploitive. The script scared me—to confront all those things and do all those things, I didn't know if I could pull it off. I didn't know if I had the energy. I didn't know if I wanted to face all those things and go to all those dark places . . . I didn't think I could balance my life and my mind and my work. It happened that I became exposed at the same time that I was playing a role about somebody being exposed. I felt beaten down. I didn't feel like a good person. I felt pretty bad."

But the writer-director Michael Cristofer—author of the Pulitzer Prize-winning play *The Shadow Box*—wouldn't take no for an answer. There was only one actress he believed could pull off the role convincingly. After agreeing to meet with Cristofer, Jolie finally relented. "We went over the script for an afternoon, and he convinced me," she said. "I think everybody involved with this film was coming from a place that was very deep inside them. She was so human to us. We all loved aspects of her, and we all identified with certain things. It became very personal."

It wasn't long, however, before she started having second thoughts. To prepare for the role, Jolie read everything she could get her hands on about the model's tragic descent, including a diary Carangi kept while she was dying of AIDS. What Jolie read terrified her.

Gia Carangi is often called the first supermodel. Born in Philadelphia in 1960 to an Irish-Italian family, Gia's father Joe ran a restaurant and a chain of sandwich bars. His wife Kathleen stayed home and looked after the kids. It was to all appearances an average middle-class family. Behind closed doors, however, the marriage was extremely volatile and often violent. In 1971, when Gia was only eleven years old, Kathleen walked out on her husband and kids.

Her fractured childhood undoubtedly took its toll. Searching for a place to belong, Gia fell in with a group of young people who called themselves the "Bowie Kids," for their obsession with rock singer David Bowie and his over-the-top style. But it was not just the glam-rock image that appealed to Gia. Bowie became the first rock star to publicly acknowledge his bisexuality at roughly the same time that she was discovering her own sexual nature.

"Gia was the purest lesbian I ever met," a friend of hers from that period told Carangi's biographer, Stephen Fried. "It was the clearest thing about her. She was sending girls flowers when she was thirteen, and they'd fall for her whether they were gay or not." Her sensuous androgynous style eventually captured the attention of a local photographer, Maurice Tannenbaum, who sent photographs of her to the New York agency, Wilhelmina Models. Despite her height of five feet seven inches, which was shorter than the requirement, Wilhelmina offered Gia a contract. At seventeen, Gia moved to New York, where her exotic look catapulted her almost overnight into the top echelons of modeling. By the age of nineteen, she had appeared on the covers of British and French *Vogue*, and U.S. *Vogue,* as well as twice on *Cosmopolitan.*

She was also a regular at Studio 54, where cocaine and hedonism reigned. In an interview with the ABC newsmagazine *20/20*, Gia admitted her rise had happened awfully fast. "I started working with well-known people in the industry, very quickly," she said. "I didn't build into a model. I just sort of became one."

She was soon notorious for hitting on other models, whether or not they were gay, as well as makeup girls, and even celebrities like Liza Minelli. "She was like a cat constantly on the prowl for other female cats," one of her conquests later recalled. "She was always that way," said Jolie after reading her diaries. "When she was about thirteen, her mother found letters she had written to girls in school." She was also known to hook up with men on occasion.

Carangi later blamed her drug abuse on the 1980 death of her agent, Wilhelmina Cooper, who had become like a mother to her. Carangi became increasingly known for her tempestuous photo shoots, where she had frequent tantrums and even occasionally passed out in front of the camera. It was clear that there was something terribly wrong. Her career disintegrated as track marks marred her arms and her reputation haunted her. She spent some time in rehab to kick her habit, only to be diagnosed with AIDS at a time when the disease was a death sentence.

Modeling agent Bill Weinberg remembers Carangi as "[a] real mess . . . [a] trashy little street kid . . . If she didn't feel like doing a booking, she didn't show up." A close look at her *Vogue* cover shoot in November 1980 reveals a number of track marks on her arms, which were still visible even after airbrushing. She was a regular at the heroin dens of the Lower East Side, where her addiction escalated to the point of catastrophe.

With her career on the rocks and nobody wanting to hire her, Carangi entered rehab and stayed clean for months. In rehab, she confided in therapy that she had occasionally prostituted herself for drug money and had once been raped by a dealer. Just when it looked like she had turned a corner, her close friend, fashion photographer Chris von Wangenheim, died in a car accident, and she began using heavily again.

By 1982, her career was virtually over. Nobody would hire her. In her last cover shoot for *Cosmopolitan*, Francesco Scavullo had her hide her arms behind her back to hide the track marks. And then she was diagnosed with AIDS, the first female celebrity to be struck by the disease. By then, she had given up drugs, but it was too late. In those days, a diagnosis of AIDS was a death sentence. Still, in her final years she came to peace, which makes her tale all the more tragic. "Even the terrible pains that have burned and scarred my soul [were] worth it for having been allowed to walk where I've walked," Carangi wrote shortly before she died in 1986.

At first, when Jolie began researching for the role, she couldn't make up her mind about the character she was going to play. She recounts,

"The first thing I saw of her was a *20/20* interview. I hated her because she was obviously really stoned and had this very affected speech and seemed very vacant. It was really hard to watch—just really sad. And then I saw footage of her talking and being herself—just this regular girl from Philly. And she's really out there and funny and bold, and I fell in love with her. That completely split personality; that was a big clue to figuring out what was going on. There were lots of articles and a lot of people had different stories to tell me. And there was her journal, her words. I really read every little thing I could find to figure out who she was.

"I think that, deep down, she was a good person with a good heart and a great sense of humor—a person who wanted to be loved, wanted more excitement, wanted more out of life. She behaved in a crazy way sometimes and really shocked people, but I think she was really just trying to reach out and communicate and connect.

"Like every single one us, she just needed desperately to be loved and understood and feel as if she had some purpose on this planet. She did lose herself, but when she found out she was dying of AIDS, she found herself again and she had time to write things down. That's more remarkable and interesting to me than the fact that she was a supermodel."

The movie was set to air in January 1998. It was evident from Jolie's comments on the press tour that playing Gia had had a profound effect on her. "The first time I saw the [finished film], I cried. I felt that I too had died. Then I saw the poster for the film, and that bothered me. It's my face and her name, but we're one and the same. I was a bit broken up by all of it."

She even hinted that she was looking at Carangi's story as a cautionary tale, frequently discussing the similarities between Gia's life and her own. "Playing her meant confronting a lot of things that I understand hurt me, so it was very difficult, but it was also this great kind of purging of all that was going on inside me," she said.

For the first time, she also talked candidly about her own drug use. "I never was involved to the extent that she, of course, was, but I certainly know the trap of it and that world," she told a group of critics. "I have this dangerous thing where I am brave, to the point where it is stupid. I will try something, and every drug could kill you. I have that fearlessness that could get me in a lot of trouble."

"She found herself," added Jolie. "She got back to her sense of humor, she forgave people, and she talked with the people she loved. She was seeing very clearly at the end of her life. There's something so beautiful about that, that she went through it all and did find herself in her last moment."

Jolie also frequently talked about the differences between the two. "I'm able to give all of myself, and I have an outlet for each side of me. Gia didn't. I have a very loving family that would accept me even if I did nothing."

It's true that her family was tremendously supportive and, at the time, still very close knit. But that didn't mean that Jolie's father approved of her sudden outspokenness. Voight was a Hollywood survivor, privy to the town's secrets and skeletons. It was only natural that he choked on his coffee when he read the interview his daughter gave to *TV Guide* while promoting *Gia*. Discussing the parallels between herself and the model, Jolie casually let slip that she had fallen "in love" with her co-star on the movie *Foxfire*. She was still a relative unknown, so the revelation wouldn't have the kind of impact it would for a major star, but it certainly wasn't the kind of admission that helps an actor reach the top. Voight was not amused.

"We've talked about it before, because I'm really outspoken, and I think he's worried about me," Jolie told *Esquire* magazine about her father's uneasiness. "Because I've talked about, you know, everything. And just being really outspoken about my marriage and, you know, being with women, and they will take it and turn it into different things.

So he's wanting me to kind of be quiet. A lot of people have wanted me to kind of be quiet. A lot of people wanted me to be quiet during *Gia*, to not say if I'd ever done any drugs, or had ever slept with a woman, which to me was being totally hypocritical. If I had, and if I could identify with the story that much more, and really saw a beautiful thing in another woman—so I thought it was nice to share what I had experienced, because I thought it was great—I didn't see why it was so bad. And especially because that's the movie. And because it's, I don't know, it's honest."

Her honesty was refreshing. But was it the best policy in Hollywood? Only time would tell.

JONNY LEAVES, JENNY STAYS

The culture of self-preservation in Hollywood dictates discretion, something gays in the town understand very well. There is perhaps no better way to illustrate the situation of homosexuals in Hollywood than to relate a conversation I had in 2007 while I was doing research for my book, *Hollywood Undercover*. At the time, I was focusing on closeted male actors and hadn't given a lot of thought to Angelina Jolie's bisexuality, even though by then she was the highest-profile actor to have ever come out of the celluloid closet. In hindsight this conversation has given me insight into many of the twists and turns in her Hollywood journey.

While posing undercover as a gay actor, I was invited to attend the weekly Hollywood Hills poker game of a group of gay Hollywood insiders who called themselves the "Queers of the Round Table." I was replacing a well-known former sitcom star—the only actor of the group— who couldn't be there that week because of a work commitment.

The first thing I told them is that I didn't believe that the actor I was replacing, a reputed womanizer, was really gay. "Queer as a three-dollar bill," came the reply from Lenny, the host, who worked as a location scout for TV and movies. "He's an actor. What do you expect?"

"What's that got to do with it?" I asked.

"All actors are gay," came the response. "Actually, that's not true, although a lot of people think they are. In reality, it's probably closer to seventy-five percent."

I found the statistic hard to believe.

"Well, let me ask you this," said Karl, a set designer. "What percentage of male hairdressers do you think are gay? And figure skaters, ballet dancers, interior decorators, flight attendants?"

"Don't forget librarians," Lenny added.

I thought about it and conceded that most of the men in those professions are probably gay, likely even more than seventy-five percent. But acting isn't the same thing, I told them.

"Honey, you are naive," said Christopher, a script editor. "Acting is one of those trades where it just helps to be flamboyant, not to mention sensitive. Gay men are just drawn to it. Tell you what, go to any drama school in this country and talk to the boys. You'd be hard-pressed to find a single straight male. And what's more, it's obvious right away. Just about every student is a swishing queen."

"Here's a good rule of thumb," said Karl. "Take the résumé of just about any movie star and look where they started out. If they took drama in college, the odds are they're queer. If they started in theater or did a stint on Broadway, especially musical theater: bingo, they're gay. And I'm not talking seventy-five percent, I'm talking ninety-five percent."

"Like who?" I asked somewhat skeptically, trying to think of a single movie star who seemed less than heterosexual.

This simple question released what felt like a verbal stampede, as all three of them started tossing out famous names, one after another, some of them A-list superstars. I'm not exaggerating if I say they went on for at least fifteen minutes.

Karl finally put a stop to it. "You know, this might go faster if we just listed the heterosexual stars." Then they started tossing out those names, and indeed the list was noticeably shorter. "Sylvester Stallone, Brad Pitt, Bruce Willis, Arnold Schwarzenegger, Mel Gibson, Hugh Grant, Colin Farrell." At the next name offered by Christopher, though, Lenny broke in.

"No, you can definitely cross him off the list. I know for a fact that he's fucking [a well-known Hollywood producer]."

I suspected they were abusing my naiveté—or perhaps their list was merely wishful thinking—so I finally interrupted the litany. "First of all, half the people you mentioned are married." This prompted shrieks of laughter from my new friends.

"He's a babe in the woods," said Karl.

The three of them then decided to give me a tutorial on the way things work for a gay actor in Hollywood. "Like we said," Christopher recapped, "drama schools are almost all populated by gays, at least the men. That much is easy to prove because at that point in an actor's career there's no reason for him to hide it. In fact, at that stage, it's almost an advantage to be gay because a straight guy is in the minority. And, by the way, that's why the sexuality of most stars is common knowledge. At some time they were openly hanging out in gay bars or cruising online, and their 'secret' is known by a large segment of the gay community wherever [they attended drama school]. By the time they head back into the closet after hitting it big in Hollywood, it's too late."

He then asked me to list the male Hollywood stars who were out of the closet. I could list them on one hand, with fingers to spare.

"Now, how is it possible that thousands of drama students— the overwhelming majority, in fact—and most Broadway actors are demonstrably gay, yet virtually every movie star is a raging heterosexual? The answer is, it's not."

Then they started with a history lesson. I expected they would begin with the obvious—Rock Hudson—but instead they cited the example of James Dean, the ultimate male Hollywood sex symbol of the 1950s, who I didn't even know was gay. "Not only was he gay," explained Lenny, but his sexuality, which he supposedly didn't even bother to hide, was causing shit-fits at the studio. They'd had plenty of experience handling gay actors before, but here they had this incredibly bankable star, worth millions, and he was cavorting around town with every fag you could think of, including another one of their biggest stars, Montgomery Clift. They were terrified the news would get out and his box-office potential would go down the crapper. So they pretty well forced him to start dating starlets, while their publicity department went to work portraying Dean as a great cocksman."

"The stakes were huge," he continued, "and there was enormous pressure from the studio for Dean to get married. Their preference was Natalie Wood, who was perfectly willing to act as Dean's beard [a companion of the opposite sex specifically chosen to distract from one's true sexual orientation], but both Wood and Dean were apparently reluctant to go along with the nuptials."

Here I interjected. Did they really think America was so homophobic that people would stop going to his movies just because they thought he was gay?

"Well at that time, yes, definitely. But that wasn't the real point with Dean," Lenny replied. "The fact is that part of his huge box-office appeal was that American girls were so in love with him that they would go to his pictures over and over again. Ironically, gay men did the same thing, but that's just an interesting side fact."

Lenny then named a superstar actor of today and drew a parallel to Dean. "Look at [one of the top box-office stars in the world]. At the beginning of his career, he had a lot of quirky roles and was never really seen as a leading man, so he didn't really bother trying to hide his gayness very much. But all of a sudden he starred in [a hugely popular film], and almost overnight he became a sex-symbol superstar. The studio surveys showed that fourteen- and fifteen-year-old girls were going to the movie over and over again, some as many as twenty or thirty times. And why? Because they liked to fantasize that they were his leading lady and that he was seducing them. If they knew he was gay in real life that was all threatened. So, the next thing you know, he's dating supermodels and going to strip joints, while his publicist makes sure the news is plastered in every newspaper in the world. Funny, though, you never heard of him having a girlfriend during the first ten years of his career."

Christopher explained that it is not necessarily homophobia per se that keeps actors closeted today, but rather this phenomenon of both men and women attending movies to fantasize about bedding the star—in short, economics. "Look what happened to Anne Heche after she came out as Ellen Degeneres's girlfriend. She had already been signed to star opposite Harrison Ford as his love interest in *Six Days, Seven Nights*. When the film came out, it completely tanked. Not because it was terrible, but because men could no longer go to her movies and picture themselves boffing her. And not long after that, look what happened. Heche broke up with Ellen and, surprise, she's straight again."

Lenny interrupted him. "Well, it's not entirely true that homophobia has nothing to do with it. Look at all the black fags who don't dare come out because the American black community is so homophobic." He names a black comedian with a penchant for transvestites. "He's not really a sex symbol; he's a comedian. So technically he could come out, but if he does, he can say goodbye to his black fan base forever. Kaput!"

At this stage, I pointed out that the star was married. I could understand why he got married; he needed a beard. But what's in it for the woman? I asked.

"Ah, that's the sixty-four-thousand-dollar question," answered Lenny. "We spend a lot of time debating that very point, and nobody can agree on the answer. In some cases, we know for sure that the women do it for career reasons. They are basically promised that if they marry a particular superstar actor, they are guaranteed that their own acting career will take off and they will be offered juicy roles because their new husband has so much clout with the studios. That much makes sense. What we don't know is how many of these women are actually lesbians."

Lenny explained that while the overwhelming majority of male actors are gay, the same is not true for females. Hollywood is not like the women's golf or tennis tour, he joked. "If seven to ten percent of women in regular society are dykes," he said, "then that's probably the percentage in Hollywood as well. Now we all know for sure who some of the famous dykes are." He named a multiple Academy Award winner who was living openly with her long-time girlfriend (they have since split up), though she has never officially acknowledged her sexuality.

"And then there's Rosie O'Donnell—a perfect example. When she started out, she was as far from a leading lady as you can get. She made absolutely no attempt to hide her sexuality. When she was starring in *Grease* on Broadway, she began a long-time relationship with one of her female co-stars. Then she's hired to front a popular day-time talk show, watched by a lot of conservative Midwest housewives who wouldn't be very keen on watching a dyke host. Suddenly, she starts talking about the crushes she has on various male actors. She constantly refers to one in particular as her "boyfriend." Then, when her lesbian friends call her on this, she tells them she's obviously joking, especially because the star in question is widely rumored to be gay. So the whole thing is an elaborate inside joke. Then within days of the show coming to an end, Rosie finally announces that she is a lesbian."

Then there were the countless women who date or marry gay actors. "The most famous Hollywood beard today," said Lenny, "is [a well-known, Oscar-nominated actress], who has been reported to be dating a number of different A-list actors over the years. Everybody in Hollywood knows she's a dyke. You can be sure that if you see an item in the gossip columns reporting that she's dating some actor, then that actor is a fag." He shot off the names of three famous actors, each of whom has been reported to be a notorious womanizer. Sure enough, all three of them had "dated" the actress in question within the previous few years.

"But what's in it for her?" I asked.

"That's easy," said Lenny. "Just as the gay rumors get dispelled whenever these actors are reported to be dating a beautiful woman—or more often when they are photographed with her in public—she gets to look like a breeder whenever it's reported that she is dating this or that handsome actor. Meanwhile, she has been dating [another well-known Hollywood actress] for years with the public none the wiser. So, it's basically a win-win situation for a lesbian actress to date or marry a gay actor. But then there's another subject we can never agree on—bisexuality."

"There's no such thing!" yelled Karl.

"Oh, shut up," Lenny replied. He explained that nobody really knew how many of these gay actors were simply dating and marrying beards, and how many of them were actually bisexual. This debate, he said, had been raging since the beginning of Hollywood.

He cites the example of Cary Grant, one of Hollywood's greatest sex symbols. Grant, he says, was reportedly in love with the movie star Randolph Scott. "Literally everybody in Hollywood knew it. They would sit there in the Brown Derby till all hours, staring longingly into each other's eyes and holding hands. They even shared a beach house together. Yet Grant was married five times. His wives had to have known about him and Scott, not to mention his lovers over the years. One book claimed that he even had an affair with Marlon Brando, another rumored bisexual. So why would anybody marry him in the first place? Were they lured by the promise of the fabulous glamorous Hollywood lifestyle and the money, or by the potential impact on their own acting careers? After all, three of his wives were struggling actresses."

I actually remembered an incident in the early 1980s when Chevy Chase was being interviewed by Tom Snyder and he said of Grant, "I understand he's a homo." Grant sued him for slander and won, although details of his affairs came out after his death. It raised the question, how does anybody prove anybody's actually gay, short of catching them in bed with a man?

Karl mentioned one of the world's most famous sitcom stars who is gay and married. "They live in this huge mansion, but according to people who have been there, he and his wife occupy half the mansion each, and they never have anything to do with each other. Very convenient, but again, why did she marry him? I hear that the way these things work is the woman agrees to put in a certain amount of time before filing a divorce. In exchange, she is guaranteed a platinum credit card for the whole marriage and a generous settlement after the divorce. Hell, I'd marry some rich dyke looking for a beard. She wouldn't have to ask me twice."

"Then there's [a recently married superstar actor], who was a little too close to being outted publicly for his own comfort. The story goes that he actually interviewed a series of women and offered them a huge sum of money, not to mention prime roles, in exchange for staying married to him for a certain number of years."

He continued, "The saddest part of the Hollywood closet for the gay stars who aren't bisexual is that they live a life of perpetual sadness. They can never really have an open relationship, so they end up having sex with high-priced Hollywood call boys for $2,000 a night."

"Unless Scientology gets its hands on them," Lenny says.

The mention of Scientology piqued my interest.

"What do they have to do with anything?" I asked.

"Well, if you pay them enough money and you're gay, they promise to convert you," Lenny explained. "Or so I hear."

Lenny was not exaggerating. Scientology has many followers in Hollywood, among them stars such as John Travolta, Tom Cruise, Kirstie Alley, and Priscilla Presley. But while the majority of the church's adherents may not be gay, part of the appeal of Scientology for some celebrities may be its alleged promise that it can turn a gay person straight through an elaborate and expensive, science-fiction-inspired regimen called "auditing." In its May 6, 1991, issue, *Time* magazine published a controversial cover story about the sect, which alleged that some of Hollywood's most famous actors had come under the sway of the Church because they were afraid their secrets would be revealed. The most shocking passage concerned John Travolta:

> Sometimes even the church's biggest zealots can use a little protection. Screen star Travolta, 37, has long served as an unofficial Scientology spokesman, even though he told a magazine in 1983 that he was opposed to the church's management. High-level defectors claim that Travolta has long feared that if he defected, details of his sexual life would be made public. "He felt pretty intimidated about this getting out and told me so," recalls William Franks, the church's former chairman of the board. "There were no outright threats made, but it was implicit. If you leave, they immediately start digging up everything." Franks was driven out in 1981 after attempting to reform the church. The church's former head of security, Richard Aznaran, recalls Scientology ringleader [David] Miscavige repeatedly joking to staffers about Travolta's allegedly promiscuous homosexual behavior. At this point any threat to expose Travolta seems superfluous: last May a male porn star collected $100,000 from a tabloid for an account of his alleged two-year liaison with the celebrity. Travolta refuses to comment, and in December his lawyer dismissed questions about the subject as "bizarre." Two weeks later, Travolta announced that he was getting married to actress Kelly Preston, a fellow Scientologist.

The controversy over Travolta was re-ignited years later, in 2006, when the *National Enquirer* published a photo of the *Pulp Fiction* star standing on the steps of his private plane, kissing a man on the lips. The man turned out to be his son's nanny.

Since my encounter with the Queers of the Round Table, I came across a University of Maryland study that indicates my poker-playing companions were less informed about gay women in Hollywood that they thought. The study found that lesbians and bisexual women are actually eight times more likely to enter theater and film than their straight counterparts.

* * * *

In view of the incredible lengths Hollywood stars have always gone to in order to hide their homosexuality, it was all the more amazing that Jolie publicly acknowledged her affair with Jenny Shimizu. What is just as extraordinary is that her career has not suffered since then but instead has catapulted her to superstardom.

Jess Search, deputy commissioning editor for independent film and video at Britain's Channel 4 television network, told the *Guardian* in 2000 that she believed there was a "mystique" about lesbians that may make them more acceptable than gay men. "It's nothing new that a male audience will find a good-looking girl more interesting if they know she's a lesbian," she said. "In general, gay women used to be seen as subcultural, something that went on behind closed doors. Now we're no longer in the ghetto, we're more socially acceptable. Men find lesbians sexy; it creates a buzz around you."

Actress Sophie Ward, who starred in Barry Levinson's 1985 film *Young Sherlock Holmes*, came out as a lesbian in 1996, and she has had a relatively successful career since then, but she admits that it has had an effect on her career. "After I came out, I certainly noticed that people were a bit wary of casting me, particularly for television parts. I think there was a feeling that I wasn't safe. Even now, I get the impression with some of the more commercial roles I'm up for that they still think I'm a bit risky. But it's very hard to tell if you don't get a job just because of your sexuality. Luckily most people in the business are strong-minded and don't get swayed by it, but I think it will take time for people to relax about me."

Still, according to the same University of Maryland study, the actresses who have come out as lesbians or bisexuals actually earn more on average than straight women in Hollywood, though that statistic may be skewed because there are so few of them and because their number includes such big-name stars as Jolie and Drew Barrymore.

* * * *

Jolie's immediate reaction to her discovery of her bisexuality may have been typical of the traditional Hollywood pattern, however. It is certain that she was having an affair with Shimizu around the time of her elopement with Jonny Lee Miller, and probably before. "We were already sleeping together when I met Jonny while on *Foxfire*," Shimizu later revealed. "She told both of us how she felt, and we all went out to dinner one night. She was honest—that's how she's been her whole life."

If it's true that Jonny Lee Miller was well aware of his wife's affair with Shimizu at the time he married her, is it possible Jolie married him with an ulterior motive? It is possible that she was treading along a well-worn Hollywood path, disguising her true nature with a sudden marriage to Miller in March 1996?

Whatever the timing, the three young actors dealt with the situation the best they could. Despite Jolie's wild reputation, it is notable that Shimizu denied that the three had ever jumped into bed together. "We didn't have a threesome," she said. "I'm not really into that—it was a friendship the three of us had. But there wasn't much conversation with Jonny; I think he was very threatened by me." Indeed, Miller later confessed to being a "horribly jealous person."

It was soon clear to everybody that the marriage was not destined to last, and few were surprised when the two separated after a year. Jolie blamed the breakup on the couple's separate work schedules: "I'm not present enough, physically or emotionally, in relationships to get serious. It's not fair to the other person that I'm so busy with my career and that I'm often distant even when I'm with someone. We were living side by side, but we had separate lives. I wanted more for him than I could give. He deserves more than I am prepared to give at this time in my life."

"It's just that I wasn't being a wife," she added. "I think we really needed to grow, and we always talked about getting remarried. Certainly, my career is first. I seem to meet a lot of men who say they are like that, but for some reason it just doesn't turn out that way."

Somewhat disingenuously, she also said the relationship broke down because she wanted to move to New York, while Miller wanted to return to Britain. He seemed to go along with this explanation when he told the *Mail on Sunday* newspaper, "I know this sounds mad, but I was missing little things like the nine o'clock news, red buses, country smells, the sound of our rock music, and Match of the Day."

However, the most accurate explanation for the crumbling marriage was probably best summed up in something Jolie told a reporter about Miller: "He really had to put up with a lot." It wasn't her career that was getting in the way of her marriage, it was her girlfriend. Judging by their later public statements, it was obvious that Jolie's relationship with Shimizu was paramount. "I would have married Jenny if I hadn't married my [first] husband," she later acknowledged.

Although Miller had occasionally gone along with Jolie's fetishes and penchant for S & M, Shimizu implied that it was she who was better suited to meet those needs. "It's not so much that we were dressed in leather capes and masks and there were chains," she later recalled to the *Sun* about their unconventional sex life. "It was emotional. I would restrain her with my arms, but we didn't get into buying stuff. We just used whatever props were available if we wanted to. She was a collector of knives and taught me about them." Shimizu added, "She's a very dominant personality. Once she displays love for you, she wants to know how much you care about her."

Of this first, ill-fated marriage, Jolie later also implied that she and Miller had been realistic about their prospects. "The first time I got married, I was young," she recalled. "I knew I wanted to be married and wanted to be his wife. And it was a great experience. But we knew it wouldn't last forever."

And, although they didn't officially divorce until 1999, by late 1997, Miller was out of Jolie's life. Jenny Shimizu, however, was not.

DARKNESS BEFORE THE DAWN

By the time *Gia* was released, in January 1998, Angelina Jolie should have been riding high. Her tour-de-force performance was almost universally acclaimed, she had a Golden Globe on her mantel, and she was being hailed as a rising star. But months earlier Jolie had tipped into an emotional abyss which she attributed to her sudden success.

"You think beauty and fame and money should make a person happy?" she challenged one reporter, who had asked her whether she was enjoying her new-found celebrity after *George Wallace*. "I don't think so, if you don't have love and you don't have people to share it with. I think a lot of people have that feeling inside, that people don't care about who we are inside or understand us."

For a while she had seemed to enjoy her burgeoning success, especially when one of her favorite bands came to call shortly after she finished filming *Gia*. "I didn't know what the Rolling Stones wanted," recalled Jolie, who had also recently appeared in a video for a Meatloaf song. The Stones recruited her to play a sultry stripper to their song "Anybody Seen My Baby." "Imagine my surprise when they wanted me to walk down the streets in basically my underwear. The great thing is that it was New York and no one cared. People in restaurants were like, 'Oh, there goes the girl from *Gia* in her undies. Pass the salt.'"

The sexy video was definitely more memorable than her next movie appearance in 1997, in the awful film *Playing God*. She plays the girlfriend of a crime boss, Timothy Hutton, in a film that features David Duchovny in his first starring role after his success with the *X-Files* television series. The movie was a critical and box-office failure, though most critics blamed the mediocrity of her character on the script rather than on Jolie's performance. The film might have been spicier: Jolie later revealed that the director had filmed two separate sex scenes, one with her and Duchovny and one with Hutton, but they were left on the cutting-room floor. "With David we were basking in sunlight, and with Tim we were fucking hard in the back of a car," she revealed. "I think they felt like they couldn't have one without the other so they cut them both." About the only good thing for Jolie to come out of *Playing God* was a brief fling with Hutton.

Almost immediately after *Playing God* wrapped, she began shooting another inexplicably mediocre script called *Hell's Kitchen*, playing a character named Liz McNeary, a second-generation Hell's Kitchen lowlife who has been waiting five years to get even with her former lover Johnny—a boxer who took the fall for a friend when a botched robbery cost Liz's brother his life. The subsequent capers and convoluted plot are embarrassingly outlandish, but, fortunately for Jolie's career, virtually nobody saw the film when it was released.

In the middle of shooting, in the spring of 1997, *Interview* magazine commissioned Jon Voight to interview his own daughter. The result is a fascinating snapshot of Jolie's perspective from that point in her still obscure life and career. After an emotional reflection on his daughter's birth and her earliest acting roles, Voight asks Angelina about the early signs that she wanted to be an actor:

> JOLIE: God, my earliest memories are of my brother, Jamie—your son—pointing the home video camera at me and saying, "C'mon, Ange, give us a show." Neither you or mom ever said, "Be quiet! Stop talking!" I remember you looking me in the eye and asking, "What are you thinking? What are you feeling?" That's what I do in my job now. I say, "OK, how do I feel about this?" And I immediately know, because that's how I grew up.

VOIGHT: You have a very strong, specific presence onscreen. I think it's a presence that will always make a difference, story-wise.

JOLIE: I have a certain energy, yeah, and it's either needed or it's definitely not needed. I know that I can stick out like a sore thumb, and there are some women I'm not ready to play. I'm curious what you'll think of some of the things I've done recently.

VOIGHT: First of all, you have *Playing God*.

JOLIE: That was very rock 'n' roll and fun and loud and say-what-you-want-to-say, dress wild and love wild. You know that fantasy. I really allowed myself to get into that world. Being the age I am, I sometimes feel like a punk kid walking onto certain sets, but I didn't this time. I felt very much a woman. As a young woman, there are parts I'll look at that may not be in the best projects, but I'm starting out in this business and trying to figure out how I can make it work. I'm having to do a lot just to keep my clothes on and not be cast in girlfriend roles. Some women will say, "I don't want to be a man; I want the opportunities I can get as a woman." Women have a certain sexuality, and I think their bodies are beautiful, and I'm not embarrassed to explore that in a film. But there are things you get offered that are vulgar and violent, just like there's a side of me that's vulgar and violent.

VOIGHT: Sometimes, to present the truth, you have to play a vulgar or violent character.

JOLIE: Yes, although in the films I've done recently, I've been learning a little more about the side of myself that enjoys being a light. I remember when I used to dress all in black, and you'd say, "Just be pretty, hold your head up, be proud. Be a pleasant person and don't cover yourself so much with all your darkness, you need to be a little crazy." Now, I have nothing against anything I've been in before, because I love all sides of me, but I have been experimenting more with that lovely woman side. In this age of feminism, I would hate for the whole gentlemen and ladies thing to be lost.

VOIGHT: What do you do when you're not working?

JOLIE: I find it hard, so I usually find a way to put myself back to work. I'll work with Tom [Bower, Jolie's partner in her theater company], or on a play. I'll read or write. And I think it's important, in between projects, for me to sit down with who I've just become and allow her to continue to evolve and find a home inside me before I go and become somebody else. But I think I also need to learn to relax and not prepare too much, just enjoy life. I notice that my characters go out to dinner and have fun and take these great trips, but I spend so much time on their lives, I don't have much of a personal life of my own. I have to sort of remember to fill out that little notebook on me.

VOIGHT: OK, Angelina, we haven't heard even a portion of the wonderful Angelina Jolie stories we know, but we've suggested some of the energy that is uniquely you. I send you much love, my dear.

JOLIE: I love you too, Daddy.

* * * *

Gia was scheduled for release in January 1998, and her parents were both confident the role was going to catapult her into the upper echelons of the business. But Jolie wasn't sure if that's what she wanted.

"I don't think I was ever more depressed in my life," she would recall. "I was at a place in my life where I had everything I thought you should have to make you happy, and I felt emptier than ever. I thought after *Gia* that I had given everything I had to offer yet I didn't find myself growing. I didn't have the strength to deal with Hollywood. I was scared of being so public with my life and I didn't want to go out like Gia. I just needed to get away and find myself."

She had almost quit the business several times before. This time she finally made good on her threat, at least temporarily. Deciding that she might be happier on the other side of the camera, she decided to move east and enroll at New York University's Tisch School of Creative Arts, majoring in filmmaking. But the move away from friends and family only appeared to make things worse.

"I didn't have close friends anymore and the city just seemed cold and sad and strange, and the subway rides—everything that was kind of romantic about New York—just got very cold for me," she recalled years later about this period. "I didn't know if I wanted to live because I just didn't know what I was living for."

She described being in a New York hotel room where she was going to use either a knife or sleeping pills to kill herself; she couldn't decide which was the best method. She even wrote a note for the housekeeper asking her to call the police, so that the poor employee wouldn't have to come across her dead body. She then spent the day walking around the city. She was about to buy a kimono, in which she would commit her final act, when she suddenly realized how crazy the whole idea was. "I didn't know if I could pull the final thing across my wrists," she recalled. In addition, she calculated that she didn't have enough sleeping pills to ensure she would die. She asked her mother to mail her some more, but then realized that Bertrand would inevitably feel responsible for her part in her daughter's demise.

It was at this point that she came up with a bizarre scheme. The girl who had been diagnosed as "unrestrained, inclined toward antisocial psychopathy" only six years earlier decided she would hire a hit man to kill her so that her death would not appear self-inflicted. "With suicide comes the guilt of all the people around you thinking that they could have done something," she explained. "With somebody being murdered, nobody takes on some kind of guilty responsibility."

She even met with a man, "a friend of a friend," who she had been told could arrange the hit. She calculated that it would cost tens of thousands of dollars to hire the assassin. She planned to put money aside bit by bit, so no one would be able to trace the murder back to her after her body was discovered. "It's so weird and so complicated and so completely insane," she later said about the plan. "And so like a fucking movie." The potential killer, she recalled, "was a decent enough person, and he asked if I could think about it and call him again in two months. [But, in the meantime], [s]omething changed in my life, and I figured I'd stick it out."

Among other things, Jenny Shimizu flew to New York, sensing that there was something wrong. The two had been having regular phone sex, and it was during one of these long-distance sessions that Shimizu sensed a cry for help. Her presence helped Jolie think straight.

Although this dark period had driven her to thoughts of suicide, a couple of years later Jolie was publicly describing it as an important chapter in her life. "That was a really bad time, because I didn't think I had that much more to offer," she told *Rolling Stone* in 1999. "I didn't think I could balance my life and my mind and my work. I was also very scared of getting public after doing [*Gia*] and seeing how undernourished her private life was, how malnourished she was, though her exterior was very glamorous. So I'd be working and doing interviews, and then going home by myself and not knowing if I'd ever be in a relationship or be really good in my marriage or be a good mother one day or if I'd ever be . . . I don't know, complete as a woman. It was a really sad time. But I think it was really good that I did that now, that I spent all those months on my own, having a very regular life, going to school at NYU, studying the different levels of how to get into this business, riding the subway back and forth and just being on my own."

She had decided that instead of ending it all, she would "live life to the fullest." While at one point in her life that would have included heavy drug use, she now insisted that was behind her. She had been awakened by Gia Carangi's cautionary tale. "Gia has enough similarities to me that I figured this would either be a purge of all my demons, or it was gonna really mess with me," she said. "Luckily I've found something that replaces a high, and that is my work." The statement is telling: Angelina Jolie was still addicted, just to something that wasn't a drug.

By the time she accepted her Golden Globe for *George Wallace* in January 1998, work was not hard to come by. Suddenly she was red hot. Scripts started to pour in and her unofficial manager and gatekeeper, Marcheline Bertrand, helped decide which ones to accept. Jolie probably would have been better off consulting her father, who had always been very selective about the scripts he chose for himself. Voight's career was also suddenly hot, with his recent Golden Globe-nominated performance in the John Grisham thriller *The Rainmaker* thrusting him into the media spotlight.

Her name change aside, interviewers never seemed to let Jolie out from under her father's shadow. But increasingly it was Voight who was asked about his daughter as he roamed the press circuit. "She's something. She's the real thing: an artist," he told one reporter proudly when asked about Jolie's rising career. "I look at her as a peer. Her work is full of detail, full of decisions, full of vision. I have heard her say in interviews that she didn't know me when I was at my height. But she did know me then. It's just that even then I was struggling," he said. "The struggle is always with us."

Another profile describes Voight's entire face lighting up when asked about his daughter. "Young men come up to me now and say, 'Oh, Mr. Voight, your work is wonderful.' I'm thinking, 'Baloney!' It's all a smoke screen. They just want to get to Angie." Voight reveals that he and his daughter have a pact. "We are definitely going to do a film together before the end of this millennium," he promised. "I would love to do a comedy with her," he said elsewhere. "She has a wonderful sense of fun, and it would be great for the two of us to play these really dopey characters, partially because we're both taken so seriously right now."

Asked whether that was also a goal of hers, Jolie was a little more circumspect, although open to the possibility. "I would have never wanted to work with him if it seemed I was getting the job because of him," she explained. "I had wanted to stay separate just to be able to prove to myself that I was worth something and able to do my job. As you grow up, your relationship with your parents changes. He's gotten to know me through the roles I've done, and I'm probably stronger now, and more confident with my work."

Even if she appeared to resent being asked about her famous father in every interview, it was clear that they were still close and that they respected each other's craft. In one interview, she even described herself as a "daddy's girl." "I talk to him, and he talks to me," she said. "We love each other. But, to be fair, I also love my mother. And, most of all, I'm my own person . . . Acting is really about life, so if we talk about careers, it isn't just shop talk. When dad was doing [the 1999 TV movie *Noah's Ark*], we often discussed how he approached the character, but it was really about our own attitudes toward religion. I was taught acting all the time; sometimes, my mom would say things like, 'Look at me, and let me see what you are in your eyes.' That's real actor stuff."

* * * *

Although her marriage to Jonny Lee Miller was over, reporters were fascinated by the most significant and lasting legacy of the marriage, her tattoos. In the years since, she has acquired at least a dozen, several of which she has had covered over by other tattoos or removed entirely. She has described her attraction to tattoos as "dark and romantic and tribal" and often gets them to commemorate personal events in her life, such as the births of her children and the death of her mother.

In one interview, she revealed the origin of her first tattoo—the Japanese symbol for death on her shoulder. "When I got my first tattoo," she explained, "I got 'death,' and Jonny got 'courage.' While he was doing *Trainspotting*, I was in Scotland and wanted to get another one, but I didn't know what to get, so I just got 'courage.' I thought, 'Oh, I'll just match his.' But it was never really me." She later eliminated both of these tattoos by covering them with new ones.

By the time *Rolling Stone* came to interview her for her first cover story, which appeared in the August 1999 issue, she was giving what the reporter described as the "obligatory tour" of her tattoos:

"OK," she says, standing up and showing her left arm, "that's my dragon, upper left." She presents the inside of her wrist: "That's an *H*. There are two people in my life who have this letter [author's note: these are often alleged to be Timothy Hutton and her brother, James Haven] who I'm very close to and who I sort of love and cherish. And this is my newest one. I got this with my mom, actually. She came with me. It's a Tennessee Williams quote: 'A prayer for the wild at heart, kept in cages.'" She regards her left forearm and smiles her holy madwoman smile.

"This is my cross," she continues, pulling down the waistband of her black pants to reveal her slender hip, "and this," she indicates a Latin motto that curves across her stomach just above the bikini line, "means 'what nourishes me also destroys me.' And this," she turns around, pulling up the hem of her black T-shirt to show a little blue rectangle on the small of her back, "is the only color I have. I'm going to turn it black. It's a window." A window on to her spine? "No," she says, "it's because wherever I am I always find myself looking out the window wanting to be somewhere else." She smiles again, her loony, beatific smile—religious ecstasy with just a dash of grimace.

Jolie appeared to have carved out a distinct public image for herself involving her knives, tattoos, and scars. The vulnerable, sensitive side that reporters had noted earlier seemed to have been replaced by a caricature of her own making. To what extent this was the deliberate crafting of a specific image is difficult to figure out. She has implied that it was a defense mechanism to help shield her from too much scrutiny: "I feel as if all that stuff has been like some sly move on my part so that people will focus on the tattoos and knives and that way [they] won't really know anything about me. Yet everyone thinks they know personal stuff about me."

Asked by one reporter what she would say in a personals ad to describe herself, she was no less forthcoming: " 'Leave me alone.' Or it might say, 'Looking for a very secret, very straight night of reckless abandon to do all the things I've never done before. Shock me and keep it private.' "

In fact, her knives and tattoos were far less important than her other passions, such as tango dancing and playing the drums. Nor did anybody know that her favorite film was Disney's *Dumbo*, the whimsical film about a flying elephant. And her secret dream, she once admitted, was to own a motel in the middle of nowhere. "It all started when I was driving by this motel in Arkansas and thought it would be perfect to have," she enthused. "I jumped out and asked if it was for sale, and they said it was. I didn't end up buying it, but I loved that there were twenty-two little rooms. I thought I could just ride motorcycles, fix up the rooms, and grease the floors and stuff. I'm still looking for another motel. It's my dream project. I love places that have funky neon signs and are really tacky. The one I liked was called Happy Hollow, and I wanted to just stay there so badly."

An *Esquire* reporter, who spent some time with her in early 1998, was expecting a knife-wielding tough girl but was surprised to discover that "she's also mushy and really close to her mom and has poetry books and lace nightgowns and wants to cook and learn French. She likes and owns a lot of lingerie, but she doesn't always wear it. In a relationship, she wears ordinary underwear and saves the fancy stuff to cheer herself up. She fears being buried alive and becoming the kind of person who dresses her dog in clothes."

Yet Jolie rarely allowed reporters to see this side of her. It didn't fit the image she was crafting or the roles she was hoping to play, none of which went along with a soft-spoken normal Hollywood starlet. And, of course, she never tired of talking about what one reporter described as "the bisexual thing." "I've been married to a man . . . " she told one magazine. "But I love women; I'm attracted to women. To me, it wouldn't matter if it was a man or a woman . . . I have been close to a woman and thought, 'I could marry this person.' "

Still, she had no intention of playing a leading lady any time soon, so presumably she had no worries that her bisexuality would affect her box office returns. If anything, she seems to have viewed it as a professional asset. "I'll probably go after a bunch of guy's roles next," she told one interviewer in late 1997. "They're not really written for women, but there are some great roles; some great army movies. I want to play a sheriff, a cowboy, an army person. I'll just keep trying for those strong roles."

She would later get that chance, but for now she signed up to play a club girl yearning for love in a romantic comedy called *Playing by Heart*, which featured an ensemble of long-established stars: Sean Connery, Ellen Burstyn, Dennis Quaid, and Gena Rowlands. When the film was released, at the end of 1998, the public could see that the twenty-three-year-old Jolie could easily hold her own with such an intimidating array of stars. More than one reviewer claimed that Jolie had "upstaged them," though the film itself was not well received. Her performance was enough to win her another award to add to her growing collection: "Best Breakthrough Performance by an Actress," presented by the National Board of Review.

Despite the stellar reviews, she remained humble and even a little embarrassed that she was being favorably compared to screen legends such as Connery and Burstyn. "I've saved the call sheet with my name against all these other actors because I was just so proud to be on the list," she said of acting with the all-star cast. "I felt like I had crashed the greatest party in history."

Jolie filled the rest of 1998 and early 1999 with two back-to-back pictures featuring two of Hollywood's hottest male actors of the moment. First up was *Pushing Tin*, a comedy about air-traffic controllers, in which she plays the wife of Billy Bob Thornton. He had recently turned in an extraordinary Oscar-winning performance in *Slingblade*, one of Jolie's favorite films. Then she worked on *The Bone Collector*, playing a rookie police officer alongside Denzel Washington.

"I begged for the part of Amelia," Jolie later admitted. "I just wanted it so badly. I loved who she was. She was very street, and there were a lot of questions about my accent, about how I'd dress. Denzel had to meet me. He had watched my films, and I was so nervous. I was filming *Playing by Heart*, and I had this pink hairdo that was all spiked up. So I tried to cover it with a scarf, [but] halfway through the dinner I accidentally pulled it off and didn't realize it. They were all staring at my head, this pink thing. Here I was trying to be like a lady, a cop, and an adult. But he approved me. and I thought that said a lot."

Asked how she chose her roles, her answer was revealing. "I do my own therapy quite a lot," she said. "My choice of characters is my therapy, from one to the next. In *Playing by Heart*, there is a need for love, someone who is not very focused on purpose and work. Playing Amelia in *Bone Collector* was next; she's a cop who is all about duty and responsibility. It was my own way of tapping every side," she said.

On January 24, 1999, she attended the Golden Globe awards ceremony for the second year in a row as a nominated actress, this time for her role in *Gia*. In a red-carpet interview on the way in, she promised that if she won she would jump fully dressed into the pool of the Beverly Hilton, where the ceremony was being staged. When she was younger, she claimed, she had jumped into the same pool while accompanying her father to an event and was kicked out by the hotel management.

Once again, when the envelope was opened, her name was called. When she got to the microphone, Jolie couldn't contain her tears on seeing her mother beaming at her from the audience. "Mom, I know you wanted to be an actress, but you gave it up to raise me. I love you." Later that evening, Jolie made good on her promise, jumping into the pool at the hotel pool in her $3,000 Randolph Duke gown.

"What's funny to me is that everyone wasn't jumping into the pool," she told *Playboy*. "It's one of those events, and the people in the room are supposed to be free and wild, but everyone is so tame and careful." The incident only contributed to her wild-girl image; it was portrayed by most media as a spontaneous, drunken lark instead of the planned celebration that it was.

Meanwhile, she was determined not to let the success go to her head. "I'm not going to get used to it too much," she claimed shortly after the ceremony, when asked how a second Golden Globe award would affect her career. "I'm aware that it will help me get another job," she said, "and that's what every actor wants—another job." There was one in particular that Jolie had in mind at that moment, and it was the job that would define her career.

STARDOM

From the moment Columbia Pictures announced they were filming *Girl, Interrupted*, virtually every young actress in Hollywood lined up for a role. Based on Susanna Kaysen's best-selling memoir, the film looked like a golden opportunity to those who had been kicking around Hollywood for years, just waiting to be taken seriously. Rose McGowan, who had co-starred in *Scream*, summed up the film's appeal after she read for a part. "It's the only decent thing out there that doesn't involve taking your clothes off," she said. It was the ideal acting showcase, and Oscar visions danced in the head of every actress under twenty-five as she lined up for a chance to read.

It is doubtful that awards were in Winona Ryder's first thoughts when she read the book, in 1993, and immediately tried to buy the film option for herself. "It catapulted me back to the first time I read *Catcher in the Rye*, and I discovered I was not the only person who knew what it was like to be lonely and alienated," she explained. "Since I read the book when I was twenty-one and fell madly in love with it, I've wanted to do this."

Angelina Jolie had much the same reaction. She wanted in. The book spoke to her in many ways; certain parts of Kaysen's life hit really close to home: in 1967, after a session with a psychiatrist, Boston prep-school girl Susanna Kaysen was put in a taxi and sent to McLean Hospital, in nearby Belmont. Reality had become "too dense" for the eighteen-year-old. Kaysen spent most of the next two years living a nightmare on a ward for teenage girls at McLean, a psychiatric hospital famous for treating the mental frailties of the privileged. It was an experience that she captured in a gripping memoir more than two decades later.

Kaysen was raised in the upper academic echelons of Cambridge, Massachusetts, and was the daughter of famed economist Carl Kaysen, a professor at MIT and former advisor to President John F. Kennedy. When her stifling Cambridge upbringing became too much to bear, Kaysen made a half-hearted attempt to kill herself by swallowing fifty aspirin. The suicide attempt brought her to McLean, whose patients have included Sylvia Plath, Ray Charles, and James Taylor, all of whom spent time there after their own famous breakdowns.

Once at McLean, Kaysen was diagnosed with borderline personality disorder and was quickly divested of any control over her own life. After a dental treatment under general anesthesia, she panicked when she awoke and nobody would tell her how long she had been unconscious; she believed she had "lost time." On another occasion, in an episode known in psychiatry as depersonalization, she bit open the flesh on her hand because she was terrified that she had "lost her bones."

"Lunatics," writes Kaysen, "are similar to designated hitters. Often an entire family is crazy, but since an entire family can't go into the hospital, one person is designated as crazy and goes inside." She believes she was the family scapegoat, sent to an institution to spare her loved ones the inconvenience of having to live with her.

Nearly a quarter century after she was finally released, Kaysen documented her experiences at McLean. In the interim, she had rarely mentioned her hospitalization, "I didn't know what to say," she recalled. When she did bring it up, "it was a good way to irritate or frighten people." But the memories of McLean kept surfacing, and finally she felt she had to record them.

In the years after her release she had discovered a significant talent for writing and had published two acclaimed novels, *Far Afield* and *Asa, As I Knew Him*. Her autobiographical account of her days at McLean was a surprise bestseller that was frequently compared to Sylvia Plath's *The Bell Jar*. As poignantly as she captured her own experiences, she managed to capture the foibles of her fellow patients, including a number of memorable and fascinating characters who had been committed for a variety of reasons.

One of these characters is a manipulative sociopath named Lisa, who, unlike Susanna, probably needed to be in an institution. Lisa was the maverick of the all-female ward, fighting for justice and defying the system. She devised diversions from the strict routines and drew escape plans and rallied the other girls to question authority—in short, she was a female version of Jack Nicholson's character Randle P. McMurphy in *One Flew Over the Cuckoo's Nest*. This is the role Angelina Jolie wanted, and she was determined to do whatever was necessary to land it. "Lisa was a very coveted role," recalled producer Cathy Konrad. "We had the pick of all the young actresses out there."

In contrast, Winona Ryder knew right from the beginning that she wanted to play the lead role of Susanna, the part she most identified with. She wanted it so badly, in fact, that she was willing to buy the rights to the book in order to land it. To her chagrin, she was beaten to it by Douglas Wick, who had produced *The Craft*.

Still, the dark, depressing story wasn't seen as bankable by most studios, and Wick was having no luck getting the film financed. That's when Ryder, in those days still a hot commodity and a bankable actress, made him a deal. She would come aboard as a producer and use her clout to get the story made. In exchange, she would be guaranteed the role of Susanna, which could be her ticket to the pantheon of serious actors that had so far eluded her.

But it wasn't mere vanity that motivated Ryder to make *Girl, Interrupted*. When she was a rising young actress, she suffered what she later called an "extra-large breakdown" and checked herself briefly into the sleep-disorder unit of a psychiatric institution. She attributed the crisis to "the pressure of working and then going through adolescence onscreen."

Because of the breakdown she had had to turn down the role of Michael Corleone's daughter Mary in *Godfather III*, which was subsequently given to Sophia Coppola. It was not a decision she had taken lightly. "I thought I was losing my mind," she later explained. "You know, when you are just so tired that you can't sleep? . . . It was a really tough year. It would be for anybody, regardless of what they're doing, whether it's cramming for exams or their parents driving them crazy or breaking up with first loves. It's the year where life is going crazy, and everything was going crazy in mine. It was amplified because it was in the papers. Every step I was taking was being written about."

During her brief stint in the institution, she recorded her innermost feelings in a journal, much like Susanna Kaysen had done two decades earlier. "I didn't get anything from that place," Ryder said. "I was so tired and just wanted to sleep. They didn't help me at all . . . I was nineteen, and I learned that no matter how rich you are and how much you pay some hospital or doctor, they can't fix you. They can't give you a certain answer. You have to figure it out for yourself. I finally realized I'm not supposed to understand everything. Life is just weird and messy, and I had to get through on my own and do my best. Choose to move on or stay miserable. I chose to move on."

Like Kaysen, Ryder had never had a chance to come to terms with the episode. But after reading *Girl, Interrupted*, she realized she wasn't crazy for reeling under so much stress. "One of the things I thought for years is that I am not OK," she said convincingly. "I thought people would think I was a brat if I complained about anything. If I said I was depressed, they'd attack me. Now I know I'm allowed to say, 'Wow, I had a hard time.' I am learning to be me."

For a long time it looked like *Girl, Interrupted* would never be made. But once she finally got the green light from Columbia to turn

Kaysen's memoir into a film, Ryder personally approached her director of choice. James Mangold had just won the best director award for his first feature, *Heavy*, at the Sundance Film Festival and was making a big-budget crime drama called *Copland*, starring Sylvester Stallone, Robert DeNiro, and Harvey Keitel.

"[Ryder] came to see me in New York while I was making *Copland* in 1996," Mangold recalled. "*Girl, Interrupted* had already gone through two writers, and I got the sense it had gone aground. It was a hard story to tell. I was so enthused by her enthusiasm that I agreed to do it, though I didn't have a clue as to how I'd get the project right, because much of the story had been told from inside the author's head. It took a while, but then, the ideas started coming."

By the time auditions began in 1998, Ryder had been working closely on the project for almost two years. It had been a constant touch-and-go with the studio about whether production would ever begin. Eventually, they were ready to cast the film. The role of Susanna was already spoken for by Ryder. To her credit, she chose the lower-key role, likely because she so identified with the character. She must have known the other roles would overshadow it and possibly attract the attention of the Oscar nominating committee. Her decision left open the roles of the other inmates. Among the most coveted were the part of Daisy, a schizophrenic victim of incest, and, of course, Lisa.

A number of high profile actresses had already publicly expressed interest in these parts, including Katie Holmes, Christina Ricci, Gretchen Mol, Kate Hudson, Reese Witherspoon, and even the singer Alanis Morissette, who had just played God in Kevin Smith's drama, *Dogma*. At that point, the only actress the producers knew for sure they wanted was the Canadian Sarah Polley, who had just impressed Ryder in Atom Egoyan's independent film, *The Sweet Hereafter*. Polley, however, passed in favor of another project, leaving the field wide open.

For the role of Lisa, Mangold didn't have anybody in particular in mind. "All I knew was that the person had to be dangerous, highly verbal, and sexy—a kind of female De Niro," he said.

Jolie had called in every favor she had owing to get a reading, but she needn't have bothered. The producers already had her on their short list. Still, nothing had been decided by the morning Jolie walked in and, without saying a word of dialogue, sat down in the chair in character as Lisa. When she opened her mouth, Mangold says, he knew he had found his sociopath.

Mangold described what he saw as one of the "greatest moments" of his life. "It was clear to me that day that I was watching someone who was not acting. There was someone speaking through her; it was a part of herself," he said. "The power coming off her, even in that cold reading, is something I will never forget. I never had someone come in and blow the walls down. She just entered the skin of the character . . . I felt like God had given me a gift."

Kathy Conrad, Ryder's fellow producer, was equally impressed. "We knew from her energy that she very much understood Lisa, and that she was inside Lisa's skin," she recalled. "She was fully realized in the audition, which is a rare thing to find. She was the perfect level of octane."

Mangold still had a few readings scheduled that day, but he had already made up his mind. "I just wanted to go to Starbucks and make a deal," he recalled. He sent Jolie's audition tape to the studio masters, who quickly seconded his choice. "She's a female James Dean for our time," said Columbia Pictures chairwoman Amy Pascal, who gave the project the green light. "I'd make any movie with her in it."

For her part, Jolie remembers what was going through her head when she finished reading for Mangold that day. "I had been shooting *The Bone Collector*, and I was so deep into that part that I really needed to do Lisa," she recalls. "She completes the other side of my personality.

She's the person who stands up and screams, the one who isn't in her head so much. I remember going into the audition thinking, 'This is so much deeper than just a part. I need to be in this movie because I am in pain.' And when I finished the audition, it was like: 'I'm done. Bye.' I just had to get out of there."

Jolie never informed Mangold or Ryder that she, like Lisa, had been diagnosed as a sociopath at a young age, though she acknowledged on a number of occasions that she identified with Kaysen's long-time affliction with self-injury. Despite her first-hand experience and teenage diagnosis, Jolie prepared for the role of Lisa by reading everything she could about her character's condition. "Since childhood I [also] was called sociopath [so] I tried to get to know what that meant," she recalled. "I came to a bookshop and asked, 'Where do you keep literature about sociopaths?' The seller answered, "Look under the heading 'serial maniac.' Well, what a good company I've got, my thought was."

She soon began to understand a little bit about the girl who her character was based on. "I realized it wasn't that people like her are haunted by dark forces; they just have certain instincts," she explained afterwards. "What it comes down to is that Lisa doesn't think there's anything wrong with her. And I don't think there's anything wrong with me, but I can get angry at things and feel that it's OK to just want to live. I thought Lisa was emotional and unhappy, but she's considered psychotic and a tough woman. For me, it wasn't about studying mental patients, but studying and enjoying life."

As to whether she identified with Lisa, Jolie was inconsistent. In the middle of the movie's press tour, she declared emphatically to a group of reporters, "I am not the girl, interrupted!" And yet she offered a more coy response to an *L.A. Times* reporter. "All of my characters are me," she said. "I have to be careful about the characters I play because they're going to be me." She was quick to add, "I've never created a character who I wouldn't want to sit down [with and] have a cup of coffee." She later dropped her guard again with reporters, confessing, "I'm Lisa. I identify with her. She was completely honest, trying to break through to people. She got involved, and she would invest in other people. She was looking for someone to talk to, to drop the bullshit and be real . . . I know where Lisa is coming from. I can scare people off pretty easily, and I know how to push people's buttons. Like Lisa, I feel that people aren't really honest with me and that makes me pull away."

Jolie later said she was especially nervous about working with *Girl, Interrupted*'s mostly female cast; she recalled her experience on the mostly female *Foxfire* as a nightmare, despite her hookup with Jenny Shimizu. "I thought it would be bad. I'm usually with men. I tried to work with a group of women once, and it didn't [work]. But I'm working with amazing actresses. And we really bonded."

That wasn't the same recollection of a technician on the film, who said the cast didn't seem to get along at all. "They were very, very icy with each other," he recalled. "I wouldn't say that Jolie was worse than the others or that she was a bitch, but she and Winona didn't seem to get on at all. Mostly they ignored each other, but they didn't seem to like each other when they did interact."

Brittany Murphy, who plays the troubled Daisy, had a similar impression of tension on the set, although she attributed it to the nature of the characters. She recalls that Jolie and Ryder, in particular, immersed themselves in their roles. "It was rare to see either of them out of character for the entire twelve-week shoot," she said afterward. "Angelina's character Lisa really hated Daisy, so she shunned me. One day, she began talking to me and then stopped cold. She stared hard at me and Angelina was replaced by Lisa, and she walked away."

Murphy did acknowledge a kind gesture by her co-star after the weeks of being ignored. "She was always teasing me about the wig I had to wear for Daisy. At the end of the shoot, [Angelina] gave me a backpack with a dog [on it] that had exactly the same hair style," she recalled. "I think it was her way of telling me there were no hard feelings. It was just part of her acting process."

Murphy had similar memories of Ryder's on-set behavior. "Winona never actually acknowledged the other actors on a day-to-day basis," she said. "She started being Susanna the moment she arrived on the set for makeup. It's not the way I'm used to working, but I think it really worked for this movie because it is so intense."

Jolie attributed the tension between herself and her producer/co-star to more than just method-acting. She acknowleged that she and Ryder just didn't get along. "Ask Winona about the night we slept together," Jolie joked afterwards about the tension between the two. "I was very sociable on the set, just not with her. That's how it ended up. And when she wasn't working, she was with Matt [Damon] a lot."

Asked whether she thought Ryder may have been intimidated by her, she was cagey. "I don't think she was intimidated by me. I don't think anybody should be intimidated by anyone . . . but maybe she thought I was going to try and kiss her." It was not the first time Jolie implied that her own lesbian tendencies may have caused some friction. "I got very close to some of the other girls," she recalled. "Quite a few of the women on the film were with girlfriends or had female lovers or were bisexual. Probably one of the few straight women on the set was Winona."

According to the technician, the real tension was between Jolie and Mangold, who, he says, clashed on more than one occasion. "When she'd yell at him, you'd never know if she was being Lisa or Angelina," he remembered, "but they definitely butted heads. It was mostly about how she would play a certain scene, with him saying she needed to be more believable, that sort of thing. He had to keep her from going too over the top with the character, and she didn't always appreciate it. But I wouldn't say she was difficult. I've seen much, much worse from actors. She really cared about her role. If there was a diva on that set, I'd have to say it was Whoopi [Goldberg, who played a kindly nurse]. I think she wanted us all to know that she was a movie star. Angelina treated everybody on the crew nicely."

As for his own impressions of their on-set tensions, Mangold said, "Angie is rebellious, volatile, and really smart. Playing this role put her in the mode of questioning authority. But if someone delivers the goods like she did, then I'm happy to struggle with the personality." He noted that she had hung pornographic pictures all over her trailer during filming, but as with their tensions, dismissed it a part of her craft. "Angie was just playing at living in Lisa's skin and pushing buttons anytime there was a button to push," he explained. "Angie is that way. She's a provocative person. She's very challenging. She's incredibly smart. She can be two or three steps ahead of you."

Jolie found the experience of playing a volatile young woman very liberating. "It was actually what I needed: to break out. Because I have been so still, and I've cared so much, and my heart's bled so much, I thought it was going to be very, very hard. Many parts of it were, especially the end. The thing is, her impulses are completely free. So I found *my* impulses completely free, more than a little weird, and I was completely open. Then you realize how much we are restricted. This character could sit at a table, could kiss somebody, throw something, spit on somebody, and just say whatever the fuck she wants. To me she was heartbreaking, and the essence of her was that she wanted somebody to talk to and be a friend. She wanted somebody to drop their fucking guard and stop with the bullshit and just admit whatever it is and be whatever you are and just stop pretending."

Watching the filming, co-producer Doug Wick was struck by Jolie's power: "She does that thing that Jack Nicholson can do. Jack can do the most dastardly things, and it's fun to watch. Angie has that kind of charisma. When Angie does dark things, rather than being repelled, you're fascinated. She has no boundaries."

Mangold later compared her passionate performance to a howitzer weapon. The description is fitting as Angelina-Lisa lets loose in one scene:

> You don't know what freedom is! I'm free! I can breathe! And you . . . you'll go choke on your average fucking mediocre life! There are too many buttons in the world. Too many buttons, and they're just . . . There's way too many, begging to be pressed. They're just begging to be pressed! You know, they're just begging to be pressed. And it makes me wonder. It makes me fucking wonder. Why doesn't anybody ever press mine? Why am I so neglected?

"There's incredible control and lyricism and pain, but also rhythms and speed—the way she jumps from here to there is just a different kind of acting," Mangold said about her performance.

By the time the film finally wrapped, Jolie was relieved to leave the role of Lisa behind her. The part seemed to have consumed her every waking moment and some of her body as well; she had lost a considerable amount of weight, and people were starting to speculate whether she had an eating disorder. "This has been a really tough time in my life. I get nervous, and I don't eat as much, even though I remind myself. I'm trying to put some weight on," she said, explaining her skeletal physique. She even told one reporter that she was so thin that her father tried to force-feed her whenever he saw her. "I'm hoping to get on a program soon. When I was in the hospital with a friend who had a drip in her arm, I was like, 'Maybe if you stick that in me, just actually inject pure protein, you know?' I would love to have my figure back. I always felt like I didn't have one."

Jolie explained that she found the adjustment from the character of Lisa back to herself very difficult. "At the end of the film there's a certain sense of them saying to Lisa, 'Nobody wants you to live, nobody likes the way you are. You'd be better off if you were sedated and tied down and shut up.' " Jolie told *Rolling Stone* that she took that personally. "If you feel that you're the kind of person she is, then it's really hard, because you're struggling with, 'Fuck, am I just damaging to people everywhere? Am I just too loud and too wild, and do I just need to let everybody live their lives and shut up and calm down?' "

Despite her difficulty with the transition, when she was offered a big-budget action film, produced by Jerry Bruckheimer, she had no hesitation. The film, *Gone in 60 Seconds*, called for her to portray a "sexy car girl" and Nicolas Cage's love interest in a story about a ring of car thieves. "There were so many women on *Girl, Interrupted* that when I got this script and saw it was going to be twenty men and me, and so many cars, I was like, 'Thank God! Testosterone! All right!' "

She was amazed that she was suddenly big enough in Hollywood to be offered such a role. On *The Bone Collector*, just a few months earlier, the studio at first had vetoed Jolie for the role of Amelia and had only offered her a contract after some intense lobbying by the producer and director. This time, the studios were coming to her. She was the actress of the moment. Her face was plastered on countless magazine covers, and the public was fascinated by her unconventional persona. But she was uncomfortable with the new media attention.

She revealed her feelings in an interview around this time with the *Today Show*'s Jill Rappaport, who showed Jolie copies of all the magazines whose covers she had recently graced. "I think there's a curse to that," Jolie explained. "That's my own personal thing—there's a curse. If it becomes too much about your personality, it's very hard for people to watch you." When asked if the new fame was "overwhelming," Jolie replied, "Yeah. But the best thing is the people I've been getting to work with, and the films I've been getting to work on. That's kind of the amazing thing."

Jolie clearly relished the work, but not the attention. Being the daughter of an actor like Jon Voight had taught her a number of important things about dealing with fame. "I learned a great lesson in having my dad being an actor," she said. "I always knew he wasn't this person everyone would say is great or bad. He was just a very regular man. When things would be successful and wonderful, it didn't make his life better. He was only happy when he was doing his work. So, I'm pretty grounded from that.

"I'm pretty scared of celebrity. As much as I'm kind of out there, I like to watch people. When I see magazine covers [of myself], I don't know who that is . . . If I wasn't working very hard and wasn't doing things that I wanted to be in, then it would kill me, because I would feel not worthy of it at all. But I'm proud of the films I've been a part of and feel that I'm doing the work as best I can. I just want to continue to work. You get to a certain [level of] celebrity where you can get pretty lazy if you're offered things that you don't need to work very hard in. I'm very focused on just doing my work."

In another interview, however, she lamented that her newfound status as a Hollywood celebrity might intimidate the people who worked with her or who met her on the sidewalk. "I want people to know that I'm so scared of people not coming up to me and saying, 'Hi.' In this business, they turn you into something that you're not. I'm not looking to shock anybody or hurt anybody. I may have tattoos and seem dark, it's just simply . . ." At this point in the interview, she trailed off and rolled up the sleeve of her black sweatshirt to reveal a tattoo she had recently gotten with her mother, a Tennessee Williams quote: "A prayer for the wild at heart, kept in cages." She became introspective. "Everybody has something that cages them. This is a prayer for everybody to just be themselves," she offered.

At this point in most actors' careers, they have already learned to cage their more honest impulses for the sake of future box-office returns.

Not Jolie. When *Playboy* magazine reported that fifty-seven percent of college women, gay and straight, claimed that they would like to sleep with Angelina Jolie, the actress was ready with a response that must have made her publicists cringe. "I guess I'm the person most likely to sleep with my female fans," she retorted. "I genuinely love other women. And I think they know that." She also hinted at her expertise in lesbian sex. "I have loved women in the past and slept with them too. I think if you love and want to pleasure a woman, particularly if you are a woman yourself, then certainly you know how to do things in a certain way."

As *Girl, Interrupted* readied for release, Jolie was excited to see Mangold's final cut, but she was not entirely happy with the results. Much of what Jolie considered her character's vulnerable side ended up on the cutting room floor. "I'm surprised that people would have compassion for a character that the film doesn't," she told *Entertainment Weekly*. "I think Mangold did an amazing job of putting the movie together, but it's a weird thing what the film says, because I don't see my character as a sociopath, but instead as someone who was very much deserving of compassion. I thought through the whole movie she was a really positive force. There's one scene where she tries to feel something, so she burns herself. They cut it, but I thought it was important. I saw her for who she was, so that's why I hate to think that it's seen as right for people like her to be locked up."

Many critics agreed with her assessment, complaining that Mangold had not adequately captured the pathos of Susanna Kaysen's memoir. "It can't help recalling *King of Hearts* and *One Flew Over the Cuckoo's Nest*, which also questioned which characters might be craziest: the inmates, their keepers, or the authorities who haven't been caged," wrote the *Seattle Times*. "By now it's become a cliché, and Mangold does little to freshen it. On this score (and others), Kaysen's book is sharper, funnier, more daring. The movie flirts with banality and sometimes succumbs.

One extended sequence that builds to a suicide is so creakily predictable that it approaches kitsch."

There was one thing, however, that virtually all critics agreed upon: Jolie had stolen the film from her co-star and producer, Winona Ryder, upstaging her and out-acting her. "Ryder seems to have misplaced the spunk of *Heathers* and evolved into a rather passive screen presence," complained the *Philadelphia Daily News*. "Things get so dull that Angelina Jolie is the only character with whom one can identify—and she's playing a sociopath," wrote another reviewer.

Still, some reviewers felt the opposite. *Time* praised Ryder's performance as "first rate" while dismissing Jolie's role as "problematic." *Entertainment Weekly*'s verdict was even harsher: "James Mangold's adaptation gets mired in snake-pit clichés, and Jolie's performance ultimately crashes and burns in a climactic hissy fit that plays like the demise of the Wicked Witch of the West."

At the box office, the film failed to recoup its $40 million budget in domestic release, but it wasn't a complete flop. The pundits were predicting that Jolie was a shoo-in for an Oscar nomination.

With her third consecutive Golden Globe award in January, 2000, the new millennium dawned with great promise for the career of Angelina Jolie. That week, a *Time* magazine profile compared her wild reputation to that of another young screen rebel, James Dean, and noted that she was the same age, twenty-four, as Dean had been at the time of his fatal auto accident. "I'll probably live to be a ripe old age," Jolie responded when asked whether she thought she'd die young like Dean. To illustrate her point, she described how she had welcomed in the New Year a week earlier. "I had a great time," she deadpanned. "I was asleep."

She was also fast asleep on the morning of February 15, 2000, when her father's old *Midnight Cowboy* co-star Dustin Hoffman strode to the podium at the Samuel Goldwyn Theater in Beverly Hills to announce the nominations for the 72nd Annual Academy Awards, alongside Academy

President Robert Rehme. The announcement made it official: Angelina Jolie had been nominated for best supporting actress for playing Lisa in *Girl, Interrupted*. She would be up against Toni Collette in *The Sixth Sense*; Catherine Keener in *Being John Malkovich*; Samantha Morton in *Sweet and Lowdown*; and Chloë Sevigny in *Boys Don't Cry*.

Jolie was in Mexico, where she was filming *Dancing in the Dark* with Antonio Banderas. When the press woke her to get her reaction to the announcement, she was nonchalant. Like many actors who have never been nominated, she had often charged that the Oscars were chosen to reward celebrities, rather than to advance the craft. "Look, it's great to be recognized for a project that you've worked really hard in," she said about the nomination. "But often you wonder how real that recognition is. Does it mean this thing is better or more important than something else? You just sometimes feel as if it's not deserved."

Secretly, of course, she was thrilled. She was very familiar with the Oscars. Though she was only two years old when her father won his "Oscar" for *Coming Home*, she had long been aware of the aura that it bestowed on him in interviews and profiles. She had gotten used to being described as "daughter of Oscar-winning actor Jon Voight," even if the statue itself was always just a funny little gold man that was kept in a goldfish bowl on her grandmother's mantel. This wouldn't even be the first Academy Awards ceremony Jolie had attended. She and her brother accompanied their father to the Oscar ceremonies in both 1986, when he was nominated for his role in *Runaway Train*, and again in 1988.

The 2000 Academy Awards ceremony was scheduled to take place on the afternoon of March 26, at L.A.'s Shrine Auditorium, and would be hosted by comedian Billy Crystal. Jolie later described it as a "beautiful day," though a week later she may have been tempted to reevaluate that assessment.

"I spent that morning with my friends who helped me get ready, and my family came over," she recalled. "They told me that it didn't matter

Angelina Jolie and Brad Pitt attend the premiere of *The Curious Case of Benjamin Button* held at the Mann's Village Theater in Westwood. Los Angeles.

Ian Halperin undercover at the Stewart and Lynda Resnick Neuropsychiatric Hospital, where Angelina was admitted.

Seen here with her brother, James Haven, Angelina Jolie, was a bit more shy at four years old than she is now.

Michael Jacobs/ZUMA/KEYSTONE Press

© Globe Photos/ZUMAPRESS/KEYSTONE Press

Angelina, age eleven, and her family at the 1986 Oscars.

Brad Pitt and his wife Jennifer Aniston on the red carpet at the 56th Annual Emmy Awards at the Shrine Auditorium in Los Angeles.

©ZUMAPRESS.com/Keystone Press

Angelina Jolie and her husband, Billy Bob Thornton, at the premiere of *Original Sin*.

© Lisa O'Connor/ZUMAPRESS/KEYSTONE Press

Photo by ABACA USA/EMPICS Entertainment/KEYSTONE Press

Angelina Jolie and her two children at Lee's Art Shop in New York on February 18, 2009.

Angelina Jolie and Brad Pitt take their adopted children Zahara, Pax, and Maddox for a trip to Lee's Art Shop in midtown Manhattan, in August 2007.

Angelina Jolie and her son Maddox spend some time in New York's Central Park on June 3, 2005.

© Globe Photos/ZUMAPRESS/KEYSTONE Press

Angelina Jolie and her father Jon Voight. Beverly Hills, Los Angeles. March 25, 2001.

© Paul Grover/Telegraph UK/ZUMA/KEYSTONE Pres

Angelina Jolie at the gala premiere for her new movie *Kung Fu Panda* at the 61st Annual International Film Festival de Cannes. May 15, 2008.

Angelina Jolie and Brad Pitt arriving at the Berlin premiere of his new movie *The Curious Case of Benjamin Button* on January 19, 2009.

one way or another and that they loved me and were proud of me. It was the greatest day of my life already."

When she accompanied her father to the 1986 ceremony, the paparazzi had taken special notice of the ten-year-old Angie because of her unusual dress, which resembled angel's wings, later described by *Rolling Stone* as "all mouth and eyes and Eighties hair, decked out in enough pearls and white lace for an entire congregation's worth of brides at a Tom Thumb wedding."

This time she chose something a little more streamlined: a black Versace gown, which *Entertainment Weekly* later described as "something Christina Ricci would look like if she'd continued wearing her Addams Family costume in public," but which Jolie loved. "It's silky," she said. "And very me." Asked to describe the most important accessory she would use to go with the dress, she answered, "A friend, and making sure my tattoos don't show."

Officially she had been single since a short fling with Timothy Hutton, though she later revealed that there was a "secret" boyfriend whom she had been successfully hiding from the world. Her date for this grand evening was, she later said, a choice between her mother and her brother, Jamie. She had already been on the awards circuit for weeks, and each time she had been escorted by her brother. So she asked him to attend this big night with her as well.

For reasons neither of them have ever explained, Angelina and Jamie decided to pass up the traditional pre-Oscar red carpet stroll. They arrived late, after the show had already started, and talked their way past security guards, who allowed them to sprint to their seats while the cameras were focused on host Billy Crystal during his opening number.

The late James Coburn had won the Oscar for best supporting actor the year before, and, following tradition, he was designated to present the award to the winner of the best actress in a supporting role category.

"It's wonderful to work in this town with so many creative, talented, gorgeous, sexy women," said Coburn, as he prepared to present the second Oscar of the evening and the first major award of the ceremony. "And I have that enviable job of getting close to one of them and presenting her with an Oscar."

After reading the nominations, followed by a short clip from each of the nominated performances, Coburn opened the envelope with a dramatic flourish, paused and looked into the camera. "And the Oscar goes to Angelina Jolie." At that moment, as the auditorium burst into applause, a tearful Jolie, still seated, leaned over to her brother while he grabbed her head and brought their lips together for a kiss that appeared to linger. On television, it was impossible to see more than their heads, so a billion viewers were left in the dark about what had transpired until photos of that kiss appeared the following day. They may have got a hint of their unusual sibling affection, however, when Jolie bounded up to the microphone and gave her much talked-about speech:

> God. I'm surprised nobody's ever fainted up here. I'm in shock, and I'm so in love with my brother right now. He just held me and said he loved me, and I know he's so happy for me, and thank you for that. And thank you to Columbia. Winona, you're amazing, and thank you for supporting all of us through this. And all the girls in this film are amazing, and Whoopi, everybody. And my family, for loving me. Janine Shrier and your sister Michelle, we love you. Geyer Kosinski. My mom who is the most brave, beautiful woman I've ever known, and Dad, you're a great actor, but you're a better father, and Jamie, I have nothing without you, you're just the strongest, most amazing man I've ever known, and I love you, and thank you so much.

An employee of ABC who had been chosen to be a seat filler—replacing invitees in their seats when they get up to use the bathroom so that an empty seat won't appear on television—described being in the audience at the moment Jolie kissed her brother. "I was sitting almost directly behind [an Emmy-winning actress] and her date; it might have been her husband. When the kiss happened, not everybody could see it. I didn't get a clear look myself, but I heard the guy lean over to [the actress] and say as clear as day, 'Do you think she's fucking him?' I think just about everybody in the auditorium wondered that after they heard her speech."

BROTHERLY LOVE

By the next morning, the kiss had been felt around the world. In the press room at the Oscars, however, Jolie was oblivious to the coming furor. Still riding high from her victory and clutching her golden statuette, a reporter asked her to explain the unusually affectionate kiss. "Can you explain the nature of your closeness to your brother?" she was asked.

"Oh God," Jolie said, suddenly a little flustered. "Well, I don't know if it's divorced families or what it is, but he and I were each other's everything, always, and we've been best friends. He's been always my strongest support . . . He's just given me so much love and taken care of me."

When he was asked about the kiss, her brother also denied there was anything improper. "I did not give Angie a French kiss; it was something simple and lovely," Haven insisted. "She was about to go off to Mexico to finish filming *Original Sin* with Antonio Banderas. I congratulated her on the Oscar win and gave her a quick kiss on the lips."

When the newspapers published a photo of their liplock the next morning, and people saw that it looked like more than just a peck of sibling affection, it set off a fierce debate and inspired many snickers. More than one outlet noted that the two had been extremely affectionate at the Golden Globes ceremony two months earlier, where Haven had also gone as his sister's escort.

Predictably, the Internet blazed with rumors, and crude jokes overflowed from the likes of the *Howard Stern Show* and *Politically Incorrect*. But the mainstream media weighed in as well, giving more than a little credibility to the speculation. "Angelina Jolie's declaration of love for her brother was just a little too creepy for comfort," wrote the *Richmond Times Dispatch*. " 'Ewww!' viewers everywhere screamed in squeamish delight, pelting their television screens with popcorn," wrote Toronto's *Globe and Mail*. "Even considering that perhaps she and her bro share the unusually close bond of children whose parents divorce, this was a tad strange," wrote the *Fort Wayne News Sentinel*.

Nearly everyone who saw the kiss experienced a strongly negative gut reaction. As a rule, American audiences are very uncomfortable with just the slightest hint of incest. Even 1995's *Clueless*, where Alicia Silverstone's Cher makes out with her former stepbrother (with whom she is not related by blood), disgusted theatre-goers across the nation. To see it happen for real was more than many people could stomach.

Perhaps the one serious media outlet that did more than any other to cast doubt on the innocence of the siblings' relationship was the *Early Show* on CBS, hosted by the respected television personality Bryant Gumbel. The morning after the Oscars, Gumbel was discussing the ceremony with his co-host Jane Clayson, herself a serious news journalist. Also joining the discussion were the show's meteorologist Mark McEwen and newsreader Julie Chen. Millions of viewers watched the four discuss the footage and photos that had emerged showing the kiss:

CHEN: And she said, "I'm so in love with my bro . . . brother . . ."

CLAYSON: Right.

CHEN: ". . . right now." And . . .

CLAYSON: And the same thing at the Golden Globes.

CHEN: Yeah. But what tipped me off was through the preshow . . . Bryant, get in on this, I know you agree with us.

GUMBEL: What? No. What?

CHEN: He was . . . the way he was holding her. She was . . .

GUMBEL: I didn't see that.

CHEN: OK, someone was interviewing her. Did you see . . .

GUMBEL: I was watching the Lakers and the kids . . .

CLAYSON: It's the way they kiss each other. I'm telling you.

CHEN: No. But did you see how he was holding her when she was doing an interview with, like, Joan Rivers.

GUMBEL: Mark, you're laughing. This is serious stuff.

CHEN: Her back . . . her back was . . .

MCEWEN: I'm laughing just because I didn't see all of that.

CHEN: . . . to him like this, and he was holding her like this . . . like really tight to him, and it was . . .

CLAYSON: Eugh.

CHEN: I was like, "I don't think brothers and sisters . . ."

CLAYSON: Didn't . . . didn't you notice that, Mark?

MCEWEN: Well, I don't know. I'm very clo . . . I'm not that close with my sister.

CLAYSON: I hope not.

MCEWEN: But I'm pretty . . . I'm very close . . .

GUMBEL: I hope not.

MCEWEN: . . . to my younger sister so I can to . . . I can understand that.

GUMBEL: I hope not.

MCEWEN: But I . . . you know, I . . . I didn't see all of that because we were busy watching other stuff.

Indeed, as the CBS crew discussed, footage and photos had emerged showing Angelina and her brother with their hands all over each other before and after the ceremony. Other journalists were quick to accept that their affection was merely the result of a bond between two children of a broken home, as Jolie had explained. "So what's up with Angelina and her brother?" asked Sandy Banks of the *L.A. Times*. "Does that relationship seem a little strange? Maybe the questions simply reflect the image that the young actress has created: an eccentric iconoclast pushing the limits of convention on matters of sex and social mores. Or maybe it's a sign of how disconnected we are from our own families, that so many of us could be made uncomfortable by the image of such strong familial love. As a woman with a brother I deeply love, I found myself moved by Jolie's tribute to Haven . . . and bewildered by the prurient tone of inquisitors who implied there must be something weird about her affection."

Dismissing the rumors, the *L.A. Times* interviewed a number of therapists who explained that it is not uncommon for siblings to be drawn closer by the trauma of divorce and for one to step into the breach and fill the role of an absent parent. "When divorce occurs, it's a very intense experience," Susan Maxwell, a West Los Angeles therapist, told the paper. "Everyone is suffering; there's a lot of sadness and grief. Your little nuclear family that has given you security has been blown apart . . . You feel a sense of abandonment. A situation like that can make the sibling bond stronger. It's the two of you against the world. It's like surviving a war. Or an airline crash. When you share an experience like that, you can come through it feeling very close, very bonded." Maxwell added that she too has an older brother with whom she weathered a family breakup. "And we're very close. We talk all the time; we understand each other. It's like we're speaking the same language."

Camille Paglia, the controversial author and social critic, had a different explanation for the Oscar kiss. "I think [Angelina] was messing with people's heads," she said. "I think she enjoys doing the unexpected." Ian Drew, West Coast editor of *US Weekly* echoed Paglia's assessment. "Only Angelina Jolie could turn that moment of Hollywood acceptance into the ultimate moment of Hollywood rebelliousness," he said.

Indeed, many people believed that the shenanigans were part of Jolie's carefully crafted image as a Hollywood wild child. After all, wrote one paper, Jolie's life has been "an open book of bizarre behavior," noting that she "sports numerous tattoos" and has "experimented with bisexuality and sadomasochism."

The controversy and speculation probably would have died down very quickly were it not for a number of new details emerging about the siblings' relationship. First, the *New York Observer* published details of the post-Oscars *Vanity Fair* party, where brother and sister partied together into the night. Frank DiGiacomo noted the "double takes" partygoers cast at Jolie and Haven, "whose cuddling appeared to surpass sibling affection. One partygoer told the *Observer* that even their father Jon Voight, who was at the party, seemed a little unnerved by their closeness."

Then the media dug back two months, to the Golden Globes ceremony, where Jolie had dragged her brother up onto the stage after winning for *Girl, Interrupted*—she wanted him to "see the view from up here." The *Fort Wayne News Sentinel* wrote, "First we see her at the Golden Globes and the Oscars, demonstrating a strange and unsettling fondness for her brother, who was her date at both events. At the Golden Globes, she led him to the stage with her when she accepted her award, their fingers intertwined, their glances not sibling-like at all, nor their kisses." On top of that, backstage in the press room at the Golden Globes, another photo had been taken of Angelina leaning backwards into her brother's chest and kissing him passionately on the lips, eyes closed, again in an embrace that seemed nothing like an innocent sisterly kiss.

Soon, news leaked that *Elle* magazine had done a recent photo shoot— weeks before the Oscars—where Jolie had showed up accompanied by her brother. The *New York Observer* reported that, during the shoot, the brother and sister had repeatedly kissed in front of the photographer and crew, posing in "their favorite scandalous pose without even being asked." Photographer Gilles Bensimon told the paper that the two first exchanged a kiss on the lips, he discreetly refrained from snapping a shot. "We don't try to use the picture in a tabloid way," he said. "But the third time they were kissing, I take the picture." Other photos from the shoot showed Haven standing with Jolie like her lover, with his hands on his sister's hips with the top of her dress open to expose a good portion of her breasts.

* * * *

It is difficult to get a handle on James Haven because he has always lived in the shadow of his famous sister and father. Jolie has always maintained that it was her brother who was most likely to follow in Jon Voight's footsteps.

In one of the few times they were ever interviewed together, a portrait emerged of the origins of their close sibling bond. "I'm so proud of him," Jolie said. "Growing up, I couldn't have cared less about movies. He had to drag me to them. Jamie always loved film. He should've been the one who was working first." Asked how she compared to her brother, she claimed the two were "almost perfect opposites." "He never swears," she said. "I swear like a truck driver when I'm angry. When it comes to the moral high ground, he wins. When it comes to being crass and loud and tough, that's me."

INTERVIEWER: Who was more theatrical as a kid?

HAVEN: That would be her.

JOLIE: Because you were always holding a camera.

HAVEN: I'd tell her to act for me. We did a version of a Subway commercial of her saying something like, "I'll punch your face if you don't buy a sandwich."

INTERVIEWER: What impressions do you have of each other as children?

JOLIE: I remember him as a happy child and then getting to a certain age and becoming very sad. When I used to have to cry in a film,

I'd think of Jamie at age six, so full of hope and happiness.

HAVEN: I'd say the same thing, a little girl who was so wonderful, and then things go wrong and cause pain.

INTERVIEWER: Once and for all, what was the deal with that Oscar kiss?

JOLIE: First, we're the best of friends. And it wasn't some odd open-mouthed kiss. It was disappointing that something so beautiful and pure could be turned into a circus.

HAVEN: It was an amazing moment. Yet it was totally misconstrued.

INTERVIEWER: Angelina, how are you as a prospective sister-in-law?

JOLIE: I've always been tough on anyone he's dated. I've been the nightmare for any girl. But if I like her, I'm fantastic.

Like Jolie, Haven also attended Beverly Hills High. One of his classmates remembers him as "more normal" than his sister: "I didn't know Angelina but Jamie was this quiet kid who was quite studious, like most of the other kids. His dad was famous, and people in that school were very conscious of those things. Most people's parents were not actors, though a lot worked in the film business or in TV or that sort of thing. We saw his dad a few times. He was this friendly parent who always would say, 'how ya doing?' to the other kids when he attended something at the school, and there was this sense that he was a famous person and that sort of rubbed off on his son."

In later years, after Jon Voight was estranged from his daughter, Haven repeatedly attacked him, calling him a bully, among other things. But accounts from the time suggest that the two were quite close. A friend of Marcheline Bertrand, who is still friendly with Voight to this day, remembers that James worshipped his father: "Forget the stuff you read today," she said. "They were a close family. Jon and Mar continued to be friends, and, when they were all together, you wouldn't know that there had even been a divorce. I think that's the most accurate way to describe the situation. Jamie looked up to his father, and they were very close, much more so than Angie and Jon. She and Jon would argue a lot, in a good natured father-daughter sort of way, or she'd get pissed off at her dad if he made a comment about her clothes or something. But Jamie got along very well with him; they'd go to a lot of movies together, sometimes with Angie, sometimes without. Jamie was his first kid, and he was older, so Jon would do stuff with Jamie that Angie was too young for at first.

"Later on, when Jamie was making films, his father would give him advice. He lived with Jon for part of that time, but I don't want to give the impression that Angie was left out. The three of them did a lot of stuff together. They even attended the 1986 Academy Awards, with his mother, and Jamie was so excited. Angie might have been a bit young to really appreciate the significance, but Jamie loved movies."

Haven was indeed obsessed with movies but couldn't figure out what side of the camera he wanted to be on. At the University of Southern California, he showed a flair for filmmaking and it looked like he might have a promising career as a director. But as Jolie's career took off, his stalled. "I'm not sure what it was," says his mother's friend. "He didn't seem very motivated," she recalled. "He was very happy when his sister started to make it as an actress, but deep down there may have been a little jealousy as well. At one point, he seemed to believe his father was favoring Angie over him.

"His father was very helpful when he was in school. He paid for the film stock, the processing, everything that Jamie needed, and of course the tuition, none of which was cheap. But Jamie may have felt that Jon had pulled more strings to help his sister than himself. I never heard him say that, but I've read some of the things that he said about his father, and it's a little puzzling to me. I was angry with Jon over some stuff as well, but I think he did right by the kids, or at least he tried to. Jon was proud of both his children and really wanted them to be happy, but maybe he did pour more attention into Angie once he saw where her career was heading."

Countless media accounts have noted the eerie resemblance between Jolie and her brother, frequently describing them as look-alikes. "Its like snogging yourself from five years earlier," said Paul Croughton, deputy editor of *Arena* magazine, about Jolie kissing someone who looks so much like herself. "I'm sure Sigmund Freud would have fun with it." Freud would have had a field day if he had known that their similar looks were not just the result of genetics. Two separate sources, one of them a photographer of long acquaintance with Jolie, confirmed that when she was in her teens, she and her brother visited a cosmetic surgeon to get their noses thinned in "his and hers nose jobs."

Still, none of this proved that they were more than very close siblings. As it turns out, their mutual fondness was quite recent. Although Jolie and her brother had been practically inseparable for almost a year, this was in marked contrast to any earlier period of their lives, when they only saw each other occasionally. Haven had never previously been a fixture in her professional career, but they had suddenly become inseparable around the time of the 1999 Golden Globes. Since then, Haven had accompanied Jolie to virtually every press interview, sometimes with their father along, but usually alone. "He was always there," recalled one photographer. "I assumed that he was just part of her entourage. In those days, the press didn't follow her around like they do now, hanging on her every move, so I don't know how much time they spent together privately. But it's like they were joined at the hip whenever she appeared at an event."

A few months earlier, Jolie had tried to buy a private island in the St. Lawrence River, near Montreal, complete with its own gothic castle, and claimed that her brother was "coming in" on the deal. And in November, only four months before the Oscars, she announced that she was forming a production company with Haven. The same month, he accompanied her to Australia on a press tour to promote *The Bone Collector*.

As the media continued to speculate and as the buzz lit up the Internet, the world appeared to let out a collective "Ick!" Jolie's promising career seemed to be under threat at a time when it should have been soaring to new heights. "Her Q rating was in free fall," said a publicist who followed the controversy, referring to the measure studios use to gauge the popularity of TV and film stars.

Haven appeared for the first time in public to defend their relationship, although Jolie's publicists may have had second thoughts about that strategy after an interview he gave one reporter. "Maybe I haven't found the right woman because my sister is too picky for me," he said when asked if he had a girlfriend. "Any woman has to go through two filters, me and then my sister. I'm a perfectionist by nature. Then, because I'm so close to Angie, it's like I've already got the perfect woman in my life, and it's hard for anyone else to live up to that."

To deflect this new controversy, Haven attempted irony when asked if he had any tattoos of his own, following the revelation that the *H* on her wrist signified her brother as well as former boyfriend Timothy Hutton. "No, but I'm thinking of getting one," he replied. And what would it be? "Angelina's name." Haven was also asked whether, given his sister's penchant to shock, they played up the incest rumors. He responded, smiling, "Oh, sure. If you guys all think that is going on, fine. Let's go, you know? It's like everyone wants to be with her, and I'm with her. Great."

"It's a really weird thing," Haven told another inquisitor. "I laughed at first, then I got angry about it. Now that I have had time to think, I think it's just that people are not used to this, so they automatically think negatively. But everyone who has jumped to this very sick thought is going to have egg on their face. They are writing all these stories that will be there forever, and they will realize in time that it is just a very close relationship, and it has nothing to do with what they are implying." When asked about Jolie's statement that she was "in love" with her brother? "The word 'love' is such a special thing," he responded. "Love and sex and whatever, they are different. I could say I'm in love with someone who is ninety years old and teaches acting and lives in Ohio."

When *US Weekly* asked bluntly if he and his sister had ever slept together, Haven said, "That's sick," before adding that in fact the pair hadn't slept together since he was seven and she was five. "I think we fell asleep in our mom's bed while we were watching television," he said.

Jolie, on the defensive, tried to use her notorious reputation for outspokenness to prove that the rumors couldn't be true. "The thing is, if I were sleeping with my brother, I would tell people I was," she insisted. "People know that about me." The strategy wasn't entirely effective, judging by the fact that the more the siblings denied it, the more reporters brought it up. The *New York Observer* even coined a new term to describe Jolie: "Incest chic."

The repeated denials had clearly not impressed the hosts of the *Early Show*, who brought up the relationship once again after the story about the *Elle* photo shoot broke.

> MCEWEN: She's real smart, says exactly what she thinks. That's why she said that whole thing with her brother . . . this was in *Elle* maybe . . . I don't know where I saw it.
>
> CHEN: You're reading *Elle*?
>
> MCEWEN: Well, I read what's on . . . you know, if somebody's on the cover I find interesting . . .
>
> GUMBEL: They didn't have *Glamour*.
>
> MCEWEN: Yeah, right. I kind of like *Glamour* myself. But she said she's very . . . people know she's very honest, and she says exactly what she thinks. And was just hugging her brother. Give me a

break.

CLAYSON: Hugging him? She gave him a big wet kiss.

MCEWEN: Well, I don't know how wet that kiss was. She did kiss him.

CLAYSON: It was wet. Whoa. It was a . . . whoa.

MCEWEN: But you know what's funny?

GUMBEL: It was a tonsil lock.

MCEWEN: Well, I don't know about that. But she kissed her brother and all of America went, "Hmm." They came right forward.

CLAYSON: Who kisses their sibling on the lips like that?

GUMBEL: Folks that . . . never mind. I shouldn't do that.

CHEN: Yeah. But I know I'm right with you.

MCEWEN: Don't say it.

CLAYSON: Don't go there.

CHEN: And it's more than just kissing.

CLAYSON: Whoa.

It was still too early to tell how the constant chatter about incest would affect Jolie's career in the long term. Her current project, *Dancing in the Dark*, had just wrapped, and she had already signed to do the high-budget action flick, *Lara Croft:Tomb Raider*. Her immediate acting prospects weren't in jeopardy, but the box-office returns of her next release could make or break her career.

Jolie's management was nervous. The decision was quietly made to keep as much distance between Jolie and her brother as possible, a decision that the pair reluctantly went along with. They were never to be photographed together in public, but it is also clear that Haven was expected to distance himself from his sister completely, publicly as well as privately. Jolie would later claim that he had decided on that course of action himself.

The damage had already been done, however. If Angelina Jolie's career was to be salvaged from the public-relations fiasco of "incestgate," it would take more than half measures. The public's perception of her would have to be changed for good. It appears that Jolie was well on her way to making that happen.

BETWEEN BROTHER AND SISTER

It's unlikely that the world will ever discover the truth about whether Angelina Jolie and her brother ever had a sexual relationship. But as a biographer trying to make sense of her life and career, I felt I had to at least try to explore the possibility instead of dismissing it out of hand. And, while a good number of people believed the two may have indeed taken their affection for each other way beyond healthy limits, very few of them, no matter how bizarre and unconventional Angelina Jolie certainly was, could bring themselves to believe that she and James Havens would violate this most ancient of taboos. It was unthinkable.

Brother-sister incest is much more common than people think, however. In a 1980 study, published in the academic journal, *Archives of Sexual Behavior*, 796 undergraduates at six New England colleges and universities were surveyed, with fifteen percent of the females and ten percent of the males reporting some type of sexual experience involving a sibling. It's not known, however, how much of this contact was consensual.

Part of the difficulty in determining the facts about consensual sibling incest is that virtually all the research in the field concerns sexual abuse. That is, coercion by one sibling over another rather than a consensual relationship. Another difficulty is that most countries have strict laws against brother-sister incest in any form, though many allow sexual relationships between cousins. In 1997, a Wisconsin brother and sister, Allen and Patricia Muth, were charged with committing incest. They were separated as kids, but when they met as adults, they fell in love and had children together. They were both convicted, Allen sentenced to eight years in prison, Patricia five. Meanwhile, in Europe, France, Belgium, the Netherlands, Spain, and Portugal no longer prosecute adults who are in incestuous relationships, while Romania is currently debating a law to decriminalize consensual incest.

The studies that have been done often focus on the psychological factors that motivate children to become involved in sibling incest. In a 1987 study conducted by the Boulder County Department of Social Services Sexual Abuse Team, twenty-five cases of sibling incest were studied over a three-year period to determine a set of common dynamics. According to the authors, the dynamics which were repeatedly observed throughout these cases were: (1) distant, inaccessible parents; (2) parental stimulation of sexual climate in the home; and (3) family secrets, especially with regard to extramarital affairs. It is not a stretch to say that the Voight-Bertrand household met most of these criteria.

Those who argue for the liberalization of incest laws usually say that consensual sibling relationships are not harming anybody. Dr. Paul Federoff, a forensic psychiatrist at Toronto's Centre for Addiction and Mental Health, has for years treated adults who have had consensual incestuous relations with siblings. The day after Jolie's Oscar-night kiss with her brother, Federoff told the *Globe and Mail* that, in his view, incestuous feelings between siblings, particularly among children and young adults, is "a common probability." More surprisingly, he said it's not necessarily a bad thing. "Sexual exploration and contact between young siblings is not uncommon or harmful provided there is not a huge age discrepancy or coercion," he says. He emphasizes, however, that he doesn't encourage incest between adult siblings. York University sociologist Ann-Marie Ambert also doesn't view consensual sibling incest as a moral problem. "Personally, I don't see anything wrong with it," she has said.

Medical historian Edward Shorter begs to differ. He argues that the prohibition against incest goes far beyond legalities and is in fact a "genetic commandment." "The general social castigation of incest has never been relaxed in any time or place," he argues. "It is an iron biological law, like the law against murder. The consequences of any indiscretion against it are engraved in our DNA."

Many experts, however, now take issue with the biological prohibition, arguing that this is largely based on the probability of birth defects and that the existence of reliable contraception means that this is no longer necessarily a factor. In addition, a number of experts take pains to distinguish consensual sibling incest from supposedly consensual parent-child incest where an uneven power-and-authority dynamic calls into question just how consensual such a relationship can ever really be. Recently, actress Mackenzie Phillips revealed that she had a "consensual incestuous" relationship for years with her late father John Phillips, founder of the Mamas and the Papas, but the fact that both father and daughter were drug addicts at the time makes her claim that it was consensual very questionable.

But what about a brother and sister roughly the same age? I was eager to meet with some siblings involved in consensual sexual relationships to get their perspective and to see whether they could shed any insight on what might have been going on with Jolie and her brother. Was their Oscar-night kiss really the moment that sibling incest came out of the closet, as one newspaper asked the next day. However, locating siblings who would be willing to talk about their relationship was easier said than done, I discovered.

Not surprisingly, the Internet has helped incestuous siblings find and communicate with each other, with countless forums and chat rooms acting as informal support groups. In such forums, siblings discuss their common ground as well as trying to educate society about what many believe is a harmless, even healthy, lifestyle.

In one of these incest forums, a man calling himself "JimJim2" discussed what happens when "two adults who just happen to be related get it on":

> You can't help who you fall in love with, it just happens. I fell in love with my sister, and I'm not ashamed . . . I only feel sorry for my mom and dad, I wish they could be happy for us. We love each other. It's nothing like some old man who tries to fuck his three-year-old. That's evil and disgusting . . . Of course we're consenting, that's the most important thing. We're not fucking perverts. What we have is the most beautiful thing in the world.

It appears as if the debate has continued in earnest all over the Internet. In an essay published on his blog, Anadder, for example, Michael Fridman outlines and demolishes most of the arguments against consensual sibling incest while still remaining queasy about the idea:

> 1. *It's unnatural*—The same old line's been used to prove the immorality of homosexuality, interracial marriage, contraception etc. Sorry. The answer's always "so what?" (being unnatural doesn't make something bad) and "no it isn't" (e.g., ten to fifteen percent of college students reported some childhood sexual contact with a brother or sister).

> 2. *It's universally condemned*—This was also used against interracial marriage etc. Again: so what? And again: no it isn't. It's universal to have some kind of incest taboo, but the limits vary a lot. In many cultures it's common for first cousins to marry (with up to fifty percent of marriages being between first cousins).

> 3. *It causes birth defects*—Finally a somewhat true statement (although apparently the best strategy is to actually marry your third cousin). But if that's reason to outlaw incest we need to

outlaw drinking/smoking during pregnancy (which we don't and it would be a big deal to do this). We'd also need to prevent two carriers of a genetic disease from procreating. Finally despite what you hear on the news, we're not living in the twelfth century. Sex ≠ babies. Two sisters having sex, or a heterosexual incestuous couple using contraception will demolish the argument.

4. *People who were brought up together shouldn't be together*— Umm, because . . .? I've heard this one before. It's priceless, the ultimate non-sequitir. This suggests that two childhood friends should avoid romantic relationships. This of course happens very often. I'm not aware of studies suggesting such couples are psychologically/emotionally worse off than the average couple. This argument is grasping at straws.

5. *It makes me personally uncomfortable*—At last, the truth! Yes, it certainly does.

But Voices in Action, a U.S. support group for victims of incest, argues strongly that there is no such thing as "consensual incest." "These teens have been brainwashed into believing this behavior is natural; it is not," states the group. "Sexual abuse is learned behavior." On the other hand, Dr. Sean Gabb of the British think tank Libertarian Alliance argues that "consenting incestuous behavior is no business of the state. It is up to individuals to make their own decisions." Brett Kahr, a senior lecturer in psychotherapy at Regent's College, London, argues that there is no proper research into the field of consensual sibling incest, writing, "Who are we to say that Joe Bloggs and his sister Jane Bloggs aren't having a perfectly good relationship and we're all missing out?"

If I was going to locate and meet with brothers and sisters who were having a sexual relationship, it appeared that the Internet was my best hope, but I was still in the dark about the logistics. Given the strict laws against incest, I wasn't sure how I could convince anybody to talk to me without being suspected of trying to entrap them. Soon, however, I discovered a phenomenon that I never knew existed called Genetic Sexual Attraction (GSA), which has given rise to a number of easily accessible online forums.

GSA is defined as sexual attraction between close relatives, such as siblings or a parent and child, who first meet as adults. In other words, they have been separated at birth, for whatever reason, then later meet and date without knowing that they are related. Those who advocate for the rights of those who commit consensual incest argue that GSA is more prevalent than one might expect.

The most famous example is a German couple, Patrick Stübing, and his sister, Susan, who grew up separately and only met as adults. Patrick was arrested and imprisoned for violating Germany's incest law, which he and his sister have been fighting to overturn for years, arguing that it hearkens back to the racial-hygiene laws of the Third Reich. But the Stübings are perhaps not the best poster children for consensual sibling incest because they have had four children together, two of whom are disabled, apparently as a consequence of inbreeding. Rather, the couple is probably a better argument to keep the prohibition against incest intact, since study after study shows a radically increased chance of birth defects and disabilities—as high as fifty percent in some cases—among children of incestuous siblings.

Despite the fact that a number of examples exist, I am not convinced that GSA is as widespread a phenomenon as its advocates claim. I suspect that it is a means for practitioners of sibling incest to claiming innocence of wrongdoing and potentially elicit sympathy from the public, which would otherwise be revolted by the idea of brothers and sisters having sex with each other (e.g., "We didn't set out to commit incest; it happened by accident. It's not our fault that we fell in love").

Nevertheless, I had no interest in locating incestuous couples who didn't grow up together. I needed to find those in a roughly similar situation to Angelina Jolie and James Haven for an accurate comparison. I started on a number of chat rooms, posing as a forty-five-year-old man who had been having sex with his sister since he was nineteen and she was eighteen. I was looking for a "support group to help us come to terms with our situation and discover if there is anybody else out there in a similar situation." I soon discovered that the majority of users on these sites were there to be titillated or expected pornography. Authentic incestuous siblings, it seemed, were not easy to find.

In the end, it was a contact that I made on a GSA site that led me to my first meeting. It started when I received an invitation for my sister and myself to meet another couple to chat. I was given a time and place to meet at a deli in Brooklyn. First, I needed to find a sister to accompany me on my charade, one who was around my age. I offered $125 to Staci, a singer I knew who had done some acting and who I thought would be able to pull off the ruse convincingly. I hadn't yet decided whether I would eventually identify myself as a journalist. My thinking was that if I let my subjects know about the book I was writing, it might get them to share their thoughts about Jolie and her brother.

The couple we met that evening I'll call Ruby and Jeremiah. When I introduced myself, I used my own name, Ian, but I introduced Staci as "Kendall." Ruby and Jeremiah looked to be slightly younger than us and, at first glance, they didn't look a lot alike, though we later learned they were brother and sister by blood. We introduced ourselves and made some small talk about the New York subways. At that first meeting, they didn't encourage a lot of personal discussion about our relationship, maybe because we were in a relatively public venue. In our communication beforehand, in fact, they had encouraged me to be "discreet." They appeared to be sizing us up, getting to know us, maybe figuring out whether we were on the up and up.

This was no small issue. Researching the New York State penal law, I discovered that there could be serious consequences to their relationship. According to section 255.25 of the New York Criminal Code:

> A person is guilty of incest when he or she marries or engages in sexual intercourse or deviate sexual intercourse with a person whom he or she knows to be related to him or her, either legitimately or out of wedlock, as an ancestor, descendant, brother or sister of either the whole or the half blood, uncle, aunt, nephew or niece. Incest is a class E felony.

Such a violation would apparently be punishable by up to four years in prison, so their caution was understandable.

While we were all digging into strawberry shortcake at the end of our meal, Jeremiah suggested we might want to attend one of their monthly get-togethers.

"A support group?" I asked.

"We don't call it that," he replied, "but, yeah, that's basically what it is I suppose. To us, it's mostly a social thing."

A little more than two weeks later, he again contacted me and invited me to an address on Staten Island the following Thursday at 7:00 p.m. Checking on Staci's availability, I confirmed our attendance and then had breakfast the next day with my "sister" to firm up our cover story.

We decided on a few basic parameters, some of which we had already agreed upon before our initial supper meeting, including what we both do for a living (I would be a technical writer, she a designer), where we come from (Tacoma, Washington), how long we've been together and whether we've ever been with anybody else since we started our relationship, etc. After that, I gave Staci the freedom to improvise as she saw fit. I agreed to pay her $400 for the evening and our "rehearsal time" and to pay for her taxi home afterwards.

On the appointed day, we took the ferry and a taxi to what appeared to be a very respectable middle-class residential neighborhood on Staten Island, complete with manicured lawns and, ironically, more than one religious grotto with a Virgin Mary statue because, we later learned, the street was predominantly Italian and very Catholic.

When we arrived, there were five other people there: the hosts, whom I'll call "Allan and Adrian"; another couple, "Shawn and Leila"; and a single woman around fifty, "Kim." We were offered white wine and an assortment of snacks was laid out in the spacious living room, which was covered with art posters. As I had assumed, the two couples were siblings. Kim, the single woman, she later explained, was in a relationship with her brother, but he worked near Chicago and lived in Skokie, Illinois, and she only saw him on occasion, which she said was "hard."

I learned that, as far as the neighbors were concerned, Allan and Adrian were married. "As long as you're not Italian, they stay out of your business, they ignore us," Adrian explained. "That's why we like it here."

It wasn't exactly like a twelve-step meeting, they were actually planning to watch a movie later on, *The Philadelphia Story*, starring Katherine Hepburn and James Stewart. But, like AA, they seemed to expect the new members to begin by telling their story. This was the part that made me most nervous, knowing that these people might be able to detect a phony couple a mile away. Staci let me do most of the talking, though she jumped in with a masterful improvisation at one point that yielded some fascinating insight.

I explained that we came from Washington State, and that our parents had divorced when we were nine and seven-and-a-half, leaving our mom to raise us, though out father was a dentist so we were well taken care of. After high school, I planted trees for a year in British Columbia and planned to go to university, majoring in sociology or creative writing. After Kendall, graduated, we both moved to New York and found an apartment in Alphabet City on the Lower East Side before eventually enrolling at the City University of New York. It was while living there that we ended up "accidentally" having sex one night. With the exception of a two-year hiatus, where we both saw other people, we had been together ever since, pretending to be married ever since our mother died of a blood infection eleven years ago.

Upon hearing our story, Kim asked whether we had ever had any "close calls." I think she wanted to know whether we had ever almost been caught. But Staci jumped in and said she got pregnant when she was twenty-eight and had to have an abortion. That, she explained, was when we broke up for awhile, "freaked out" about our flirtation with disaster. A little while later, after they had shared their own experiences, they all said they knew siblings who had also had abortions, though none of them admitted to an accidental pregnancy themselves. Allan and Adrian, however, said they knew a "friend of a friend" who had become pregnant with her brother's child, and, for whatever reasons, decided to have the baby, presumably well aware of the risks. "The baby was normal," explained Allan, "but it was still fucking stupid."

Maybe I was expecting some kind of *Penthouse Forum* scenario, but none of the people there that evening shared how exactly they had first ended up having sex with their sibling, though each said it had happened in their teens, apparently at a much younger age than what I had claimed for Kendall and myself. Like my friend in college, and like my own concocted tale, it just sort of happened, they implied.

At one point I said, "I'm so relieved to see we're not alone. We never met anybody else who was like us, and we thought that maybe we're freaks, though we knew there were people out there from reading about it on the Internet." They all nodded knowingly. There were so many questions I wanted to ask, but I had to be careful not to come off like a journalist, and I found myself biting my tongue to avoid appearing too inquisitive.

They didn't tell us their own hometowns, but Kim said, "You'll find that most people like us move as far away as they can from wherever they grew up. I have no idea what the statistics are, nobody does really, or where sibs mostly live. But I think a lot of them move to New York. It's such a huge city that it's just safer here. I'll bet that more sibs live here than anywhere else in America." *Sibs* is the term they use to describe people like themselves. I noticed that the word *incest* was hardly ever used.

Each of the other five siblings said they felt alone for years until they found other people who were in a similar situation. "I've gone to therapy for some of my so-called neuroses," says Shawn, "but I never once told her about Leila. I would have obviously liked to talk about it, and I'm sure it would have been OK, but I just couldn't bring myself to do it. I don't feel safe. It's not that I thought she'd turn us in, but it's that I know how people judge what we're doing. She'd turn it into some psychological hang-up and start looking at everything through that filter. And, you know, I am neurotic, but I don't think it's got anything to do with me and my sister. It's sort of the opposite, if you know what I mean. It's Leila who makes me feel grounded and sort of gets me through all my crap." Leila herself barely said a word all evening when we talked about these things, but she did nod vigorously when Shawn said this.

Hoping to inspire a conversation along these lines, I said, "Yeah, people think we're deviants, but it seems totally normal to me. We've been together longer then most married couples I know, and we're still happy. We fight sometimes, but that's normal too, right?"

"Exactly," Adrian chimed in. "We consider ourselves married. I think this link we have makes our 'marriage' more successful. It's not about blood but maybe some sort of special connection that we had from growing up together or something like that. You know, I know a lot of sibs who break up, or who actually get married to other people, so it's not like it's a guarantee. There's all kinds of problems that come about from trying to hide it, and it gets stressful. You guys haven't had any real close calls, but we have, believe me."

I asked what kinds of close calls they've had, but Shawn just said, "family stuff." They are all passionate about the fact that all incest is seen as deviant or a form of child abuse. They convincingly argue that consensual sibling relationships are in a category by themselves, though at one point Adrian dismisses the concept of GSAs. "What are the odds?" he snorts contemptuously.

"The thing that screws us up," says Kim, "is that there are so many cases of incest involving rape or coercion or father-daughter stuff. That stuff's sick. There's also sick stuff going on in our world sometimes. I knew a girl who had started having sex or at least doing sexual stuff with her older brother when she was eleven and he was sixteen. She realized years later that this was the equivalent of rape, even though he didn't technically force her. But they never had anything like what me and my brother have or what these guys [pointing at the others] have. This is the real McCoy. There's nothing sick about it. This is about love."

By this point in the evening, I'd decided that I couldn't reveal what I was actually doing there because I didn't think they would appreciate the deception. But I really wanted them to talk about the subject at hand, so I took the plunge: "It totally sucks that we can't talk like this to other people, that we know we're going to get judged by society or arrested. How are we going to ever change people's attitudes if we can't talk about it? I remember watching the whole brouhaha over Angelina Jolie and her brother and thinking that she's about to come out of the closet about consensual sibling incest, and we got so excited. We thought people's attitudes were going to change."

At the mention of Jolie and her brother, everybody seemed to brighten up. "They're totally sibs," Allen said. "It's so obvious. I wish she'd have the balls to admit it." Only Adrian was skeptical. "Maybe," she said.

I asked whether they thought the backlash against the Oscar kiss would be different today, now that Jolie is known as "Saint Angelina." "Back then she was already considered a freak," I said. "There was the blood and the knives and the lesbian thing. She wasn't exactly the right poster child for consensual sibling incest."

"I didn't know any other sibs at that time," said Kim. "But I remember that Lars [her brother] and I thought she was getting ready to out herself, that she was testing the waters or whatever. We always want to do that. I always want to blurt it out to somebody, thinking that they'll understand that it's normal, [that] they'll see me and know I'm not a freak, that we love each other like anybody else."

Kim suggested we go to the computer in the den and check out the kiss on Youtube. We all gathered around Allen's laptop, and he wondered what search term to use. "Put in 'Jolie Oscar brother kiss 2001,' " Kim said.

"2000," I corrected her.

A couple of dud videos came up before he finally found the right one. At the conclusive moment, however, it was impossible to even see the lips make contact.

Allen googled it and found the photo in question, the one showing the smooch.

"They're totally tonguing," Kim yells out, excited. Adrian pointed out that there was no tongue visible. Leila seemed amused by the debate but remained silent.

Some other photos came up, including one of the siblings with their hands all over each other either before or after the Oscar ceremony and another from the Golden Globe press room of Jolie leaning back into her brother's arms and appearing to kiss him passionately, like a lover.

"That one proves it," Kim said. "That's more lovey-dovey than the Oscars."

That's when Adrian piped in with her theory.

"Here's what I've always thought about those two," she said. "I believe they had a powerful quasi-incestuous attraction to each other and that there was sexual tension galore, but that they probably never acted on it, even if they wanted to." And, although we'll probably never know for sure, that's roughly the same conclusion that I had come to.

In the end, however, it was irrelevant whether Jolie and her brother had ever slept together. The public perception of their possible incest was doing incalculable damage to her career and something had to be done before it was too late.

BILLY BOB

The new gossip started with a blind item—a vague and unsupported reference to a celebrity—leaked to a New York newspaper at the height of the incest allegations: "Which Oscar-winning actress is earning a reputation as a home-wrecker?"

It just so happened that Angelina Jolie was back in Mexico filming *Dancing in the Dark* with Antonio Banderas. It was only natural that readers assumed that the item referred to her and Banderas. His notoriously jealous wife, actress Melanie Griffith, was reportedly steaming when she read the item, assuming that Jolie had stolen her man.

Not a soul knew that Jolie was actually three months into an affair with Billy Bob Thornton, who at the time was engaged to Laura Dern. The affair was apparently so secret that not even the usual insiders had a clue it was going on. Hence, the surprise when in the second week of April, the *New York Daily News* reported that Jolie was dating the Oscar-winning *Sling Blade* actor. The paper also reported that while bowling with Matt Damon, Matthew McConaughey, and Thornton at an L.A. bowling alley, she was spotted with a new "Billy Bob" tattoo on her left arm. "She said she'd just gotten it," a friend of Jolie told the paper. "She said she'd always loved him."

The timing of the leak, of course, couldn't have been more convenient. E! Online correspondent Ted Casablanca had just said of Jolie's relationship with her brother, "That's not Hollywood. That's creepy!" And, more significantly, *Saturday Night Live* was beginning to make fun of Jolie's allegedly incestuous relationship on a weekly basis, threatening to make her a laughingstock. In one *SNL Weekend Update* segment, "Angelina" and her brother engage in a slobbery make-out scene after denying incest, followed by an admission that they had sex and the appearance of a deformed child with a human arm sticking out of its head and something foul oozing from its mouth.

But if the timing of the revelation of the affair was convenient and even suspicious, it was also effective. As the *Daily News* put it, the news that Jolie was involved with Billy Bob Thornton served to "quash the incest rumors." She needed to change the subject and she had done so very quickly. Indeed, before long, it seemed that America had completely forgotten the Oscar-night kiss and could only talk about Jolie's new love.

At first glance, Billy Bob Thornton may have seemed a rather unusual man to fall in love with. Exactly twenty years Jolie's senior, the forty-four-year-old Thornton was raised in Hot Springs, Arkansas, in a shack that had neither running water nor electricity. His mother was a professional psychic; his father, a teacher and basketball coach. After years of slogging it out in small roles, Thornton finally rose to attention as a regular cast member of the CBS sitcom *Hearts Afire*, starring John Ritter, from 1992 to 1995.

As a struggling actor, Thornton had worked as a waiter and had once served the legendary filmmaker Billy Wilder, director of classics such as *Double Indemnity* and *Some Like It Hot*. After chatting for a few minutes, Thornton asked for advice, at which point Wilder suggested he try his hand at screenwriting. He heeded Wilder's advice, and a few years later wrote the quirky independent feature *Sling Blade*, which he also starred in and directed. The film won him an Oscar for best adapted screenplay and made him a star, vaulting him to the top echelons of Hollywood.

Thornton's personal life was not as successful. Before he met Jolie, he had been married and divorced four times. His fourth marriage, to *Playboy* model Pietra Cherniak, ended in a messy divorce in 1997, and her allegations, despite being unproven, might have caused wife number five to think twice before tying the knot. In her divorce petition, filed in Los Angeles Superior Court, Cherniak made a number of troubling accusations against Thornton:

> Respondent's and my relationship has been characterized by his physical violence and his verbal, emotional, and mental abuse of me. The abuse, particularly physical abuse, has become more severe over the past twelve months. Respondent needs help. I am terrified that my filing this proceeding has jeopardized my life, and that Respondent will now follow through on his threats to kill me. I need protection, and I ask that this court grant the orders I have requested.

In her affidavit, Cherniak maintains that Thornton told her he was diagnosed by a psychiatrist as a manic depressive, and that he was taking lithium on a daily basis. But a month or two after they got married, she said he told her he couldn't take lithium anymore because it blocked his creativity and made him "feel like a piece of driftwood." When she was seven months pregnant, she charged, he became extremely violent for the first time, throwing or pushing her onto a coffee table. Then, three months after their son Willie was born, Cherniak says Thornton punched her in the eye while she was holding the baby, then got on his knees and "begged for forgiveness."

In her documents, she describes how three weeks before she filed for divorce, Thornton began to choke her. With his hands around her neck, she says he looked her in the eyes and said, "I am going to kill you. I'm going to kill you, and then I'm going to go to prison, and the children will be orphans."

Thornton countered that it was his wife who was abusive, charging that she was trying to up the terms of their divorce settlement now that he was rich and famous, having recently won his Oscar for *Sling Blade*. The judge granted each party a restraining order against the other.

Depending on who you talk to in Hollywood, Thornton is completely nuts or merely eccentric. Either way he is definitely odd. His eccentricities include some curious phobias, including his famous aversion to French antiques. "It's just that I won't use real silver," he told the London *Independent*. "You know, like the big old, heavy-ass forks and knives; I can't do that. It's the same thing as the antique furniture. I just don't like old stuff. I'm creeped out by it, and I have no explanation why . . . I don't have a phobia about American antiques. It's mostly French, you know, like the big old, gold-carved chairs with the velvet cushions. The Louis XIV type. That's what creeps me out. I can spot the imitation antiques a mile off. They have a different vibe. Not as much dust."

Whether he's nuts or not, he has admitted to some mental-health issues aside from manic depression, including a battle with obsessive-compulsive disorder. But even his detractors admit that he's creative, funny, and highly intelligent—all traits that Jolie valued in a man.

According to the official story, spread jointly by Jolie and Thornton after they went public in a whirlwind media blitz, they had heard of each other for a long time before getting together. Geyer Kosinski, one of the people Jolie thanked in her Oscar speech, was her long-time manager and used to be Thornton's agent. He told Billy Bob that he should meet Jolie because they had a lot in common: a mutual affinity for tattoos, for example, and an untamed wild streak that frequently defied Hollywood conventions. Two years before they officially met, they were at an event together, but Jolie reportedly deliberately avoided him. Then they were signed to co-star in the film *Pushing Tin*, a comedy about air-traffic controllers, which was filmed in Toronto in the spring of 1998. On the day she arrived to begin filming, the two got into the same elevator, though they still had not been formally introduced. Thornton later recalled that meeting: "I said, 'I'm Billy Bob. How are you doing?' and then we came out of the elevator, and I just remember . . . you know wanting something to not go away? Wishing the elevator had gone to China. It's like a bolt of lightning. Something different happened that never happened before."

Jolie offered a similar recollection. "Something went wrong with me in the elevator," she recalled. "Chemical. I really walked into a wall. It was the elevator. I kind of knocked it as we were both getting out. He got into a van, and he asked me, 'I'm trying on some pants, you want to come?' And I nearly passed out. All I heard was him and taking off his pants. I just said 'no.' And I went around the corner and sat against a wall, breathing, thinking, 'What . . . was . . . that? What the fuck was that? Jesus, how am I going to work?' I was just confused. I became a complete idiot."

The two claimed that one night in Toronto, after filming, they had dinner together, but not alone. Thornton was with his assistant, Jolie with a friend. But across the table, they talked and a connection was made. "We were not able to be together at that time," Jolie said. "We never at that time said one day we're going to be together. We couldn't," added Thornton about that initial spark. "But I know now that it was impossible not to be together." "We would say strange things," she said. "We would just randomly be talking about something in our lives, like the difficulty of living with people, and he'd say, 'I could live with you.' I thought . . . not that I wasn't good enough for him, but that I didn't know how centered in any way or together or solid or good for anybody I was. So I wouldn't have assumed that that would be a great thing if we were together."

At the time, Thornton was dating actress Laura Dern. Consequently, after *Pushing Tin* wrapped in late 1998, Jolie and Thornton had no contact for months until they began talking by phone. Then, in April

2001, after persistent media reports confirmed that Jolie and Thornton were now a couple, the syndicated Rush and Malloy column asked Thornton's publicist, Michelle Beaga, to check on the status of his romance with Dern. She confirmed that they had indeed "broken up" but claimed that she didn't "know any more than that."

Dern had met Thornton in 1997 when they both appeared on the landmark episode of *Ellen* where star Ellen Degeneres comes out as a lesbian for the first time, confessing to the character played by Dern. Dern and Thornton later co-starred in the 2001 film, *Daddy and Them*, which was written and directed by Thornton. They had both talked openly of their engagement. Only a month before his affair with Jolie became public, Thornton had given an interview to the magazine *Men's Journal* about Dern, saying, "I'm now happily involved with someone who's my best friend. We have a dog and a yard, and I have my kids part of the time, and I feel that I've become a good father, and it's something I'm proud of."

The couple split after Dern heard about the affair with Jolie, although apparently Thornton called Dern on May 1 to say he wasn't serious about Jolie; he was "just doing his thing." Four days later, however, he married Jolie. Dern told *Talk* magazine later that year, "I left home to work on a movie, and while I was away, my boyfriend got married, and I've never heard from him again. It's like a sudden death."

Dern is the daughter of veteran character actor Bruce Dern and the versatile, three-time Oscar nominee Diane Ladd. Ladd was said to have been fond of Thornton, but just after his publicist confirmed that he and Dern had broken up, Ladd was quoted in mid-April as saying, "Billy Bob Thornton is a real Dr. Jekyll and Mr. Hyde. I'm shocked. Billy Bob told me he wants my daughter to be his wife, and I know they've talked about having kids. I don't know how to make sense out of it."

By the end of April, Thornton and Jolie had gone public with their relationship, and there were hundreds of articles reporting that wedding bells were imminent. On April 28, E! Entertainment News's Hollywood correspondent Ted Casablanca reported that the two had eloped, but his information turned out to be incorrect. Nevertheless, a week later, on May 5, Thornton and Jolie drove to Las Vegas where they were indeed issued a marriage license at the Clark County courthouse. That same afternoon, they headed to the Little Church of the West Wedding Chapel, which hosts more than six thousand ceremonies a year, many conducted by an Elvis-impersonating minister who sings two songs by the King and performs the ceremony for the bargain price of $575.

Thornton and Jolie stuck to the more traditional $189 beginning package, which included a bouquet of red and white roses. "They came in like anyone else," recalled chapel owner Greg Smith. For their wedding music, the couple chose "Unchained Melody" by the Righteous Brothers. For the nuptials, the bride wore a blue sleeveless sweater and jeans, while the groom sported jeans and a baseball cap.

"He identified himself as Bill Thornton when he made the reservation," said Smith. "I didn't know it was him until they got here." The wedding entourage included none of Jolie's friends or family, only Thornton's pal, cinematographer Harve Cook, who served as his best man. Cook was the video assistant operator on *All the Pretty Horses*, a film Thornton had recently directed.

Soon, the couples' hyperbole reached a deafening roar. "I'm madly in love with this man," Jolie told *Talk* magazine afterward, "and will be till the day I die." "You know when you love someone so much you can almost kill them? I was nearly killed last night," Jolie told *US Weekly.* Thornton rolled up his pant leg for a reporter to reveal a colorful mushroom on his right calf with the name "Angie" written inside.

"It was all very over the top," recalled a correspondent for the *Hollywood Reporter* who says that "everybody in town was rolling their eyes when this stuff started to come out. It all sounded so contrived, like they had one of their scriptwriters churn it out."

Indeed, even publicists who earned their living generating this kind of coverage seemed to believe there was something amiss. In an unprecedented move, the venerable Hollywood public-relations firm of Baker Winokur Ryder (BWR), which represents A-list clients such as Leonardo DiCaprio, Brad Pitt, Chris Rock, and Michael J. Fox, quietly dropped Jolie from their stable. "Why on earth would anyone want to end a working relationship with the beautiful Oscar winner?" asked *New York Magazine*, which broke the story. Jolie's former representative at BWR, Cari Ross, told the magazine, "It wasn't working for me, so I told Jolie's manager Geyer Kosinski that I needed to back out." Kosinski's company, Industry Entertainment, immediately put their own spin on the unusual move. "Angelina decided she just didn't need a publicist," said Industry's Anne Woodward.

It was not, ostensibly, an opportune time to lose her publicist, but perhaps Jolie knew what she was doing. Publicly outing her affair with Billy Bob Thornton had succeeded in pushing talk of incest out of the media. The whispers were silenced, and her brother's name was barely mentioned in conjunction with hers after mid-April 2000. James Haven, the person closest to Jolie for more than a year, the man she had recently described as her "best friend" and "strongest support" had apparently been banished.

* * * *

On June 1, 2000, *New York Post* columnist Liz Smith, known for her vast network of Hollywood friends and sources, reported a rumor that she had recently heard about Jolie and Thornton's wedding: they were actually "just good friends." The marriage was "basically Billy Bob's way to keep an eye on Angelina because he feared she might fall over the edge somehow, and she agreed she needed looking after."

Indeed she did. Although there appeared to be little basis for the rumor, a story had already been circulating that Jolie had indeed fallen "over the edge" before her marriage to Thornton. Something happened between May 1, the day Thornton told Laura Dern he wasn't serious about Jolie, and May 5, the day Jolie and Thornton got married. The London *Daily Mail* was the first to break the news, citing sources from the Stewart and Lynda Resnick Neuropsychiatric Institute at UCLA in Los Angeles. The sources claimed that Jolie had checked herself in at the beginning of May. For seventy-two hours, she had been put on a psychiatric hold, the maximum somebody could be held under California law without being formally committed. Hospital insiders told the paper, "She said she was afraid she would hurt herself. She was very angry and thought she might kill herself if she wasn't treated." Jolie's spokesperson confirmed to the British paper that she had checked into the UCLA psychiatric hospital, but not because of Billy Bob Thornton. Rather, Jolie was treated for "exhaustion."

But a year later, Jolie broke her silence about the incident in an interview with *Rolling Stone*. She claimed that the psychiatric stay was indeed related to her relationship with Thornton. "What happened is we didn't know if we were going to be able to be together," she told the magazine. "I remember him driving somewhere and not knowing if he was OK . . . We had wanted to get married, and then for all these different reasons we thought we couldn't. We both were just . . . are just, it's a beautiful kind of love, but it's also a little insane, and I for some reason thought something had happened to him, and I lost the ability to . . . I just went a little insane . . . All I can say is, it was not about other people. Neither one of us didn't love the other. All I can say is, it's just that life just explodes sometimes . . . Maybe part of me needed to shut down for a few days to process everything before; I don't know."

She claimed that just before the incident she had been with Thornton in Nashville. When she returned to Los Angeles and was picked up by her mother at the airport, she started weeping. "And I just couldn't stop crying," she said. "I don't know what it was." She started stuttering, and soon she was unable to speak. A doctor was called and she was taken to the hospital. "Basically I thought he was gone," she said. "So they took it as I was going through the actual trauma of having lost, like a woman who lost her husband. I couldn't really speak."

The coincidence of being committed to a mental hospital only a month after she won an Oscar for portraying Lisa Rowe was not lost on Jolie, nor on her fellow patients. "Some of them were aware of me, some of them had seen *Girl, Interrupted*," she said. "In some weird way it's nice to know that everybody's insane. I mean, to a lot of young girls, to all of us, there are these pictures in magazines of people that have their shit together where their lives are perfect. I think that somehow it was refreshing for these people that were struggling with the different things I've struggled with in my life to realize that it's not about . . . Certain things don't make it better; there isn't some other side of life. People aren't any different."

When she was released from the hospital on May 4, Jolie told the magazine, her mother tracked down Thornton against her daughter's wishes. "I think he had been looking for me," Jolie said. Twenty-four hours later, the two were married. It was a romantic and touching account. But was it just a little bit too Hollywood?

* * * *

Ever since I had started to follow Jolie's biographical trail, there was one constant. Virtually everybody I talked to in L.A.—including ardent defenders of the actress, reporters, publicists, actors, and industry employees—was skeptical of her relationship with Billy Bob Thornton from start to finish. "It was just a little too coincidental that everything started leaking just as the brother rumors were running rampant and just when she needed a diversion," said one reporter. "Nobody's ever been able to find a single person—a friend, a relative, nobody—who saw any hint of this great love before the 2000 Oscar ceremony. Not a single hint before the controversy began, and then suddenly a week or two later they're madly in love. Give me a break. Go out and find me anybody who believed that was real. Fantasyland."

After posing as an actor for more than a year and seeing the unbelievable lengths to which celebrities go to maintain their image or to hide a secret, I had no trouble believing the cynical implications of the people who insisted the Thornton relationship was a giant smokescreen. But there was one nagging question that kept me from buying the story. What was in it for Thornton? It is a question that I still cannot answer with satisfaction to this day.

One thing was clear. Jolie had, without a doubt, been committed to a psychiatric hospital in the spring of 2000. I wanted to know why. One of my journalistic heroes was a woman named Nellie Bly who, in the late nineteenth century, was a reporter for the *New York World*. She feigned insanity to expose the conditions of the Women's Lunatic Asylum on New York City's Blackwell Island, now known as Roosevelt Island. Bly practiced mimicking mental illness and got herself diagnosed by a respected psychiatrist as "undoubtedly insane," which allowed her to be committed to the asylum for more than a week, experiencing the brutal conditions firsthand. Her account of her stay in the asylum, which she turned into the book *Ten Days in a Madhouse*, caused a sensation and led to significant and lasting reforms to the American mental-health system.

Inspired by Bly's example, I was determined to gain some insight into Jolie's experience by infiltrating the Resnick Neurospsychiatric Hospital, where she had been committed in May 2000. I wasn't sure what I expected to find or what I could possibly discover nine years after the fact, but I did have a way in. A year earlier, while I was posing undercover as a paparazzo for a documentary, Britney Spears had suffered her much-publicized breakdown and had been committed to the same hospital by her father, very much against her will. Unfortunately, I was in New York that day, so I missed most of the drama. But upon my return, I cultivated a number of relatively low-level contacts at the hospital, including security personnel and orderlies, some of whom still worked there when I returned a little more than a year later. It was one of these hospital employees who facilitated my deception.

"You have to be careful," he told me when I informed him of my plan. "Most of the people who come through here have had a referral from another hospital. If you just show up, they won't take you unless you have the right symptoms." He explained to me that I would have to claim to be suicidal or in danger of hurting others in order to be admitted. Armed with this nugget of information and a little background about the hospital, I was now ready to venture in.

When I arrived at the hospital the next morning, the place turned out be a whole confusing complex of buildings, but I finally located the right one. A security guard was stationed at the entrance and asked me where I was going. I told him that I was feeling suicidal, and he immediately directed me to the emergency ward, pointing down the hall. Instead of heading directly to emergency, I decided to look around and found a cafeteria where I decided to get a bite to eat. There were various food stations replete with all kinds of healthy foods—salads, juices, vegetarian selections. I opted for a chicken salad and mango juice. This was in marked contrast to Nellie Bly's description of the food she was served at the asylum: "Gruel broth, spoiled beef, bread that was little more than dried dough, and dirty water that was undrinkable."

I sat and ate at an outdoor terrace that was populated mostly by doctors and employees. Next to me was a man about thirty-five years old named Reeve, who said he was following up as an outpatient. I asked him what he was in for. "If it wasn't for this place I'd be dead," he said, explaining that he had gone through a messy divorce that left him almost catatonic with depression. "I had nowhere to run, nowhere to hide except here." He told me he was still depressed but that "it's under control now." I told him I'd heard of celebrities checking in here. Had he ever seen any?

"I know Britney Spears was here last year," he said. "My doctor told me all about it. It was a zoo. There were camera crews everywhere. She apparently turned the hospital upside down because everyone was trying to sneak in to get photos of her here. Supposedly, a photo of her in the unit would have fetched a million dollars. I heard they even stuck her in a padded room at one point."

After lunch, I met another patient in the men's room, a guy named Mark. I told him I'd been depressed since Kurt Cobain died, and I'd never gotten over it. It was the one area of mental illness where I had some familiarity, having authored a book about the rocker's death, with particular emphasis on the sixty-eight copycat suicides that took place in the aftermath. These were mostly depressed teenagers, and I was in my forties, but I played my best pitch. Lately I'd been thinking about finally ending it all, I told him. Was it worth checking in? Could they help me?

"Damn right. You'd be crazy not to. I shit you not," he said emphatically. "This place ain't like *One Flew Over the Cuckoo's Nest*. Everybody thinks it's going to be like that." I asked him whether he'd ever seen *Girl, Interrupted*, but he'd never heard of it. It turned out, however, that he is a fan of Angelina Jolie, having seen *Wanted*. "She kicks ass," he said. "They'll get you straight here, but don't, like, expect overnight results. It takes time," he added.

He told me that he did the three-day emergency program a while ago and now is strictly an outpatient, though he never told me what brought him there in the first place. "The group therapy sessions are incredible. They help you bring out everything that has been hidden inside. It's like a big self-disclosing session, but with other people. It's hard to tell personal stuff at first, but you get used to it. You walk out feeling like you're not nuts and that you're not alone."

I finally headed over to the emergency ward, where there were some desks with receptionists behind them. There was a bit of a line, so I sat in the waiting area. After a couple of minutes, a doctor came up to me, a resident I assumed, and asked me, "Are you OK?" I told him I was having some problems, that I wasn't sure I could "handle things." He told me I was in the right place and said I should fill out the forms when my turn came and they'd "take care" of me. When it was my turn, a woman who I didn't think was a nurse handed me some papers to fill out. When I asked her about the request for a medical ID number, she asked me how I was going to pay. I told her I was Canadian, and I didn't think I was covered by insurance. When I asked if I could pay in cash, she said that without insurance, it would be very expensive—"thousands of dollars"—if I was admitted. She gave me a number to call, saying that it would be much cheaper to visit as an outpatient. I finally left, vowing to call my travel-insurance company to for information about my coverage. I discovered later that unless I was brought to the hospital in an ambulance under special circumstances, I was probably not covered.

I had been planning a possible documentary to accompany my book, and I realized that I would need footage of the hospital as well as scenes of me inside the ward gathering information. This was no easy task, given that I had seen signs all over the hospital forbidding cameras on the premises. There was also a State of California privacy law providing stiff penalties for anyone who published photos or video footage showing the face of a hospital patient. Nevertheless, I needed some visuals. That meant I would have to sneak in not only myself but a cameraman on my next visit. I had a friend who was an accomplished video operator and still-photographer. I had used him before on a number of similar projects. He is an actor who once had a significant role in a made-for-TV movie playing a famous comedian, but he was now struggling, and I knew he could use the work. Fortuitously, he had just recently begun development of a reality-show pilot where the participants were given mini video cameras—the size of a credit card—to record their experiences. He agreed to accompany me on my next visit after I assured him it was safe.

We headed back five days later. At first, he seemed to regard our undercover day at the hospital as an adventure. But it wasn't long after I snuck us in that he began getting nervous. He was posing as my brother who had decided to bring me in because I was acting erratic, and he feared that I would harm myself. Once inside, he seemed to clue in that this was a place where people can be held against their will for weeks or months at a time.

Again, we were directed to the emergency room, but I was determined to sneak onto the inpatient floors to see what goes on there and to get some footage for my film. We were both nervous, especially since some of the security guards were armed. A little while later, we managed to get into a part of the hospital where, I imagine, I would be sent if I were admitted for a seventy-two-hour observation. Here the patients mostly seemed to be in their own zone, preferring peace and quiet. Each of the patients wore their own clothes, so it didn't feel like a typical hospital ward. In one lounge, we sat next to an outpatient named Roy. His story was the most gripping I had encountered since I arrived.

He told me he had been in a state mental facility for years in the early nineties before being let out. Now, he was coming here regularly for treatment. He wasn't shy to talk about his experiences. "I received electroshock in the state hospital," he said. I thought they had stopped that practice years ago. I had a vague notion that electroshock was akin to bleeding with leeches, but he disabused me of that. "They still use it even today. It's safer than it used to be, but it still messes up your head.

You have to consent to it. They tell you it's going to help you, but they ask you to consent while you're in no state of mind to make decisions. I suffered memory loss and more mental damage than I had before I was admitted.

"Here, it's completely different. They don't do things like that. They are genuinely concerned about the patients' well-being. I wish I could have been in a place like this back then. That place totally screwed me up. They just pump you full of meds; that's how they keep the patients under control. Here it's all voluntary; you're allowed to refuse meds."

When we finally got to the emergency ward, a receptionist again asked me to fill out a form. I told her I didn't feel up to it because I was feeling dizzy. She asked an attendant to look after me. Two minutes later, I was lying on a hospital gurney in a small narrow area just off the ward.

While lying there for about forty-five minutes, I was able to observe and hear what was going on. Everything seemed rather calm for a so-called nuthouse. It was a much different environment from what I had expected. At one point, I overheard a doctor talking to another staff member about a patient who was supposed to be released that day. To my surprise, the doctor was going on about how he feels strongly that the patient didn't need medication and that he was ready to re-enter society.

Meanwhile, I was dying to get off the gurney and explore some more. Finally, an attendant came in and asked how I felt. I told him I was feeling much better. My "brother" hadn't been permitted to accompany me into the area, but he managed to come in briefly and check on me as I was leaving, permitting him to get some footage. Again, I told the receptionist that I had no insurance coverage. Again, I was given a number to call and then I prepared to leave.

Everywhere I had gone in the hospital, I had tried to work Angelina Jolie into the conversation. Less than half the people I talked to knew she was once a patient there, although almost everybody knew that Britney Spears had been, and several people told me that some TV actor I had never heard of and whose name I forgot to write down had been in recently and attracted some attention.

Shortly before my third planned visit to the hospital, I finally had a breakthrough of sorts, thanks to one of my original contacts. He knew I was digging for information about Jolie's stay and said he had found me somebody who was willing to talk, an employee who once worked on something called the "psychiatric intensive care unit." I envisioned our meeting as a cloak-and-dagger operation, since not long before, an employee of the same hospital had been indicted for accessing and selling celebrities' medical records to a national media outlet for $4,900. I wasn't sure what I would do if somebody offered to sell me the records from Jolie's stay, but $4,900 seemed like a bargain to me.

At the appointed time and place, the employee met me in a designated outdoor area near a building called the Ronald Reagan Medical Center in the same complex. When we met, I made some small talk about how I had once acted as a stuntman in a TV movie about Ronald Reagan. Unimpressed, she proceeded to tell me she had a story for me about Jolie, whom, to my disappointment, she had never met.

"I'm watching *Larry King* with a staffer who had been on the unit when Angelina Jolie was a patient here," she said. "Suddenly King asks her about her time here. So we listen to her telling the whole story about her boyfriend, Billy Bob Thornton, and how she couldn't live without him, how she thought she'd lost him and all that, and my friend turns to me and says, "That was a fictional story. She's a very good actress. None of that was true." Or something along those lines. I remember she used the word fictional. I think I asked her what part wasn't true but that's all she would say. That was years ago." She agreed to give me the name of the woman, who now worked in another hospital, also in California. I tried to get in touch with her, but she never returned my calls.

My so-called undercover operation was decidedly less successful than Nellie Bly's. I now had a better idea about the reasons for Jolie's stay—that is to say, which were not the reasons. But I was not a lot closer to finding out what they were. Short of obtaining those medical files, we will probably never know for sure.

However, if I were forced to make an educated guess about the most likely cause, based on my own investigation, I would point to the times she let her guard down during the interviews she did in the months following her wedding to Billy Bob Thornton. During this period, she publicly professed to be happier than she had ever been. In a July 2001 interview with *Rolling Stone*'s Chris Heath, for example, she appeared to confirm what insiders have repeatedly said about the period following the Oscar kiss, when incest-gate was raging out of control and everybody around Jolie was telling her she needed to distance herself from her brother to salvage her career: " 'It was a difficult time for my family,' Jolie says. 'I haven't talked to Jamie for a few months. I think he . . . and I'm not sure . . . but somehow he made a decision to . . . to . . .' She pauses and begins to cry, 'not be around me so much, so we wouldn't have to answer stupid questions.' "

Some of the elements about the official story just didn't add up. If she was secretly dating Thornton for months and was madly in love, as she claimed, it is understandable that she may have kept the news from the world. But her own brother, who she's always claimed was her rock, who she shared everything with since they were children, has acknowledged that he didn't know about the affair or even the wedding until Jolie called him to tell him about it after the vows had been exchanged. "I asked her if she was happy," he recalled, "and she said, 'Yes, this is it.' "

Even more puzzling is Jolie's claim that she went straight to Thornton's hotel after the Oscar parties and talked with him in the garden. "He was in his pajamas, and he'd just put the kids to sleep," she told *Rolling Stone*. But Liz Smith of the *New York Post* told me that she was at the same parties and that she saw Jolie still going strong at a post-Oscar event well after 2:00 a.m. that evening. Others present had similar recollections, and a number of media accounts said she partied into the early hours of the morning, clutching her Oscar all the while. Jolie had to be at the airport at 4:00 a.m. for an early morning flight to Mexico, where she was scheduled to resume filming *Dancing in the Dark* that day, so the timing in her oft-repeated account just doesn't mesh with the chronology. Moreover, she also told *Rolling Stone* that "soon after that," her brother helped her pack so she could go off and get married. Yet James Haven, of course, has always claimed that he had no idea about the wedding until after it took place.

It appears that the account of her months-long, secret, pre-Oscar relationship with Billy Bob Thornton—revealed only after incest rumors started to swirl—is filled with many unexplained holes. On the other hand, maybe Angelina Jolie had actually found her soul mate and true happiness, as she would profess repeatedly over the next year. It certainly looked that way, at least for awhile.

SEX, BLOOD, AND LARA CROFT

Before anybody had a chance to catch their breath, the new couple seemed to be everywhere, professing their undying love for each other. "They were like Romeo and Juliet with tattoos," gushed one paper. Indeed, Americans couldn't pick up a newspaper or magazine without reading about the new Hollywood lovers.

"I'm so alive," declared Jolie to NBC. "All my life I've been thinking, I'm really just half alive. I thought I was crazy. Half the time I thought I was crazy. Then I met him, and I thought, maybe I'm crazy. But he is also. I'm so proud to be his wife; it's everything that I am. I've always been very, very much alone, and sort of felt like I was surviving that way and was self-contained and had my secret world in my head, and nobody ever really connected to me. I met him, and I loved life. I met him, and suddenly everything that I wondered about made sense, and everything that I wanted in life and hoped life could be . . . were the things that were possible."

Declaring Thornton her "soul mate," Jolie told another inquiring reporter, "He is the most amazing person I have ever met. He is really a free spirit, bold, really strong and passionate and wild and all those things. But he is also a very kind person, a really good friend . . . I never felt grounded before in my life . . . Suddenly, I'm more content, more alive, and my life has taken on meaning. He is my strength. Now, being centered and safe, I feel more alive than ever and really free." Calling Thornton the "sexiest fucking creature who ever lived," she declared, "I am madly in love with this man till the day I die."

It seemed they just couldn't stop talking about their sex life. After Thornton told an interviewer that he had to restrain himself from squeezing his new wife to death while she slept, adding the sex is almost "too much" for them, Jolie shared her reaction. "You know how you love someone so much you can almost kill them? I was nearly killed last night, and it was the nicest thing anyone ever did to me," she said.

There is a "sixth sense" to their lovemaking, Thornton eagerly told another reporter. "The other day we were mentioning how I needed to get one of those heart monitors on me, because I'm convinced I'm going to have a heart attack mid-thrust." Jolie responded, "He kissed me the other day, and I nearly fainted. I swear on my family's lives."

As if sensing the unspoken cynicism, they both took every opportunity to publicly guarantee that their love would last. "The fact of the matter is that I can't prove to you that we're going to stay together forever, but we are. If I see you again in five years' time, you will be able to say, 'How's everything going? How's your wife?' and I will say, 'Great.' The difference is that, in the past, I was never in the right spot."

When words alone didn't placate the cynics, they stepped it up with almost constant mention of their fabulous sex lives, including the occasional live demonstration. At the 2000 MTV Music awards, for example, they were stopped by a reporter on the red carpet and asked, "Billy Bob and Angelina! What's the most exciting thing you guys have ever done in a car?" Thornton, stopped, thought about it a moment, then replied in his down home Arkansas drawl, "We just fucked in the car."

When the *New York Daily News* noted that many people were waiting for their relationship to crash and burn, Jolie responded, "We might. But it'll be from sex." "He's an amazing lover, and he knows my body," Jolie offered. On another occasion, she complained to reporters about suffering from rug burns as the result of having sex on their pool table. To a British newspaper, she revealed that Thornton was such a stud in bed she couldn't walk after sex. "Before I know it, I'm in a corner across the room breathing heavily," she said, "and I don't know what happened, and I'm trying to get back on the bed, but I can't walk."

Asked whether her new-found love meant that she had sworn off women, she responded, "When I was twenty, I fell in love with somebody who happened to be a woman. I wanted to be close to her because I had feelings for her. The reality is, I love people. If Billy was a woman, then I'd be a lesbian. Simple. If I was a man, we'd be a gay couple."

While Jolie had gained a reputation for her penchant for unusual sex in previous relationships, she never spoke in detail about the sexual specifics and was not known for public displays of affection. She had also frequently expressed her discomfort at being portrayed as a sexpot. In February, 2000, only three months before she married Thornton, she told *Esquire* magazine that she had cried at a *Rolling Stone* cover shoot because they tried to force her to wear a lacy camisole, which she considered to be "verging on lingerie." Her "glammed up expression" in the final cover photo, she explained, was not the result of makeup, but tears. "The cover . . . I was totally red-faced from crying. Because I felt like a whore." She had often expressed similar consternation at the media's attempts to play up her sexual persona, even if she brought some of it on herself by openly admitting to S & M, bisexuality, and past use of knives during sex play.

Yet now at virtually every public appearance and media interview, she worked in the topic of her sex life with Thornton in graphic detail. She made sure to give almost each reporter and photographer a visual demonstration. "They kiss, and as they talk, discussing the day's details, she absent-mindedly traces her index finger up and down the zipper of his pants," one profile described about an evening at home with Thornton and Jolie.

At public events, the two were often all over each other, making sexually suggestive gestures or implying that they couldn't wait to have sex. At the Golden Globes one year, the *Los Angeles Daily News* reported that the "couple smooched their way down the red carpet." After they groped each other for reporters at the premiere of *Gone in 60 Seconds*, author Robin Gorman Newman, who is known as the "Love Coach," was quoted by one newspaper disapprovingly: "I would think the ones really having great sex are not the ones doing that." Newman may have known what she was talking about. After they broke up, Thornton gave an interview in which he implied that his sex life with Jolie wasn't everything he had made it out to be at the time. "Sex doesn't have to be with a model to be good," he said shortly after Jolie was named *Esquire* magazine's sexiest person in the world. "Sometimes with the model, the actress or 'the sexiest person in the world,' it may literally be like fucking the couch."

At the time, however, one couldn't have helped thinking that the pair was trying too hard to be the poster couple for amazing sex. "It just seemed so contrived," said one entertainment reporter who followed Jolie off and on for years. "It's like when the cameras, especially TV, were on, they'd put on this whole semi-pornographic show, but when they got inside, they practically ignored each other. There were literally pools among journalists about how long they would last."

The paparazzi were thrilled about the colorful visuals but most of them wondered what was going on. "Jolie never gave us that kind of shot before with her husband. She was always quite dignified, especially considering her wild rep. And then suddenly she's practically having intercourse with Billy Bob for our benefit," said a freelance British photographer who covers Hollywood for a London-based newspaper. "You had to wonder what the hell was going on with those two. I suppose it's possible he brought out the exhibitionist in her."

Even if the Hollywood establishment was skeptical about the constant public sex play, it made good copy, and no one dared to express their doubts in print. In Britain, however, the media were a little more candid and were not afraid to mock the couple's persistent public canoodling. "The more nauseatingly and insistently two stars proclaim their togetherness, the closer they are to coming apart," wrote London's *Evening Standard*. "Witness Pamela Anderson and Tommy Lee, Jennifer Lopez and Puffy, or America's Sweetheart, Julia Roberts, who has declared her eternal devotion to everything that moves, and several things that don't. Meanwhile, celebrity couples that evidence staying power, like Tom Hanks and Rita Wilson, tend not to conduct interviews with their legs coiled around each other's heads." The paper called Jolie and Thornton's shenanigans "marriage as performance art."

For good effect, the two occasionally threw in other bizarre tidbits to spice things up for reporters. First, Jolie revealed that Thornton often wore her panties to keep her close to him. He later confessed that some patrons caught him in her underwear while working out at the gym. Then the couple announced that they were wearing amulets containing each other's blood around their necks. "We exchange each other's blood all the time," he confessed. "For my birthday she gave me a will with our grave plots next to each other. That's pretty great, huh?" Jolie raised the stakes even higher: "And he signed a contract in blood with a notary public saying that we'd be together for eternity." Then she added, "Some people think a big diamond is really pretty. My husband's blood is the most beautiful thing in the world to me."

At one point, Thornton even summoned a nurse to the Louisiana set of a film he was shooting, *Behind the Sun*, and asked her to draw two vials of his blood and mix it with an anti-clotting agent. He explained that he wanted to write Jolie a love letter using his own blood. "I'm not really one for jewelry, but I love his blood," Jolie told reporters at another public event, fondling the glass globe pendant that contained her husband's hemoglobin. "If I could drink his blood, if I could devour every part of him, I would. He's my soul."

Perhaps because they had originally eloped, depriving reporters a chance to hear about their impending honeymoon night, they decided to get married again, this time at the Beverly Hills home they purchased for $3.8 million from the Guns n' Roses guitarist, Slash. "We want to get married in different countries, in different ways, different customs," Jolie told the *L.A. Times*. "We love getting married," Thornton chimed in.

Reporters were especially eager to know if Jon Voight approved of his daughter's new mate, who he had co-starred with in the 1997 Oliver Stone film, *U-Turn*. "My dad likes him," Jolie said. "I wasn't sure how it would work out. I mean, they are fellow actors. But my dad loves me so much, and he's never seen me so happy, so of course he likes him. They worked together, you know? I think it's funny that they both did *U-Turn* and they were so damn weird in it. We joke about that. 'Yeah, that's my family in that movie, the two strangest people!'"

More than one skeptical member of the media wanted to know whether Thornton could make a marriage work, considering his four previous divorces. "In terms of relationships, this may be the first time in my life that I haven't failed," he responded. "Angelina is everything to me as a human being, as an artist and as a partner."

But even early in the marriage there were whispers, true or false, that not all was as it appeared on the surface. As early as the summer of 2000, the *New York Daily News* reported that Jolie and Thornton were already talking divorce. At the same time, the paper cited a witness who saw Jolie emerging from the S & M club, Hellfire, which she and Jenny Shimizu had been known to frequent at the height of their affair.

Meanwhile, Jolie had been signed to appear in an action-film adaptation of a popular video game, *Lara Croft: Tomb Raider*, playing the title role. According to one apocryphal account, it was Lara Croft who had come between Jolie and her first husband, Jonny Lee Miller. The story had it that he had become so addicted to *Tomb Raider* on his Sony Playstation that he never spent any quality time with his wife. "When they called me about [playing] Lara Croft, I said, 'Oh God, not her,'" Jolie recalled. And even though video games likely had very little to do with the breakup of her first marriage, it can be argued that it was indeed Lara Croft who led to the end of her second.

* * * *

When Jolie was in the fifth grade and attending El Rodeo Elementary School in Beverly Hills, the school faced a budgetary crisis and announced it was forced to lay off nine teachers. One of those on the chopping block was Angelina's favorite phys ed. teacher, Coach Bill Smith. Jon Voight later described the campaign organized by his ten-year-old daughter to overturn the school board's decision. "Angie's friends and Angie got together and decided they would fight for him and they started this campaign 'Save Our Smith,' " recalls Voight.

Smith himself also remembers Angelina's role very well. "She's picketing, she's walking down the street with her sign," he recalled. "They came up with the idea for a bake sale where they could sell cookies and cakes and stuff to raise money for my salary. They really were like a little army. They were very focused on doing something good for somebody." The crusade worked. Of the nine teachers facing layoffs, only Smith kept his job.

"I think that was maybe the beginning of something for her so that she felt she could affect things, she could make a difference," said Voight, who was himself actively involved in a number of political causes, including the rights of American Indians and Vietnam veterans.

Jolie arrived in Cambodia in the fall of 2000 to do the location shots for *Tomb Raider*. But what might otherwise have been a simple romp in a tropical paradise ended up exposing her to what she later called the "horrifying depths of human suffering." When she returned to Hollywood, she would find it difficult to look at her life the same way again. She had, as she would soon declare, now "found purpose."

BRAD AND JENNIFER

As the sex life of Billy Bob Thornton and Angelina Jolie was splashed all over the papers throughout 2000, another high-profile celebrity couple was also making headlines, albeit in a decidedly more dignified manner. In July, just two months after Jolie eloped to Las Vegas with her new soul mate and pledged to be with him "forever," Brad Pitt and Jennifer Aniston tied the knot in Malibu. The lavish ceremony overlooking the Pacific Ocean reportedly cost more than a million dollars to stage. "Great location, great script, terrific casting," noted *People* magazine, declaring that the wedding had all the elements of a Hollywood production.

The two were first seen together in public on a dinner date over two years earlier, in March 1998. The event was brokered by their respective agents, which wasn't all that unusual in Hollywood; most public dates in the town are designed by publicists to get their clients' photos into the weeklies and generate mutually beneficial gossip. What was unusual was the that the two immediately hit it off. "He was just this sweet guy from Missouri," Aniston later recalled.

Pitt then called Aniston the day before she was due to leave for London to shoot the Ross-Emily wedding episodes on *Friends*, in the first week in April. He left a message on the answering machine offering to help her pack and bring her coffee, but he didn't hear back from her. "I was so nervous that I never called him back," she told Oprah Winfrey. "I pretended I got the message too late. When I got back from England, we had a date." After that first real date, when they hung out at Pitt's bachelor digs in Los Feliz listening to music, Aniston claims she fell in love. "We both knew [right away] . . . it was weird," she recalled. "The first time [he] kissed me, I stopped breathing. He literally took my breath away."

They spent the next few months hanging out together, long before the media knew about their romance. They played poker, watched TV, and enjoyed each other's company in what she would later describe as a "love nest." "From the second date, we just huddled into this little house," she recalled. "We wound up sitting on the couch and ordering in, having steak and mashed potatoes. That's how it all began. It was one of those weird feelings where you just kind of know. You feel like you're hanging out with your buddy. There was something very familiar about it. This was just very much meant to be." Aniston also said that she first knew they were destined to be together because her dog, Norman, adored him.

It wasn't until mid-June 1998 that the public got wind of their romance, when the two were seen kissing each other backstage at the Tibetan Freedom Concert in Washington, D.C. The next day, the *Washington Post* reported that the two were "all cuddly" together. And although their spokespeople insisted that they were just "good friends," the *Post* said a more apt description would be "touchy-feely friends."

With the cat out of the bag, the tabloids and entertainment weeklies had a field day contemplating a romance between the two A-listers. When Aniston finally confirmed the pairing, her breathless enthusiasm was like that of a teenager who had fallen in puppy love with the high-school quarterback. "Brad's the cutest guy on earth, and he's so deep and spiritual," she reportedly told one reporter. "I love being in his arms. I want to have his baby." It wasn't long before the media were speculating on a wedding date. After filming *Seven Years in Tibet*, the story of an Austrian mountain climber who becomes close to the Dalai Lama, Pitt had immersed himself in Tibetan Buddhism, and there were reports that he wanted to be married in a Buddhist wedding ceremony. "He'd like to go the whole Tibetan nine yards, having the wedding high on a mountain top, in traditional robes, with the Dalai Lama looking on," a friend of his told the Auckland, New Zealand, *Sunday News*.

Pitt finally proposed to Aniston in November 1999, and the two began planning a lavish summer wedding. Four months later, the couple attended the *Vanity Fair* post-Oscar party, where Joan Rivers approached the bride-to-be and loudly demanded to see the ring. Pitt held out Aniston's hand, prompting Rivers to announce, "It doesn't get any better." A few feet away, Jon Voight looked over to see what all the commotion was about. Next to him stood his daughter Angelina Jolie, clutching the Oscar she had won earlier in the evening.

* * * *

Like Angelina Jolie, Jennifer Aniston was born into a show business family of two actors. And like her future rival, her childhood was shaped by divorce and a womanizing father. Aniston was born in Sherman Oaks, a suburb of Los Angeles, in February 1969. Her father, born Yannis Anastassakis in Crete in 1933, had had his name changed to John Aniston when the family moved to the U.S. when he was two. He began his acting career on Broadway in the late 1950s. By 1962, he had moved to Hollywood, where his ethnic good looks got him roles. When he appeared as "Greek number 2" in a 1964 episode of the World War II drama *Combat*, he befriended another young actor of similar descent, Telly Savalas, who was a guest star on the episode. The future *Kojak* star and Aniston became best friends, and Savalas was named the godfather of baby Jennifer when she was born five years later.

By then, John Aniston had met and fallen in love with a struggling actress named Nancy Dow, who was divorced with a three-year-old son. When they finally were married, Savalas acted as best man. Neither

Aniston nor his wife were particularly successful as actors, however, with each only able to find work in small roles on sitcoms and crime dramas. By the time Jennifer came along in 1969, Dow's career highlight was probably an appearance in 1966 on the *Beverly Hillbillies*, while Aniston continued to be typecast as Greek characters on shows such as *I Spy* and *Mission Impossible*.

Like Marcheline Bertrand with Jolie, Dow devoted herself to raising her daughter and supporting her husband's career. After several professional setbacks, Aniston decided to change careers and become a doctor. Although he passed his pre-qualification exams, the forty-one-year-old couldn't get into medical school in the U.S. because of his advanced age, so he looked abroad. He decided to sell the family's small home in the San Fernando Valley and move to his homeland, Greece, where he was accepted into the University of Athens medical program.

After a year of study, however, his plans were thwarted when Turkey invaded Cyprus, forcing the closure of the island's university and prompting an exodus of Greek students back to Athens, where they were given preferential treatment in admissions. Foreign residents were asked to withdraw for a year, and the Aniston family was forced to move back to the U.S. As luck would have it, almost as soon as Aniston started auditioning again, he was offered a part on the long-running daytime soap opera, *Love of Life*, which was shot in New York.

The family settled in Manhattan, where, for the first time in his career, Aniston had a steady income, and his daughter Jennifer became a real New Yorker. Whenever Telly Savalas flew to New York for location work, he would hang around at the Anistons' Upper West Side apartment where he taught young Jennifer to play poker and eventually how to smoke cigars—both skills that endeared her to Brad Pitt years later. Despite her closeness to her godfather, though, Jennifer got to see enough during the family's brief time living in Greece to make her vow never to marry a Greek man. "Women are still second-class citizens," she later explained, "pregnant in the kitchen while the men sit around drinking ouzo and smoking cigarettes after dinner instead of helping with anything. And Greek men are well known for being philanderers." Her father, it seemed, was no exception.

Unlike Angelina Jolie, who was too young to remember her parents splitting up, Jennifer Aniston has vivid memories of the time she returned from a friend's birthday party when she was nine and her mother told her that her father would not be around for a while. John Aniston had fallen for his *Love of Life* co-star, Sherry Rooney, and had asked his wife for a divorce. Dow was devastated. Although she tried to keep it from her daughter, who didn't see her father again for almost a year, it didn't take long for Jennifer to figure out what was going on.

"It was awful," she recalled. "I felt so totally responsible. It's so clichéd, but I really felt it was because I wasn't a good enough kid . . . She didn't say he was gone forever . . . but I just remember sitting there, crying, not understanding that he was gone." For his part, John Aniston acknowledged the effect his affair had on Jennifer. "I knew the divorce was hard on her," he later said. "I'm sure I could have done a lot of things to make it easier, but it was very difficult."

After John moved in with Rooney, Jennifer would visit him on weekends at their home in New Jersey, just across the Hudson River. But whereas most weekend dads fill their kids' visits with fun activities, John had a different style. Jennifer later recalled being sent to her room when she was twelve for not being interesting enough. "My father told me I had nothing to say," she remembered. "He made me leave the table."

In fact, Jennifer had a lot to say. Her mother had enrolled her in an expensive Waldorf school—dedicated to the principles of the Austrian philosopher and educator Rudolf Steiner—which encouraged children's artistic side and nurtured the imagination. John paid the annual $15,000 tuition, and Jennifer thrived in the creative environment.

When she was only nine, one of the young Aniston's paintings was selected to be displayed in an exhibit at the prestigious New York Metropolitan Museum of Art. Shortly after that, her mother took her to a Sunday matinee performance of *Children of a Lesser God* on Broadway, and Aniston decided on the spot that she wanted to be an actress. When she enrolled at the Waldorf school, at age eleven, in 1981, she joined the school's drama club, where her first performance was in an eighth-grade Nativity play as an angel. In 1984, at fifteen, she applied for one of the few available spots at New York's High School for Performing Arts, known as PA, the school that had inspired the Alan Parker movie *Fame* a few years earlier. Three thousand New York children were competing for only seventy spots. After a rigorous audition process, she was accepted.

But unlike Jon Voight, who was thrilled at his daughter's career choice, John Aniston was dead-set against Jennifer following in his footsteps. "My father did not want me to be in this business," she later recalled. "It's so full of rejection." John Aniston doesn't dispute her recollection. "Well, I wasn't terribly thrilled," he said, well after his daughter had become famous. "I don't think a father who knows anything about this business would be thrilled to have a daughter who is in it."

After Jennifer graduated from PA in 1987, she took acting classes to hone her skills for what she still assumed would be a stage career, since the High School of Performing Arts usually prepares its students for a career on Broadway, not Hollywood. She also took night classes in psychology, thinking that she might want to be a psychologist if acting didn't work out.

Going to auditions by day, she soon landed her first professional role in an off-off-Broadway play called "Dancing on Checkers' Grave." Between auditions, she worked as a bicycle messenger and a waitress to pay the rent at the West Village apartment she had moved into when she was eighteen. She soon landed her second professional role, in an off-Broadway production called *For Dear Life,* which lasted all of forty-six performances. It didn't appear as if Broadway was her calling.

Finally, in 1989, she decided to abandon her stage ambitions and head to Hollywood, where her father had recently moved to take on a new role, as a Greek villain, in the popular soap opera *Days of Our Lives.* Although she never dressed in a chicken suit, her first years in the town were remarkably similar to Pitt's. While waiting for an acting breakthrough and living with her father and his second wife, Aniston waitressed and took a variety of unrewarding jobs—telemarketer, messenger, and receptionist. Her first real Hollywood role was in a made-for-TV movie called *Camp Cucamonga,* starring John Ratzenberger of *Cheers* fame. She also was cast in the pilot of a sitcom called *Molloy* and won a part on *Ferris Bueller*, the television spin-off of the Matthew Broderick hit film comedy, *Ferris Bueller's Day Off.* At a party during this period, Aniston was introduced to an unknown young actor named Matthew Perry, who would later play Chandler on *Friends,* and the two hit it off as friends immediately.

When she wasn't working, which was most of the time, Aniston liked to lounge around the house watching TV and eating mayonnaise sandwiches. It soon showed on her figure, which, as those around her noticed, had gotten noticeably rounder. She once described herself as being the physical product of her heritage: "I am a Greek woman, and that figure is big tits and a big ass." According to her, it was at that point that her agent took her aside one day and informed her that the reason she wasn't getting more parts was because of her weight. She promptly went on a diet, cut out the mayonnaise sandwiches, and almost immediately lost thirty pounds. The figure may have been greatly exaggerated, but there's no question that she suddenly appeared with the trademark body that would turn heads even after she turned forty.

"I was just as happy before I was thinner," she says. But casting agents were quick to notice the change, and she was soon offered parts in projects like the horror movie called *Leprechaun*, then an ensemble comedy series called *The Edge*, on Fox for the 1992–1993 season, and in a sitcom called *Muddling Through*, which aired for one season.

When she heard from her friend Matthew Perry about a show he was auditioning for called *Six of One*, Aniston asked her agent to get her a reading. It was an ensemble sitcom with a cast of three men and three women. The parts of two of the women, Monica and Phoebe, had already been cast, but the last one, Rachel, was still open. Though nobody anticipated just how big the show would eventually become, a number of young actresses wanted the part desperately. Among those vying for the role were future stars Elizabeth Berkeley, Denise Richards, and Tea Leoni. But when Aniston came in and read for the part, she immediately shot past her rivals; her poise and her natural flair for comedy so impressed the casting director that two hours after her audition, she received a call at home from the producer telling her the part was hers.

Before the pilot was shot a few months later, in the summer of 1994, the title of the show had been renamed *Friends Like Us* and then just *Friends*. The pilot episode was not well received by viewers, scoring a weak forty-one out of one hundred on the crucial "program test report," and for a while there was doubt that NBC would pick it up.

On that first report, it was Monica alone who had attracted favorable reactions from viewers. It was assumed that Courtney Cox, already familiar from her role on *Family Ties* as Alex Keaton's girlfriend, would be the star of the new series. "None of the supporting cast members reached even moderate levels with the target audience," read the report.

Before the first season was over, however, Aniston had been designated the breakout star of the new hit series. She would prefer to think it had to do with her acting or personality, but it appears instead to have had something to do with her hairstyle. Mid-season her hairstyle had been changed to a bob that framed her face in a unique way that had never really been seen on screen before. "It looked terrible on me," she later recalled. But the millions of American women who soon flocked to their salons requesting the "Rachel" seemed to disagree.

The success of *Friends* made a sort of America's sweetheart out of Aniston, whose down-to-earth openness attracted millions of admirers. She had no steady boyfriend and, being something of a homebody, she managed to keep her private life out of the tabloids. Her only visible baggage, it seemed, was an estranged parent—one more thing that she and Angelina Jolie appear to have had in common.

In 1996, Aniston's mother, Nancy Dow, had given an interview to a TV talk show, ostensibly about the pedagogy used at Waldorf schools. But when the show aired, there was no mention of Rudolf Steiner's educational philosophy. Instead, Dow chatted about her famous daughter and her success on *Friends*. That evening, Aniston called her mother, furious about her "betrayal." The two stopped speaking to each other. Then, to make matters worse, Dow came out in 1999 with a tawdry, self-serving "memoir" entitled *From Mother and Daughter to Friends*. The book was not particularly negative about her daughter, though it contained some embarrassing episodes from her childhood, but it disparaged Aniston's friends—whom Dow referred to as the "hip crowd"—and their bad language and wild behavior. The book angered Aniston even further, and any hope of a reconciliation seemed to vanish.

By the time *Friends* had been on the air for three seasons and Aniston was a full-fledged superstar, she had been single for an extended period. Shortly after the show first aired, she had briefly dated the dreadlocked lead singer of the Counting Crows, Adam Durwitz, but their fling was brief. In 1997, she was set up on a date with actor Tate Donovan, whose idea of a romantic evening at first appeared somewhat unusual. "He said we were going to dinner, and I got my hair done," she later recalled. "I put on this major dress. Then he took me to a strip-mall food court. Later, Tate told me he did it to see if I was one of those stuck-up girls."

Donovan couldn't handle the fishbowl life that came from dating an A-lister who was followed everywhere by paparazzi. He broke it off a month later, but the two soon resumed the romance, and Aniston realized that he was in a different league from some of the men she had dated in Hollywood. "He's a nice guy, a good guy," she said about Donovan. "I reached that point where I'm not going to deal with the bastards anymore."

They dated for more than two years, and she even arranged for him a guest role on *Friends*, playing Joshua, a passing love interest. By the time the shows were filmed, however, their relationship was somewhat shaky in real life, and Donovan later provided a revealing glimpse into Aniston's lifestyle at that point in her career.

"We were fighting when I was on *Friends*," he revealed in 2003. "We were already breaking up. Our split didn't happen suddenly. It was in the cards for a while. She likes top-notch hotels and luxury; I like B & Bs and riding my bike. That's the most shallow version of it, but it's indicative of our personalities." His explanation doesn't ring true, however, and may be based more on bitterness about being dumped than reality. Those in the industry usually describe Aniston as down-to-earth and approachable, not a typical Hollywood diva stuck on material things.

There may have been another reason for Donovan's post-breakup bitterness. The *Friends* episodes featuring Donovan aired in April 1998, the same month Aniston had returned from London and gone on her first real date with Brad Pitt.

* * * *

With his *Thelma and Louise*-driven escape from obscurity in 1991, Pitt had become a genuine movie star by the time he started dating Jennifer Aniston in 1998. In 1992, Robert Redford directed him as one of two fly-fishing brothers in *A River Runs Through It*. In that film, Pitt delivered what the *Los Angeles Times* called "a career-making performance," high praise for the acting skills of someone who could have easily coasted by on his looks. "It's like tennis," Pitt said of working with Redford. "When you play with somebody better than you, your game gets better."

Two years later, Pitt starred with Tom Cruise in the 1994 vampire epic, *Interview with the Vampire*. "I hated doing this movie," he later told *USA Today*. "Hated it. Loved watching it. Completely hated doing it. My character is depressed from the beginning to the end." He also hated working with Tom Cruise, who had attempted to recruit his co-star to his controversial church, but Pitt was having none of it. "He thought Cruise was a shallow asshole," a former crew member said ten years later. "He made no secret of his disdain and he never socialized or hung out with Cruise when they weren't filming."

Vampire producer David Geffen, not usually given to hyperbole, issued a prediction at the time: "Brad is one of the most attractive and talented men in the world. He's going to be one of the biggest actors out there." Indeed, that year saw Pitt earn his first Oscar nomination for playing an erratic mental patient in the sci-fi thriller, *12 Monkeys*.

That same year, he fell in love with twenty-two-year-old Gwyneth Paltrow, who played the role of his soon-to-be-decapitated wife in the grisly thriller *Se7en*. At first, she said she resisted his advances, assuming he was just another horny Hollywood Lothario. "And then I started getting a crush on him," she told the *L.A. Times*. "I'm like, 'Are you sane? You can't get a crush on Brad Pitt. Get hold of yourself.'"

Pitt, however, seemed smitten from the start. When he won a Golden Globe award for his performance in *12 Monkeys* in 1996, he thanked Paltrow as "my angel." After a long courtship, during which they were Hollywood's darling glamour couple, Pitt proposed in December 1996, while filming *Seven Years in Tibet* in Argentina, and the two kicked off a long, public engagement. "Brad's the good one and I got him," Gwyneth bragged. "I can't wait, man," he told *Rolling Stone*. "Walk down the aisle, wear the ring, kiss the bride. Oh, it's going to be great."

But in June 1997, as abruptly as it began, it ended. Pitt broke off the engagement. No explanation was given but, from all appearances, there was no other woman involved. "It's not because of any one specific event," his publicist said at the time. Pitt, it appears, had simply fallen out of love.

By the time Aniston and Pitt started dating seriously, they had both just come off recent long-term relationships. That didn't seem to affect their courtship, possibly because their friends on both sides, by all accounts, seemed to sense they were meant to be together.

"You go through a lot of different relationships with friends, but never was I absolutely positive like I was with Brad," recalled Aniston's close pal, *Veronica's Closet* star Kathy Najimy, about the moment she knew Pitt was the right one for Aniston. "I saw how much he loved her. I went home, and I was weepy about it. She was one hundred percent herself with him, and that's all I really wish for my friends."

Before the wedding, Pitt's own friend, *Little Odessa* director James Gray, told *People* magazine about a dinner he had with the engaged couple when Pitt was trying to quit smoking. "They finish each other's sentences; they're two peas in a pod," he recalled. "Jennifer was telling him to wear his patch. She's trying to get him not to smoke, but she smokes. He says, 'Don't smoke either, honey!' And she says, 'Well you quit first!' They're perfect together." "Marrying Jennifer was the pinnacle for him," echoed Marcia Gay Harden, Pitt's co-star in *Meet*

Joe Black. "Sexiness isn't just about the single bachelor and good looks. There's something gorgeous about his commitment."

After the two were married in 2000, their friends continued to publicly marvel about the strength of their relationship. "They just made each other really happy, and it was completely obvious," Pitt's long-time friend Catherine Keener told *Rolling Stone*. The only time they spent apart was when Pitt had to go on location for a film. The separation, according to onlookers, was hard on both of them. When Pitt spent five weeks in Real de Catorce, Mexico filming *The Mexican* with Julia Roberts, the film's producer Lawrence Bender told a reporter about his star's unhappiness on the set. "He was like, 'I gotta get back and see my girl.' They're just lovebirds. There's nothing else you can say."

Aniston's *Friends* castmates were equally enthusiastic about her marriage to Pitt, who was a constant visitor on the set and even guest-starred on an episode, playing a former schoolmate who hates Rachel. "Jennifer's a lot more peaceful now, like a woman who's in a good relationship," Lisa Kudrow told a reporter. "There's not a lot to say about them because there's no problems. They're both light-years ahead of themselves. You know how your grandparents have a certain perspective about life? They've got that now."

Although Aniston's philanthropic efforts at the time can't be compared to those of her future rival, she was heavily involved in social causes long before she met Pitt, including children's charities and equality for gays and lesbians. Pitt too was starting to come into his own as an activist during the marriage, actively involving himself in the 2004 presidential election campaign on behalf of Democrat John Kerry.

They usually kept their causes separate, but in 2004 the couple signed on to lend their celebrity to an international movement called *One Voice, a* grassroots campaign to bring Israelis and Palestinians together and work towards peace in the Middle East. Soon after they joined,

Pitt and Aniston issued a joint statement about their commitment to the cause. "The past few years of conflict mean that yet another generation of Israelis and Palestinians will grow up in hatred. We cannot allow that to happen." They told the media they believed most people in the region wanted a negotiated settlement with an end to violence and imagined that by appealing to "ordinary folk," they could help bring the warring parties together.

Personally and professionally, things were going very well for them as 2004 began. All that was missing was a baby.

THE FEUD

In his brilliant 2006 essay, "The Many Faces of Celebrity Philanthropy," Joseph Epstein recalled an old joke about a young Hollywood star seeking to ornament his rising fame with a charitable cause. The star instructs his agent to find a charity for him to associate with. "Morty," he says to the agent, "you gotta get me my own charity. Bob Hope and Bing Crosby have their charity golf tournaments. Doris Day works for protecting animals. Danny Thomas has St. Jude's Children's Hospital. Jerry Lewis has Muscular Dystrophy. It works for them, Morty, it'll work for me. Get on it right away." A week later the agent calls back. "You've found my charity?" the young star asks. "It wasn't easy," the agent replies, "just about everything was taken." "What was left for me?" the star asks, with hope in his voice. After a brief silence and a clearing of the throat, finally the agent says, "Acne."

The point of the joke, explained Epstein, is to show the artificiality of celebrity giving, "the emptiness of it all, reducing it to the low status of little more than a good career move. Is this unfair? Of course it is. I, for one, am certainly not prepared to say that Doris Day doesn't truly love stray dogs. Nor am I ready to quip, as the comedian Lenny Bruce did, that Jerry Lewis damn well ought to work for muscular dystrophy, since he caused it. (Bruce would here make a claw of his fist and go, 'Gnang, gnang.')"

Indeed, as any celebrity publicist will tell you, Hollywood philanthropy—associating an actor with a humanitarian cause—is one of the most effective methods for repairing or transforming a tarnished image. So it was hardly a surprise when *Time* magazine sounded a mocking note at the news, in August 2001, that Angelina Jolie was appointed a United Nations Goodwill Ambassador. "Snicker if you will—it's certainly understandable—but Angelina Jolie actually earned the title of goodwill ambassador for the UN High Commissioner for Refugees," the magazine wrote, noting that a baby in Sierra Leone had recently screamed in terror at the sight of the actress, supposedly because of her white skin. "It certainly couldn't have been that vial of husband Billy Bob Thornton's blood on the chain around her neck," *Time* wrote. But the mocking didn't last long. People soon started to realize that Jolie was not just any fly-by-night celebrity pretending to care. She appeared to be genuine in taking up a cause that was near and dear to her heart.

It all started when she flew to Cambodia at the end of 2000 to film *Lara Croft: Tomb Raider.* While there, she was taken to see the plight of refugees on the Thailand-Cambodia border where she expressed shock at the conditions they faced. "Growing up in the States, I learned about American history, and that was the extent of it," she told the *Scotsman.* "I focused on what was affecting us, not the rest of the world."

Jolie had long admired Audrey Hepburn, whose reputation as a screen legend was cemented towards the end of her distinguished career when she was appointed a UNICEF goodwill ambassador by the United Nations. Hepburn then traveled tirelessly, dedicating the last years of her life to helping impoverished children in the world's poorest nations.

The significant difference between Hepburn's appointment and Jolie's is that the UN had approached Hepburn to become a goodwill ambassador because of her long-stated commitment to children, whereas it was Jolie who approached the UN to offer her services. Jolie has asserted that she merely called them up asking for information and that they then asked her to come aboard. Others, including the UN itself, have claimed that Jolie herself offered to become an ambassador.

There are also a number of conflicting stories about how she first became interested in the plight of refugees. At first, she claimed it was her trip to Cambodia that opened her eyes to the issue. But in 2003, when she was promoting her newly released film *Beyond Borders*, she gave an interview to *Newsweek* in which she shared a different version. She stated that her initial interest began in 1998, when the film about international aid workers was first under development but was struggling to find financing:

> Five years ago, I read the script for *Beyond Borders*, and I was so moved by the content and curious about a world I knew nothing about. I felt a responsibility to start to educate myself as we all should, as we grow up. When I found out the film wasn't going to go forward, I was really sad because I had wanted to take that journey and understand what that was about. Then it dawned on me that I could educate myself and travel to these parts of the world and see for myself what was happening. And so I read many different books on different organizations and different chapters of the UN. And I was shocked when I read about how twenty million people are displaced today. I couldn't understand how that was possible. I called [the UN office in] Washington and, at the time, I had been following stories about Sierra Leone, so that was the first place we discussed me going, so I could observe and help.

Whatever her original motivation, it was soon obvious that her new-found interest in humanitarian issues was sincere, especially when she put her money where her mouth was, donating $1 million of her own money and traveling to dangerous hotspots in Africa and Asia to educate herself on the issues.

In the past, the UN had only designated non-controversial celebrities to the post of goodwill ambassador—people like Danny Kaye, Richard Burton, Sophia Loren, and Muhammad Ali. Now, they explained that the appointment of celebrities like Jolie and another recently appointed ambassador, former Spice Girl Gerri Halliwell, was meant to appeal to a new demographic: teenagers. "The UN is often seen as a boring bureaucracy by young people," explained a spokesperson.

At the ceremony where she was formally appointed an ambassador, Jolie broke into tears as she described her encounters with Afghan refugees in Pakistan during a recent trip. "It's still very hard to talk about. It is the worst situation, I think, because there is no end in sight for the needs of these people," she said emotionally. "But I was surprised to sit down with these women and their children and talk with them, and they were so kind and warm and funny and generous and hard-working and grateful for any little help they could get, and they are living in a situation [where] I don't think anybody in this room could survive for more than a few days."

Whereas a year earlier Jolie talked ad nauseum to the media about her sex life with Thornton, she was now single-minded about a different topic. The constant talk about sex, blood, and underwear had been remarkably effective in changing the subject from incest, but she had nearly become a caricature. She was no longer being offered the kind of serious roles that had won her three consecutive Golden Globes. Instead, she was being offered mediocre action movies from people wanting to capitalize on the new image she created for herself in her huge box-office success *Lara Croft: Tomb Raider*. Her management was worried that she had lost her momentum, and numerous Hollywood insiders have reported that she was urged to transform her image or at least stop the embarrassing public antics with Thornton.

While there seemed to be no question that she had an authentic concern for her cause, she now worked her new passion into almost every interview. Publicly, she started to reject the material values of Hollywood and talk about how she could channel her fame to help others rather than for personal profit. She discussed how her trips abroad had helped give her a new perspective about her fame. "You know, what's funny is that I thought I would come back with a lot of anger or a lot of distance," she said about her first international trips on behalf of the UN. "But instead, I felt bad for people who were focused on material things or fame. I just wished for them to not be so caught up in those things and hoped they would realize that all that stuff doesn't matter, and this stuff does."

Returning from a UN trip to Africa in 2001, she told reporters that she had undergone a transformation. "I had gone from being in an African jungle to sitting on a first-class flight home," she recalled. "Though I was covered in dirt, I felt real and at my most beautiful. And suddenly, I was surrounded by people who knew me as an actress. I think my appearance was upsetting to all of them, in their suits and makeup, looking at magazines. I felt sick because I started flipping through the articles about parties, film ratings, who has this, who's the hottest that. I felt like I didn't want to return to that world."

The media also began to notice that she and Thornton were spending less time together. When they did appear, the subject of their sex life never came up anymore, much to the disappointment of the gossip-columnists and paparazzi. In the past, they had always been able to count on the couple to give them something colorful.

Thornton later lamented that when she first came back from filming *Tomb Raider*, Jolie was a different person from the wild child he had married. Jolie later described his increasingly wary attitude to what he assumed was a hobby. "He would say, 'Why are you going to do these things? What do you think you're going to accomplish?'" It wasn't just her husband who was wondering what she was doing. "It seems crazy to some of my friends that I want to leave the warmth and safety of my home. But I had to believe I could accomplish something. They asked, 'Why can't you just help from here? Why do you have to see it?' I didn't know how to answer them."

Meanwhile, Thornton was devoting more and more time to his own hobby, the blues-and-roots rock band that he recorded with on weekends, frequently spending more time with his bandmates than with his wife. Both spouses stopped wearing the infamous amulets around their necks bearing drops of each other's blood.

Jolie's parents, who both had strong social consciences, were more supportive of what she was doing. They were also deeply worried about her safety, especially before her first trip to Sierra Leone and Tanzania in February 2001. Just before she was scheduled to leave for Africa, Jon Voight called the American office of the United Nations High Commission for Refugees and tried to persuade them to cancel her trip. In the journal she kept of that trip, later published as a memoir entitled *Notes from My Travels*, Jolie recalled her reaction when she learned of his behind-the-scenes maneuvering. "I was angry with him," she wrote, "but I told him that I know he loves me and that as my father he was trying to protect me from harm. We embraced and smiled at one another."

Bertrand was no less concerned, Jolie admitted in her journal: "My mom looked at me like I was her little girl. She smiled at me through her teary eyes. She was worried. As she hugged me goodbye, she gave me a specific message from my brother, Jamie. 'Tell Angie I love her, and to remember that if she is ever scared, sad, or angry, look up at the night sky, find the second star on the right, and follow it straight on till morning.' That's from *Peter Pan*, one of our favorite stories." Whether her travels were causing tension in the marriage or whether she was trying to distance herself from the couple's crazy antics of the year before, Jolie was rarely seen in public with Thornton any more except for high-profile events. Now, instead of talking to reporters about their sexual antics together, she began to talk about how she spent a lot of time with Thornton's kids. "Billy Bob has two beautiful children," she told one magazine. "They're just turning seven and eight. They are still babies, and they live with their mother . . . She is wonderful about me getting to know them because they spend a lot of time with us and we want to spend more and more time with them."

The media began to take the bait. The talk about her "stepchildren" begged the obvious question: Did she want some of her own? It was a question that started to be asked by just about every reporter. At first, she was noncommittal, but then started to hint at a future adoption. "We are a family already," she told an inquiring journalist. "But when they are older, I think we will adopt quite a few children."

In July 2001, after she had signed on to play Lara Croft for the second time, she was asked by *E! News Daily* correspondent Greg Agnew whether *Tomb Raider* was becoming a "franchise." Her response was telling. "I have this year and a half, two years between them in case I do . . . get pregnant." When Agnew asked if she was considering pregnancy, she responded, "No, I've never wanted to be pregnant. I've always wanted to adopt." He pressed on, curious to know whether she would adopt in the United States or go abroad. She refused to go there. "We've talked about it a lot, and I'm sure you'll know. Everybody will know," she replied cryptically.

The question was much on her mind during this period. According to a friend of Thornton's, Jolie had looked into the possibility of an American adoption but had been told her odds were slim, given her controversial past. "I think she talked to a lawyer at one point," he revealed. "She wanted a newborn, not an older child, and she was told that she and Billy might have difficult being accepted as prospective parents because of their issues."

Indeed, when Jolie publicly contemplated adoption for the first time, it came just a year after she had spent seventy-two hours in a psychiatric institution. Thornton himself also had some mental-health issues in his past, and they had both admitted to previous substance-abuse problems. On top of that, Thornton had been accused by a previous wife of extreme physical and mental abuse. Not, perhaps, the ideal candidates for adoptive parents.

Still, I was curious if those issues would actually disqualify them from the adoption process, so I decided to put it to the test. Posing as a father who wanted to adopt a baby with my wife because of infertility problems, I approached a California-based organization called the Adoption Network Law Center, which specializes in "legal-adoption assistance."

Talking to an agent named Robin Elcott, who specializes in newborn and domestic adoptions, I told her my name was Billy Bob Jackson and that my wife and I wanted to adopt, but we were afraid that some of our personal problems might disqualify us. I told her that I had recently been in a psychiatric ward for seventy-two hours, under observation for some mental-health issues, and that both my wife and myself had struggled with drugs and alcohol in the past but that we were now clean. Would that rule us out?

"It's safe to say that your chances would be lower," she explained. "You would have to pass a home study, which gets into a lot of details financially, physically, and emotionally." However, she emphasized that we would not automatically be disqualified. "If you had ever been arrested, it would be another matter," she explained. "But it's on a case-by-case basis, and they would look at your current circumstances before making an evaluation."

I asked whether I would have a better chance adopting abroad. "Not necessarily," she said. "It depends on the country. In some foreign countries, mental illness is actually an official exclusion, so you would have a better chance adopting here than in those countries." Even for a foreign adoption, she explained, a home study would be required.

In August, Jolie appeared on CNN's flagship talk show, *Larry King Live,* where she was asked about her plans. Again she hinted that she was thinking of adopting, but this time she referred to orphans, implying that she was thinking of a foreign country where, unlike the U.S., orphanages still exist:

KING: Want a family?

JOLIE: Yes.

KING: Working on it? Would you like to get one soon? Have you thought about when you might want one?

JOLIE: Well, I've always wanted to adopt. I've always felt it was . . .

KING: You don't want to give birth?

JOLIE: It's not that. It's that I've just . . . I think some people have certain callings in life. Certain people are maybe meant to give birth and it's wonderful. And some people . . . Ever since I can remember, after hearing about different kids that need homes or different orphans or different, you know, not a baby necessarily, but little kids . . . I've just always known that I would love [an adopted child] as much as I would love my own. So I'd be a great mother to adopt a child.

One of the countries that doesn't automatically exclude adoptive parents because of mental-health issues is Cambodia, where Jolie had filmed *Tomb Raider*. She often said that during those weeks on-set, she had fallen in love with the people there. It was soon apparent that she had her sights set on adopting a Cambodian orphan. At first, Thornton sounded like he was on board with the idea, and he even accompanied his wife in September 2001 to fill out the forms required by the U.S. Immigration and Naturalization Service to start the process of foreign adoption.

The couple underwent and passed their home study and announced to friends that they would be travelling to Cambodia to visit an orphanage and choose their new baby. "Somebody told me that if you're going to adopt an orphan, you should adopt from a country you love, because that's the only history you're going to share with them," Jolie later explained of her decision to adopt from Cambodia.

But Cambodia also had another appeal, at least at that time: its relatively lax adoption criteria. According to the internationally respected Cambodian human-rights non-governmental organization, LICADHO, corruption and poverty had in recent years turned Cambodia into a "magnet for wealthy, childless foreigners," with as many as a thousand adoptions rushed through annually, most of them to the United States.

When she visited Cambodia in November 2001, the UN announced that the purpose of her trip was to visit returned refugees on the Cambodia-Thailand border. But according to local photographer Chor Sokunhea, "We all knew why they were here: to adopt a baby at an orphanage she had been to when she made the movie." She did indeed take a trip to an orphanage in Battambang, and by the end of their two-hour visit, Jolie knew she had found her son. He was the last child she saw, a three-month-old boy named Rath Vibol, who she said was from "a very poor village." "I went into an orphanage and decided I'd not go for the cutest child but just go to the one that connected to me," Jolie later recalled. "He was asleep, and he woke up and smiled. As soon as I saw him smile, I felt like this kid wasn't uncomfortable with me. He seemed okay in my arms."

Before the adoption could be completed and the parents could bring the boy—renamed Maddox Chivan by Jolie—back to the States, there was still a significant amount of red tape to cut through, not the least of which was getting the U.S. visa required to bring him home. That process suddenly got very complicated in December when the first reports came to light that illegal networks in Cambodia were buying infants from destitute mothers and selling them to orphanages. "The key is money," explained Naly Pilorge, deputy director of LICADHO. "Americans are paying $10,000 to $20,000 [for a child] in a country where the average income is $250 a year . . . That comes to something like $7.5 million a year, all under a cloak of humanitarian assistance."

The news prompted the U.S. government to ban the adoption of Cambodian orphans by Americans. An exception was made, however, for applications processed before December; those would be decided on a case-by-case basis. This meant that Jolie and Thornton were still eligible.

Less than three months later, Jon Voight, who had just been nominated for an Oscar for his portrayal of Howard Cosell in the biopic, *Ali*, attended a luncheon honoring Oscar nominees. After lunch, he let the news slip. "Angelina adopted a Cambodian baby. I'm a grandfather today," he said. Indeed, the Cambodian authorities had suddenly approved the adoption, and baby Maddox was brought to an ecstatic Jolie, who was in Namibia filming *Beyond Borders*.

Meanwhile, to the frustration of the new parents, the U.S. embassy in Cambodia still hadn't issued Maddox's visa to enter the U.S. "I'm certain Thornton and Jolie both know that . . . they must complete the proper procedures in accordance with U.S. law before bringing the child into the U.S.," the U.S. ambassador to Cambodia, Kent Wiedemann, said.

Finally, at the end of April 2002, the embassy's special investigations unit approved the adoption, and Maddox was cleared to travel to his adoptive land. Then, after Jolie finally returned with baby Maddox to begin her new role as mother, she was suddenly engulfed by an adoption scandal that was now rocking Cambodia. In June, human rights agencies in Phnom Penh, the Cambodian capital, charged that Maddox was not an orphan at all but that he had been "bought" from his destitute mother. Equally alarmingly, they charged that his adoption had been fast-tracked after "substantial bribes" had been paid to senior government officials. "I'm sure that this child was not a real orphan and was not abandoned," Dr. Kek Galibru, head of LICADHO, told the London *Daily Mail*. There was an allegation that Maddox's birth mother was paid approximately $100 to hand over her son, a small fortune for a poor Cambodian.

Maddox's adoption had been facilitated by American businesswoman Lauryn Galindo, a Hawaiian-born former professional hula dancer who had been working as an adoption agent in Phnom Penh since the early 1990s. It was Galindo who had personally brought Maddox in March from the Cambodian orphanage to Walvis Bay, Namibia, where she delivered him to Jolie. Galindo later denied that she had paid money for children or been involved in any illegal practices. "When people ask me what I do, I don't say adoptions, I say humanitarian work," she told the *Cambodia Daily* newspaper. "I didn't come here to steal children. I came here to do what I could to help." Pressed further, she admitted that half of the $9,000 fee she charges American couples for processing an adoption was handed over to government officials. She denied that this is akin to bribery. "It's OK to give tips," she explained. "It's fine because these guys can't live on their salaries . . . I'm really happy to share the wealth." Quizzed by reporters about the controversy, Jolie insisted that the adoption was legitimate and maintained that she and Thornton had hired private investigators to determine Maddox's lineage. She has never released the results of that investigation, however, nor the documentation that she was given about Maddox's origins.

Behind the scenes, Jolie immediately hired a team of lawyers to fight any attempt to return Maddox to Cambodia after the U.S. government hinted that she might have to do so. "I would never rob a mother of her child," she insisted. "I can only imagine how dreadful that would feel. Maddox is my baby, he is by my side all the time, and I think I can give him so much. I can no more imagine living without him than not breathing." Her efforts appear to have been successful, and no further action was taken.

Two years later, however, when the allegations had been long forgotten, Jolie's adoption agent, Lauryn Galindo, quietly pleaded guilty in U.S. federal court to fraud and money laundering in the falsification of documents to obtain visas for Cambodian children purported to be orphans. It is uncertain to this day whether Maddox was one of the orphans whose papers she had falsified, but Jolie was never formally implicated in her case.

The indictment leveled against Galindo, in fact, concerned only adoptions processed between 1997 and 1999, more than two years before she helped Jolie obtain Maddox. But it does provide a rather revealing insight into her modus operandi. In one 1998 case, according to the charges, Galindo faxed her sister the medical records of a child to be adopted with a handwritten note: "Father dead, mother very poor." Four months later, she allegedly told the adoptive parents to give the birth mother $100 and to donate $3,500 to the orphanage that had been holding the child.

This may be significant, given that at the height of Maddox's adoption process, Jolie announced that she was making a sizable donation to the orphanage. "Before I adopted Maddox, I decided to do something financially to help the whole orphanage," she explained at the time. "I can't bring every kid home, but I can make sure that life is better for a big group of them." Now people wondered whether that contribution was demanded from her as a condition for taking Maddox.

What would a baby-buying scandal do to Jolie's new image as a humanitarian and a mother? Just four days after the first American paper, the *Boston Globe*, broke the story of the adoption scandal and Galindo's role in it, Jolie neatly changed the subject once again, suddenly announcing to the media that she and Thornton had split up.

"You have to hand it to her," a Hollywood publicist said recently, laughing. "There sure are a lot of coincidences involved in that marriage. It started when she was accused of shagging her brother, and it ended when she was about to be accused of purchasing her baby. She came through both times smelling like roses, and the media played into her hands both times. It's like in magic where the secret to the trick is misdirection. Angelina is a master magician. I wish I was half as good as her at my profession. She's probably the most talented image consultant on the planet."

The publicist, however, didn't give all the credit to Jolie herself. "My hunch is that the real mastermind is Geyer," she speculated. "That's his department. He takes good care of her. She brags about how she doesn't have a publicist, but she doesn't need one. She has Geyer." She was referring to Jolie's long-time manager, Geyer Kosinski—one of the people she thanked on Oscar night—who has helped her navigate many different crises while acting as her gatekeeper, spokesperson, and damage-control artist.

Whoever was responsible for keeping the adoption scandal from tarnishing Jolie's reputation was certainly skillful. Other than a single headline in the *New York Post*, "Did Angelina Buy Her Baby?" the story was virtually ignored in the United States, and most Americans are still unaware that she was caught up in a potentially devastating scandal.

Meanwhile, details appeared about her breakup with Thornton. It seemed as though Jolie would emerge from this, too, unscathed, while Thornton would be portrayed as an insensitive Hollywood boor, unsupportive of her attempts to save the world. At first, Jolie explained that the two had simply chosen different paths. "What went wrong, or not even wrong but what wasn't meant to be was he was focusing on his music, and I was upstairs reading. I went through a change in my life and started paying more attention to the news and learning about other countries and becoming more politically active. I was saying, 'OK, well, listen, you're going to finish this song and I'm going to Washington and I'll see you on Monday,' and then I'd come back and we wouldn't discuss what he wrote in the studio and we wouldn't discuss what I learned in Washington, and then two weeks later it would be, 'OK, I'm going to Sierra Leone and Tanzania . . .' "

Soon, however, her accusations became harsher, and she accused her ex of failing to support her humanitarian activities. "He's never been to a refugee camp," she told *US Weekly* in July 2002. "I asked him to come, but he chose not to. You learn what a person is about by their behavior. And sometimes what they do hurts you."

Despite Thornton's public claims that he planned to raise Maddox with Jolie, it was clear that this was a smokescreen when it emerged that she had put only her name on the adoption papers. It was a hint that the marriage had been over already for some time. When news of their separation emerged, the two had only been seen together in public four times in the previous five months, although Thornton had accompanied her to Cambodia to choose Maddox and then to Namibia where they took possession of the new baby. The last time she saw her husband, she revealed to *US Weekly*, was on June 3, the day before her twenty-seventh birthday. They had a huge fight. "It was ugly," she said. Since then she hadn't spoken to him. Jolie officially filed for divorce from Thornton on July 17, 2002.

* * * *

Less than a month after the end of that relationship, her world was turned upside down by another man she loved. In the beginning of August 2002, Jon Voight contacted the producers of *Access Hollywood* and asked if he could appear on the show to send a message to his daughter. The next night, he shocked America with what he had to say. Breaking down in tears, an emotional Voight declared, "I've been trying to reach my daughter and get her help, and I have failed. I'm sorry, really. I haven't come forward and addressed the serious mental problems she has spoken about so candidly to the press over the years. But I've tried behind the scenes in every way. You can be sure that's been my agenda. They're very serious symptoms of real problems . . . real illness. I don't want to look back and say I didn't do everything I could."

He then described an incident that he says happened while Jolie was wrapping up shooting *Girl, Interrupted.* "I went to New York, and I went on the same mission, you know, to be with her and try to get her and try to get her help. She said, 'You can't help me! You can't help my pain!' And I saw it, you know, and I said, 'Angie, we can. We can get help for this.' "

He blamed the people around her for failing to get her the help she so desperately needed: "When the money train is running everybody wants to be on it and nobody wants to make adjustments, and I'm angry about that. And I'm especially angry at her manager who has been with her and seen everything. I begged him to help me many times, and always he has turned her against me."

He was referring, of course, to Geyer Kosinski, who in July had ordered Jolie's bodyguards to block Voight from stepping forward and giving his daughter a hug when they both attended a gala celebrating the ninetieth anniversary of Paramount studios. In an effort to discredit him, somebody later leaked a false story to the media that the bodyguards stopped Voight from physically manhandling his daughter, despite numerous witnesses saying he had done nothing improper.

Voight ended the shocking interview by saying his biggest heartache was not being able to see his newly adopted grandson, Maddox, and knowing that the interview would likely put at risk a future relationship with the boy. "Of course I want nothing," he said, breaking into tears again. "I want nothing more than to hold my baby in my arms, and keep her from harm . . . At least she knows that somebody's out there, trying to get help."

The next day, Jolie issued a terse statement in response. "I don't want to make public the reasons for my bad relationship with my father," she stated. "After all these years, I have determined that it is not healthy for me to be around my father, especially now that I am responsible for my own child." Jolie's mother immediately rallied to her daughter's defense. "I'm shocked," Bertrand said. "There's nothing wrong with Angelina's mental health. Mentally and physically, she is magnificently healthy."

Many people, including those who knew the family well, were blindsided by the suddenly public family drama. A friend of Voight's, who said he has helped the actor in his charity work, reported in 2007 that Voight has always refused to tell anyone what sparked the feud. "It didn't seem to be a single incident that set it off, as if something suddenly happened that caused them to fight. I know Angie was peeved at her father for leaking the news of Maddox's adoption to the press before she had a chance to announce it for herself, but that was just a squabble. They always bickered good-naturedly and occasionally she'd tell her dad off, but honest to God, they got along great. We [his friends] always speculated that he found something out about her that freaked him out, but we could never figure out what it was. It made him sad. He loved those kids so much, and then he lost both of them. Jamie took it badly. And he was so excited about meeting his grandson. He would talk about changing [Maddox's] diapers and how he hoped he hadn't forgotten his technique."

The feud was all the more surprising to those who had been following Jolie's career closely. They knew very well that, contrary to later media reports, Jolie and her father had never before been estranged. Her consistent public statements over the years amply demonstrated that she and her father were close. She repeatedly talked about how much she loved him, and time and again, she called him a great father in interviews. She had always made it clear she did not like being asked about being the daughter of Jon Voight because she didn't want to be measured against her father, but she never shied away from expressing her appreciation for him.

They fought occasionally, and she seemed to resent his frequent lectures over her public behavior, even how she dressed, but that was normal father-daughter stuff. There had never been any extended period since childhood when the two weren't in contact, except when their work took them to different places for lengthy blocks of time. The media seems to have gone along with the post-2002 mythology created by Jolie and her brother about their relationship with their father. It is common today to read descriptions of Jolie's family life that claim he "abandoned" their mother when they divorced and that Jolie has been estranged from her father ever since. It is almost impossible to find references to the fact that Bertrand and Voight had joint custody and that the children were for years raised by their father as much as they were by their mother. It is even rarer to find mention that for years Voight traveled once a month across the continent, after their mother moved to New York, to spend time with his kids.

Today, Jolie likes to tell reporters that she and her father "were never close." But a smattering of her own statements over the years belies this, notably what she told an interviewer in 2001: "I never remember a time when I needed my father and he wasn't there." And of course there was her Oscar acceptance speech, in front of a billion viewers in March 2000, when she said, "Dad, you're a great actor, but you're a better father."

In another odd twist, after the feud began, it was often James Haven who went on the offensive in interviews to discredit their father, despite having been even closer to Voight than his sister. In 2007, Haven told *Marie Claire* magazine that he had devoted himself to the cause of abused women after watching Voight inflict "years of mental abuse on his mother." He also said Voight had failed to provide financially for Bertrand and the children. And yet Jolie herself had frequently given interviews over the years mentioning that Voight and her mother remained "best friends" even after they divorced. In 2001, just a year earlier, she had talked openly of how much fun she and her dad had when, at her request, he played Lara's father, Lord Croft, in the first *Tomb Raider* film.

Family friends of both Voight and Bertrand had confirmed many times that everybody got along very well over the years and that they didn't even seem like a broken family. In interviews, Bertrand frequently stated that Voight was an excellent father and a good friend to her. "Nothing means more to Jon than the children," she told *People* magazine in 1993.

According to a friend of Voight's who has witnessed the vicious public feud play out, "Jon was very hurt by what the kids were saying about him. He knew that they knew it wasn't true. But what did he expect after what he said about Angie on television? He crossed a line, it seems to me. In this case, he probably should have kept the dirty laundry hidden."

Brad and Angelina

The only time I ever met Brad Pitt was on December 8, 2004. I was shooting a documentary in Hollywood and was trying to get some footage of George Clooney. With the help of my publicist, I had hatched a plan to crash the premiere of his film *Ocean's Twelve*, scheduled for December 8 at Grauman's Chinese Theater. I had acquired two forged passes, one for myself and one for my cameraman. They read "Red Carpet Access Only," meaning we couldn't watch the film itself but could be present when the film's cast appeared and walked in.

When the stars began to arrive in their limousines, we were in position, though publicists and handlers kept elbowing us and pushing us back to make room for their clients to make their entrances. When Clooney arrived with his mother and his girlfriend, he was immediately surrounded by TV cameras from various entertainment shows and local stations, all of whom get priority at these events, so I was never able to get close enough to talk to him.

I stood there for a while, frustrated. Then I caught sight of one of the film's other stars, Brad Pitt. He was standing a little ways away, keeping himself at a safe distance from the media and the crowds. All the cameramen, including my own, were being muscled away en masse, but, thanks to my forged pass, I was allowed to stay where I was. After a while, having watched most of the rest of the cast walk past on the carpet, I found myself about two feet away from where Pitt stood. He was waving to the crowd and refusing to talk to the media, who were cordoned off at a slight distance. Seizing my chance, I quickly introduced myself as a struggling actor who had just had a bit part in Martin Scorsese's film, *The Aviator*, which was about to be released. Pitt commented that he'd love to work with Scorsese and seemed quite willing to continue chatting with me. Not having anything specific to question him on, I asked if he had any advice for an actor like me. His answer was immediate, and sounded almost rote: "Take classes, work your ass off, and if you haven't made it by thirty-five, give up." Then he gave me the once over. His expression changed to a sheepish smile. "Oh, I guess you're already over thirty-five," he said affably and shrugged. "What can I tell you?"

In retrospect, I might have asked him a different question. As I was talking to him, in fact the entire time he was on the red carpet, fans kept screaming at him, "Where's Jen?" But a few from the media were yelling another question: "Where's Angelina?"

When the stars finally headed in to watch the film, I asked a photographer from *Splash* what was up. "He's been banging Jolie for months," he answered. When I asked how he knew, he told me that he had been at the Cannes Film Festival the previous May, where Pitt's affair was all people could talk about, even though Aniston had flown there at the last minute to be by her husband's side. He said he had spoken to all kinds of people who had witnessed the two "all over each other." When they started filming [*Mr. & Mrs. Smith*], the paparazzo elaborated, she was seen going into Pitt's trailer for hours at a time and coming out with a "just-fucked look." At one point, they were spotted holding hands in public; that was the story that fueled the first rumors. He said they had apparently "cooled off" at one point, but he didn't know whether it was because the affair had ended or because the two had decided to keep their distance after rumors started to circulate.

A month after this conversation, Pitt and Aniston formally announced their breakup, though it would be several months after that before Pitt made his relationship with Angelina Jolie official.

* * * *

Aniston met Jolie only once. It was on the *Friends* lot, just before Pitt was about to begin filming *Mr. & Mrs. Smith,* a tale of husband and wife assassins who are hired to kill each other. "Brad is so excited about working with you," she told her husband's new co-star. "I hope you guys have a really good time." At that point, there was no indication whatsoever that there was trouble in paradise. Aniston and Pitt were constantly being asked about their relationship, and their answers always sounded very sincere, even if a bit sickly sweet. "Brad and I were driving, and we saw an old couple driving," Aniston told one magazine. "The lady was at the wheel, and her hands were shaking. He touched her hand, and he seemed to say, 'I've loved you for 7,000 years, and I still do.' I hope that's Brad and me one day."

For his part, Pitt seemed committed to making that happen. "I never thought being married would make me feel this way," he told one reporter. "It's an amazing feeling. I look at Jen and think . . . she's my wife . . . Marriage is great. It's made me feel very good about taking this kind of journey together with a terrific woman who wants to share my life and share the journey with me."

According to friends and co-workers, the only time she and Pitt bickered was about architecture and design. Pitt was a fanatic about modern design, particularly the Arts and Crafts movement, while Aniston was a traditionalist, in keeping, perhaps, with her Greek heritage. It made for some fun disagreements, even occasional tension, while they were renovating the massive $14-million Beverly Hills mansion they had bought together and had been renovating for more than a year. But for the most part, friends always said they seemed the ideal couple.

Pitt and Aniston had formed a production company together, Plan B Entertainment, and had just secured the rights to the memoir of Mariane

Pearl, entitled *A Mighty Heart*, about how her husband Daniel, a reporter for the *Wall Street Journal*, had been murdered by terrorists. Aniston was set to play Mariane in what was assumed to be the perfect vehicle to launch a serious acting career.

In 2003, Pitt told an Australian newspaper that he and Aniston were starting to think of having children. "Jen and I are in the negotiation phase," he said. "We're still practicing. But everything's going well, and I'm looking forward to the future." Asked whether he preferred girls or boys, his answer was immediate: "There's no question about it. I love girls. I want little versions of Jennifer. That's my dream."

It was clearly Aniston's dream as well. She had already designated a large light-filled space in the corner of the couple's Beverly Hills mansion as a nursery for their expected baby. Aniston referred to the space as the "Room" and supervised its transformation from beginning to end during the extensive renovation process, which is reported to have cost approximately $300,000.

One of the contractors who worked on the renovations confirmed that Aniston had very specific demands about what she called "the nursery": "Brad was more hands-on with the renovations. He had all kinds of ideas and fancied himself an architect. But Lady Pitt supervised the nursery room, which had to be constructed specially to fit the space. It wasn't just a room where you'd stick a crib and a mobile. It was quite elaborate, and she had very specific ideas about it.

"They never decorated it as far as I saw, though," explained the contractor. "We're talking 2003, I think. Maybe they were waiting to know whether the baby would be a boy or a girl."

* * * *

Many rumors have surfaced surrounding the relationship and breakup of Brad Pitt and Jennifer Aniston. One such rumor has it that, near the end of *Friends*, Aniston had suffered a miscarriage during the early stages of a pregnancy. Another says that, at one point in 2003, Aniston had quit smoking for an extended period because she was pregnant, though a version of the same rumor says that she had quit because she was "trying" to get pregnant. She had also been taking a daily folic-acid supplement at the time, which is commonly used to prevent birth defects when a woman is trying to conceive or is already pregnant.

In June 2004, MSNBC reported that an inside source told them that Aniston was pregnant and that an announcement was expected later that month. It was a little over a month after she had flown to meet Pitt at the Cannes film Festival. "This is something Brad and Jen both want," a source told the network. More significantly, Aniston's spokesman refused to deny the report, as would be expected if it weren't true. Instead, he merely said, "I keep hearing that rumor." But the announcement never came.

Babies had been on Aniston's mind since well before she married Pitt. "I love everything about them. Their backs, necks, smell, all their fits," she told *Cosmopolitan* in 1997. "I want to be a young mom too." In 2001, she told a magazine that she wanted three children. Brad wanted seven, she added, but that wasn't in the cards. "Not unless he gets a mail-order bride," she joked. "But I'll give him the rest. I hope I'll be a good mom. I love kids."

On a number of other occasions, she made it clear that she and Pitt would settle down and have kids as soon as *Friends* ended. That was always planned to happen at the end of its ninth season in 2003. When a reporter from *Vogue* asked her when she and Pitt planned to start a family, she asked with a laugh, "Do you all want to be there when we conceive? It will happen when *Friends* is over." But in the middle of what was expected to be the final season, the producers suddenly announced that the cast had agreed to film one more. But there was a catch. The tenth season would only contain eighteen episodes instead of the usual twenty-four. At the time, word leaked that it was Aniston who had insisted on the shortened season. The media picked up on the report and assumed that she wanted to finish the series so she could embark on a film career.

According to a former employee of Pitt's, films were not, in fact, the reason Aniston was anxious to leave her *Friends* family. Aniston had always promised to stop after nine seasons so that they could start a family. But the other cast members were itching to do one more and pressured Aniston to go along. She reluctantly agreed, but only for eighteen episodes, a compromise she reached with Pitt, who hadn't wanted her to do a tenth season at all.

Part of the reason that the media speculated about Aniston's desire for a film career was that she had already signed to do a number of future film projects even before *Friends* came to an end. This seemed to be a sign that establishing herself as a movie star was foremost in her mind and that she had no immediate plans to take a hiatus to start a family. But the media didn't necessarily have it right.

"That's something that all female actors do," a friend of Pitt's says. "A film can be shot in a few weeks, depending on the complexity of the production. It's not like a TV series, which commits you to months of filming at a time. And if you check her film contracts, they each had a clause that allowed her to withdraw in case of pregnancy before production began. The production companies are insured against that very possibility. The idea that Jenny had decided to put aside her baby plans in favor of a film career is a crock of crap. She wanted to have kids. You could tell. She'd say she couldn't put it off much longer or it might be too late."

* * * *

Just before Pitt began filming *Mr. & Mrs. Smith*, Aniston told an interviewer, "I had a period in my life when was younger when I was jealous, but I don't feel that now." *Friends* was scheduled to wrap the last episode of its ten-year run in January 2004. Around that time, Aniston was interviewed on ABC's *Primetime Live* by Diane Sawyer, who asked about having babies. She said she would "definitely love to have two" children now that *Friends* was coming to an end. "I've liked working right now," she told Sawyer. "But I also feel that this'll be probably the most important job I'll ever do, having a baby. That deserves time like my career deserves time."

But on the set of *Mr. & Mrs. Smith*, sparks began to fly between Pitt and his new co-star almost as soon as filming began in L.A. in November 2003, according to those present on the set. "They both went after each other," a film employee told Mara Reinstein and Joey Bartolomeo, senior writers for *US Weekly*. "It wasn't like she was just after him and seducing him. They wanted each other. It was pretty obvious."

After a shoot at an L.A. restaurant in February, the cast and crew of *Mr. & Mrs. Smith* partied on the rooftop at the city's chic Standard Hotel. Shortly afterwards, reports emerged that hotel staff had witnessed Pitt and Jolie kissing long after filming had ended and the crew had gone home. Reinstein and Bartolemeo later confirmed those rumors. "It was just the two of them in a roped-off area on the rooftop, near the patch of grass," an employee told the reporters. "They wanted time alone, and the staff made a booth space for them. I know for a fact they kissed."

Jolie's representatives denied anything unprofessional had taken place, but the reports were already getting back to Aniston, who started to panic at the prospect of losing her husband. For the public, however, she adopted the pose of ignoring the rumors and assuming they had been fabricated. Aniston joined Pitt at Cannes in May. Shortly afterward, his representatives reportedly sent a message to Jolie to keep her distance for the time being.

Meanwhile, Pitt was making his admiration for Jolie known. "I've never seen someone so misperceived in the press," he had told reporters in April. "Jolie's really a delightful human being, a dedicated mother and really quite normal. [She's] dedicated to her work with the UN. There's actually a real lightness to her."

Rumors were flying, as gossip columnists were drawn to the increasingly numerous accounts of Pitt's alleged dalliance with Jolie. As with all Hollywood couples, stories of affairs, impending separation, and divorce had dogged Pitt and Aniston ever since they were married, but now there was an added bit of intrigue: the "other woman" was Angelina Jolie.

Jolie herself was very sensitive to the position she was in. Just three years before, she had stolen Billy Bob Thornton away from his fiancée of long standing, Laura Dern, and her career had suffered. Her careful efforts to recast her image since then were only now slowly starting to bear fruit. She couldn't jeopardize that. If Dern had made a sympathetic victim, then Aniston would be even more so. An affair with her supposedly happily married husband would stain Jolie as a "home-wrecker" again, perhaps permanently jeopardizing her valued female fan base. She had to tread very carefully to protect her carefully built and brand new persona as a humanitarian and loving mother.

The first hints of how Jolie planned to do that soon emerged. "Insiders claim Pitt's desire to start a family and his wife's reluctance to give up her career have caused "intolerable pressures," wrote one newspaper. Many such stories began to appear as the year progressed, all citing "insiders" and all hinting that Aniston was selfishly denying her husband the family he so desperately craved.

Mr. & Mrs. Smith took a hiatus from April through the end of July 2004 so that Pitt could film *Ocean's Twelve*. After filming resumed in August, the crew flew to Italy to shoot the European scenes. While there, reports filtered out about how much fun Pitt was having playing with Maddox at the Hotel Santa Caterina in Amalfi. But Jolie remained consistent in denying the rumors, and in November gave an interview to *Allure* magazine. "I wouldn't sleep with a married man," she insisted. "I have enough lovers. I don't need Brad."

Six weeks later, however, on January 7, 2005, Pitt and Aniston broke up. "We would like to announce that after seven years together, we have decided to formally separate," their press release began. The decision was the result of "much thoughtful consideration," and it was not caused by "any of the speculation reported by the tabloid media," the couple insisted, assuring their public that they would remain "committed and caring friends with great love and admiration for one another."

As soon as the breakup was announced, public sympathy, especially women's, sided almost exclusively with Aniston. The Hollywood boutique Kitson reported that by the following summer, its "Team Aniston" T-shirts were outselling "Team Jolie" T-shirts by a margin of twenty-five to one. Jolie's Q score began to plunge; her negative evaluations, in particular, were much higher than they had been six months earlier. In *Entertainment Tonight*'s annual "Red, White, and Blue" poll on July 4, asking Americans to name their favorite celebrities, Aniston came out on top by a wide margin. Jolie was selected number eight, while Pitt came in at the bottom of the rankings at number ten.

Jolie's camp had been prepared, however. A day after the announcement of the breakup, the *New York Post* ran the first of what would become a steady drumbeat of stories, all with the same theme and all without a single source, allegedly delivering the real story behind the breakup of Hollywood's golden couple. "It's about children," a "pal" of the couple told the *Post*. "[Aniston] just doesn't want kids right now, and he wants kids." Each time the story was repeated, it was an "insider" who assured the reporter or a "friend" of the couple. "A pal said Aniston doesn't want to take the time off to have a kid and she doesn't want to endure the physical effects that giving birth will have on her sexy body," said another report. "Three main reasons have emerged for the breakup: Aniston's refusal to have a baby, Pitt's relationship with Angelina Jolie, and Aniston's obsession with her career," wrote yet another.

Pitt, for his part, had been photographed by paparazzi strolling hand in hand with Jolie on an African beach. At the same time, carefully leaked accounts began to emerge of Pitt's stellar relationship with Jolie's young son. "With the paparazzi snapping away, Pitt stepped into what looked suspiciously like a paternal role with Jolie's adopted Cambodian son, Maddox," *Vanity Fair* later noted.

Pitt would still not confirm whether he and Jolie were an item. He continued to say that she was a not factor in the breakup and denied that the two had slept together while he was married. Jolie told the same story. Interviewed in March 2005 for *Marie Claire* magazine, Jolie tried to squelch the persistent rumors that she had Pitt had been having an affair for months before the separation. "To be intimate with a married man, when my own father cheated on my mother is not something I could forgive," she said. "I could not, could not, look at myself in the morning if I did that."

By the time Aniston gave a tearful interview in the September 2005 *Vanity Fair*, she was on the defensive. The issue broke all sales records for the magazine. In it, Aniston decried the stories that had been circulating as sexist and cruel. "A man divorcing would never be accused of choosing career over children," she said. "That really pissed me off. I've never in my life said I didn't want to have children. I did and I do and I will! The women that inspire me are the ones who have careers and children; why would I want to limit myself? I've always wanted to have children, and I would never give up that experience for a career. I want to have it all."

Vanity Fair writer Leslie Bennetts tracked down most of the couple's mutual friends to determine what had really happened. Most of them told her that Pitt "virtually checked out" of his marriage as soon as he began working with Jolie. "He was gone," a friend told Bennetts. They also dismissed the myth that Pitt had been obsessed with having children while Aniston kept putting it off. "When Brad and Jen were in the marriage, having a baby was not his priority—ever," another friend told Bennetts. "It was an abstract desire for him, whereas for Jen it was much more immediate. So is there a part of Brad that's diabolical? Did he think, 'I need to get out of this marriage, but I want to come out smelling like a rose, so I'm going to let Jen be cast as the ultra-feminist and I'm going to get cast as the poor husband who couldn't get a baby and so had to move on?'"

Yet there was something else that could have been a factor for both parties. Jennifer Aniston had been thought to have been pregnant twice recently, in 2003 and in the late spring of 2004. Rumor had it that both pregnancies had ended in miscarriages. Was Aniston unable to have children, or was her insistence on maintaining an ultra-thin, camera-friendly figure interfering with her efforts to have a baby? Such things put uncommon stresses on marriages. It is difficult to say, but perhaps Pitt was vulnerable at that point in time and simply unable to resist the force of nature known as Angelina Jolie.

Pitt does not in fact seem to have been complicit in what was proving to be a mean-spirited but effective campaign to shift public opinion against Aniston. Jolie, however, was. By now, she was an accomplished veteran at what one publicist called "misdirection"—deflecting a crisis by changing the subject—and she appears to have used those skills to good advantage once again. "It was Angelina who came up with the whole story about Jennifer not wanting to have kids," a source connected to the publicity department at 20th Century Fox, which produced *Mr. & Mrs. Smith*, said in February, 2009. "She was convinced that is the story that would resonate with all these women who saw her as a man-stealing bitch."

According to a journalist who worked for the *Hollywood Reporter*, insider stories about Jolie, even the most innocuous, usually emanated from the office of Jolie's manager, Geyer Kosinski, or from her brother, James Haven, who had become an aggressive defender of his sister's interests in the press for quite some time. His days of distancing himself to avoid the incest rumors were long past. "That's the way things are done in this town," the journalist said. "There's nothing particularly wrong with it. Unlike the tabloids, we need to know where the information is coming from before we'll print it, how reliable it is. If we quote an "insider," we know who that is and whether they are genuinely in the loop. Every celebrity has some trusted authorities they use to get their information to us or into the mainstream gossip columns like [the *New York Post*'s] Page Six."

And it was working. As 2005 drew to a close, Jolie's Q score began to climb again. Millions of women now believed that Pitt had left Aniston because she had chosen to put career over children. *Vanity Fair* called these stories as misogynistic as they were false and noted that mutual friends believed Pitt could have done more to refute the false rumors. "To some, this looks like sheer hypocrisy," the magazine chided. Others took Pitt to task for continuing the charade that he hadn't cheated on Aniston while he was married, although Aniston's close friend and castmate Courtney Cox chose to give him the benefit of the doubt. "I don't think he started an affair physically, but I think he was attracted to her," she told the magazine.

Others were appalled by a recent photo spread in *W* magazine featuring Pitt and Jolie as an early-1960s-style married couple. The pictures had been shot in March, the month Aniston filed for divorce. "He's missing a sensitivity chip," Aniston said, referring to Pitt's continuous public flaunting of the relationship.

A former employee of Pitt's put a different spin on it, however, defending Pitt's continuing denials. "Of course he was sleeping with

Angelina most of that time, but he didn't hide it because he was a prick," the man said. "He hid it because he was too nice a guy. He didn't want to hurt Jen. He still loved her, and he didn't know how to break it to her. In fact, for a while there he genuinely thought of ending the thing with Angelina and going back to Jen. I'm not sure what finally happened or why he decided to end it, but would you rather he did what Billy Bob did to the Dern chick? Was he a coward for not telling Jen sooner? Probably. But what would you do in that situation? It wasn't easy for him. I doubt if he forgives himself to this day."

Pitt had long suspected that the stories about Jen were being leaked by his new girlfriend, and he was, according to my sources, furious, ordering Jolie to desist from her whisper campaign. He was still visibly upset when *GQ* magazine asked him in its June 2005 issue about the rumor that Aniston didn't want to have kids. "That was one version, and total bullshit, by the way," he responded forcefully. In an ABC *Primetime Live* interview that same month, Diane Sawyer asked him the same question. This time he was even less equivocal, dismissing the reports as "ridiculous bullshit" and "completely fabricated." By then, however, the damage had been done.

A New Image

On January 8, 2005, the day after Brad Pitt and Jennifer Aniston publicly announced their breakup, a little girl named Yemsrach was born in a small Ethiopian city called Awassa. Six months later, with Pitt by her side, Angelina Jolie flew to Addis Ababa where the girl—now her new daughter—was handed over to her by adoption authorities. *People* magazine landed an exclusive interview with Jolie and broke the news with a cover story, announcing that the girl had been orphaned by AIDS. "Her name is Zahara Marley," Jolie told the magazine. "Maddox and I are very happy to have a new addition to our family."

A month before, in June 2005, Jolie had appeared on CNN describing the first time she saw the death of a child in a refugee camp. "I saw him dying," she recalled. "And, you know, it was my first trip, my first moment, and being somebody from the States and with a bit of money, I thought, well, we'll just airlift him and take him to the hospital. I can solve this in a second. And then you suddenly . . . it was that moment where you look around and realize that there are, you know, hundreds of thousands of people in the exact same situation and that a lot of these kids were going to die. And then I went home, and I thought, 'I should have at least taken one.' "

She said it was Maddox who had ultimately helped her decide on the adoption. "My son is in love with Africa, so he has been asking for an African brother or sister," she said. Earlier, Jolie had publicly declared that she wanted to create "a rainbow family." "That's children of different religions and cultures, from different countries," she explained.

"Actually, I'd love to have seven, a small football team."

For a while it seemed that the first color to join Maddox in the Jolie family rainbow would be white, not brown. The London *Daily Mail* reported in December 2004 that she had been "scouring" Russian orphanages the previous month, looking for a child. "We were told she wanted a child of Slavic appearance," said one of the directors of "Baby House 13," an orphanage outside Moscow. "She wanted a blond baby with blue eyes." Orphanage officials said Jolie had her heart set on a blonde, blue-eyed baby named Gleb. "Miss Jolie took him in her arms and kissed him," the orphanage director said. "Then she asked her translator to tell the staff: 'I've found my son.' "

But before the adoption could be made official, she also visited another Russian orphanage, "Baby House 22." That center's chief doctor, Natalia Kostyushina, told a similar story. "Like the heads of other baby orphanages, we knew that Jolie was interested in boys with a Slavic appearance only," she told the paper. "As I understood it, on the first day of her visit she was trying to see as many kids as possible and on the second day was planning to make a decision. One of our kids was playing with his toys in the playpen when Angelina entered the room. She looked at him and he smiled, as if he recognized her. She then rushed to the playpen, took him out of it, clasped him to her bosom and started to whirl him around. They both laughed, and it looked like a happy mother with her beloved son. It was a very moving scene. After that, we had no doubt that she would take our boy as her son. But to our regret, it didn't happen."

A pattern was emerging, the *Daily Mail* reported. When the paper spoke to the director of yet another orphanage, they heard a familiar story. "She showed interest in one of our children, too, but most were deemed not suitable for her," revealed the director. "It was something of a circus the way it happened, as if we should all drop everything because this rich and famous American single mum needed another child. There are more than four million children in Russia, many of them abandoned by their parents, but there are rules in place to make it difficult for Westerners to adopt only 'healthy' babies. Instead they are encouraged to adopt those with serious sicknesses or disabled ones."

In the end, Jolie left Russia without a child, later explaining she didn't think Maddox was ready yet for a sibling. "I was going to adopt this other child in Russia, but it didn't work out, so I may adopt another in about six months," she said at the time. In fact, Jolie reportedly had learned that dealing with the Russian bureaucracy meant months of red tape before she could bring a baby home, and she had abandoned the plan. Was she hoping to adopt another baby at the time to distract from the imminent breakup of Pitt and Aniston?

When she finally adopted Zahara over half a year later, watchers were astonished at how quickly she was able to gain approval from the Ethiopian government, a process that usually takes between six months and a year. Zahara's adoption was approved a week after Jolie filed her request, according to Hadosh Halefom, head of the country's state-run adoption agency.

Dr. Tsegaye Berhe, medical director of the Addis Ababa orphanage, told a British newspaper that Pitt was with Jolie when she arrived to claim the baby and that they looked just like a married couple. "They were like any couple looking at their child for the first time. Angelina wiped a tear from her eye." he recalled. "They were so happy. Then they turned to me and said, 'This makes us a whole family.'"

Zahara had been described as an "AIDS orphan" in every media account of the child's adoption. Jolie herself called Zahara an "AIDS orphan" on June 23 in an interview with Anderson Cooper of CNN. But in August 2005, new details emerged about the baby's circumstances that brought to mind the controversy surrounding Maddox, who was not an orphan as was originally claimed.

Europe's largest English-language newspaper, the *Sun*, discovered that the baby's mother was not in fact dead, and that Zahara was not an AIDS orphan after all. Girma Degu Legesse, an employee of Wide Horizons for Children, the private agency that facilitated the adoption, admitted to the newspaper that he knew that Zahara's real mom was only "missing," not dead. Attempting to justify the deception, he claimed, "Some Ethiopians believe that disappearing and dead is the same."

The *Sun* tracked down the real mother, Mentewab Dawit, who described the circumstances behind Zahara's birth. She explained that she had been staying with her grandmother in a small village called Shone while she attended school. One night, when her grandmother was away on business, she was walking home in the dark after a day of work selling onions at a local market, when a man approached and attacked her.

"He pulled a dagger and put one hand on my mouth so that I could not scream. He then raped me and disappeared," she later told Reuters. When she discovered she was pregnant, she claimed, she didn't tell anybody at first. "I feared the consequences of being raped in a community where rape is considered a taboo, even if what happened, happened forcibly," she said.

Her daughter was born on January 7, which in Ethiopia is Christmas day. She was named Yemasrech, which means "good news," though she was later renamed Tena Adam, the name of a local herb. When Mentewab's mother, Almaz, learned that she had given birth, she came and brought her daughter and the baby back to Awassa, a small city about three hours south of the capital. There, Mentewab worked as a laborer for a construction company, barely subsisting on the inadequate wages. "Sometimes all I had was a piece of bread all day," she said, explaining that the uncle they had been staying with eventually asked them to move out. "My baby was crying all the time because she was hungry. I thought she was going to die, so I ran away," she said.

The grandmother, Almaz, claimed that soon afterwards she took the baby to the local council and told them that her daughter had run away and left the baby with her. "She was really skinny. I was even thinking she could die," Almaz claimed. "I said to them, 'Please take the baby before she dies.'"

At this point, the details become murky. Almaz had been introduced to a local "fixer," who arranged adoptions for a local agency, and he "agreed to take the baby." "He promised he would keep in touch. He said he would bring back the baby to visit after five months and he would send me a picture," claimed Almaz. "He also promised to introduce me to the family that would adopt her." She said she never actually told the fixer or the authorities that her daughter had died or that the baby was an orphan. "But then [the fixer] came to me and told me the baby had been adopted and taken abroad," she said. "He said, 'There will be journalists coming to you and you must deny the whole story and say it is not your granddaughter.'" "He brought this woman who claimed Tena Adam [Zahara] was her daughter. He tried everything to get me to say that it's not my granddaughter. He even threatened that he'd put me in jail and have me tortured."

When the *Mail on Sunday* checked into the fixer's credentials, they discovered that he had been claiming that he worked for the adoption agency that brokered the Jolie adoption, Wide Horizons for Children, and had even distributed business cards claiming that he represented it. But when the story broke, the agency said he was not an employee but was instead employed by an orphanage in Awassa. The agency did not deny it was the fixer who had originally brought Zahara there. "What he has done is tantamount to kidnap," Mentewab told the newspaper. "He took my daughter and just disappeared with her saying I was dead."

When the report originally emerged, it prompted a brief stir, with some media falsely claiming that the birth mother was demanding that Zahara be returned to Ethiopia. But Mentewab was reportedly thrilled when she learned that it was Angelina Jolie who had adopted her daughter. "She will have a better life with Angelina," she told the *Daily Mail*. "If she had stayed with me she could have died. I'm happy to see my daughter in a better life, in a better place. The thing that makes me upset is that Angelina is saying I'm dead. I'm alive and have never had AIDS." She also expressed a desire for Jolie to bring her daughter to visit her birthplace and family. "She must know her country, she must know her family, that's where her identity is," she added.

To this day, Jolie has apparently not brought Zahara to meet her birth mother or to visit the city of her birth, although she has brought her to Ethiopia on more than one occasion.

Given the controversies surrounding the birth of Maddox and Zahara, it was a little unusual to pick up the newspapers in January 2007 and see Jolie criticizing Madonna for illegally adopting a Malawian baby. The pop singer had been at the center of a media storm for several months after she announced that she and her husband, Guy Ritchie, planned to adopt a Malawian boy whose mother had died in childbirth. Aid groups inside the country and abroad had criticized the singer for suddenly announcing that she was planning to adopt an African child. Malawi, it turns out, usually required an eighteen-month residency before a child could be adopted, making it appear that Madonna was somehow flouting the law or that her adoption was being "fast-tracked."

Despite Jolie's public admonition, however, there was nothing illegal about Madonna's adoption. The procedures were being strictly monitored by the Malawian courts to ensure compliance with the country's laws. In January, Malawi High Court Judge Andrew Nyirenda issued an "interim order" allowing the singer and her husband to take the young boy, David Blanda, back to England, where they had to undergo a rigorous vetting process before the adoption could be finalized. Two years later, the adoption was finally approved. The official report submitted by the child welfare officer to the court described Madonna as a "perfect mum" for David.

A number of media accounts noted that there had been no similar backlash when Angelina Jolie had adopted Maddox and Zahara. "I think Angelina Jolie's adoptions were thought of differently because she's always shown an interest in children and in doing good in the world, whereas people felt like Madonna just flew in and suddenly got herself a child," Anastasiade Waal, of the human-rights group Civitas told the Cox news agency. "What has annoyed people in Britain is that Madonna's action seems whimsical and that she appears to have flouted the law."

In fact, there was nothing whimsical or illegal about Madonna's decision to adopt from Malawi. For months, she had been quietly traveling to the country on behalf of an organization she had founded called Raising Malawi, dedicated to "offering lasting solutions to the orphans of Malawi." She had chosen to focus her efforts on Malawi when she learned that it was one of the world's poorest nations, with more than a million orphans in a country of only twelve million people and where malaria, drought, poverty, and AIDS had decimated the population.

Months earlier, the pop superstar had announced plans to raise $3 million to build child-care centers, orphanages, and support aid projects in the poverty-stricken country. She was already working closely with international aid experts such as Columbia University economist Jeffrey Sachs, as well as local development officials on the most effective ways to help the people. Long before Madonna announced her adoption plans, in fact, an Associated Press writer visited the village of Mphandula and interviewed the locals about her efforts. "The village headman here has never heard of Madonna the pop star," AP reported, "but he has heard of Madonna the philanthropist."

Madonna had even dedicated one hundred percent of the royalties from a children's book she had written to her Malawi charity. The book, *The English Roses*, became an international bestseller. She vowed to match every dollar donated by the public with a dollar from her own pocket, putting her money where her mouth was, just like Jolie herself. Unlike Jolie, however, Madonna did not publicize her efforts in advance. She chose to travel without a media entourage or photographer while she visited the country and traveled to remote African villages. She didn't seem to need the services of a certain Trevor Neilson.

* * * *

Whether it arises from a sense of noblesse oblige or as an attempt to avoid appearing too greedy, there is a long tradition of philanthropy among American millionaires. For more than a century, many of the nation's greatest universities, hospitals, museums, and social-welfare organizations have relied on the generosity of wealthy benefactors from the world of business.

During the 1990s, as Microsoft cornered the software market and Bill Gates became known as the richest man on the planet, some people began to notice that while he had amassed a fortune of many billions of dollars, the computer entrepreneur didn't give very much of it away. He did give to numerous charities, but his donations were relatively paltry compared to his net worth.

The criticism came to a head in 1998, when Ralph Nader took Gates to task in an open letter urging him to sponsor a conference on the "unequal distribution of wealth" in America. In Nader's letter, he noted that Gates was worth more than the combined wealth of the poorest forty percent of Americans, excluding the value of their cars. "His wealth is highly publicized," Nader later told an interviewer. "His social responsibility is yet to be developed."

The response from Gates's philanthropic advisor, Rose Berg, was only minutely reassuring. Berg said Gates and his wife Melinda were "just beginning their philanthropy and plan to give most of their money away." Indeed, the billionaire and his wife had established a foundation and were busy making plans to distribute huge sums of money. Yet in the public eye, he was being portrayed as a greedy capitalist, which is a disastrous position for somebody under scrutiny from the U.S. government for monopolistic business practices. Gates needed to change his image.

Enter Trevor Neilson. Plucked directly from the White House, where he had worked in the travel office arranging President Bill Clinton's trips abroad, Neilson was a well-connected Democrat. This was considered a definite asset, given that Microsoft was being investigated by the U.S. Justice Department at the time. But Neilson also had a flair for public relations, which he employed aggressively after he was appointed director of public affairs and director of special projects for the Bill and Melinda Gates Foundation.

Very soon after Neilson was appointed, long, flattering profiles began appearing in the media about the philanthropic efforts of Gates and his wife, and soon every American had heard that Gates was planning to give away his entire fortune before he died. By the time Neilson left Microsoft to work for Angelina Jolie as her "philanthropic advisor," the Gates Foundation was the largest charitable foundation in the world, and Gates had given away more money than anybody else in history.

Neilson's specialty wasn't deciding where philanthropic dollars could be spent most effectively; it was advising benefactors on how to use their giving to enhance their public image. This became clear when Jolie launched her thinly veiled broadside on Madonna over the adoption of baby David. Assuring the media that she was "horrified" by the attacks on the singer, Jolie proceeded to dig the knife in. "Madonna knew the situation in Malawi, where [David] was born," she sniffed. "In that country, there isn't really a legal framework for adopting. Personally, I prefer to stay on the side of the law." Of course, Madonna had in truth adopted the baby legally and had not flouted any of Malawi's laws, as Jolie implied. So why did she appear to undermine the humanitarian efforts of another celebrity? The answer is Trevor Neilson.

"Neilson is a genius," another Hollywood philanthropy advisor gushed. "This is the same guy, remember, who turned Bill Gates from Scrooge to Albert Schweitzer. He practically created Brangelina. Pitt and Jolie may hate the term *Brangelina* when it's used by the tabs to gossip about their lives," she explained, "but it's become a very, very powerful brand. It's practically synonymous with goodness in the public's mind." She credits Neilson with intertwining the couple's philanthropy with their acting careers, which she says is another example of his genius. "Their philanthropy is the source of their power," she explained. "I can't name another example of that phenomenon in my entire career, and I've been doing this since the eighties."

As for Jolie's apparent 2007 attack on Madonna: "That was Angelina's way of saying, 'There's not enough room in this racket for the both of us.' She was saying, 'Get out of my way, bitch, you're horning in on my turf.' " The attack on Madonna came just as Jolie was solidifying her image as "Saint" Angelina. "Madonna was starting to work on some of the stuff that Jolie thought she had a monopoly on. Africa was her domain. I think Madonna was starting to hang out with Bill Clinton and his foundation, and that was another area that Brangelina thought was their territory. I'll bet Neilson had a hand in that."

Why did the whole world know about Jolie's globe-trotting humanitarian efforts, while Madonna was attacked as a dilettante? "That's easy," she said. "Angelina brings the cameras along, and there's nothing wrong with that. She'd argue that by conducting her missions in the public eye, she's helping bring the world's attention to very important issues. Can you argue with that? Do you think most of her fans had ever heard of Namibia before she went there? Do you think they ever thought of anything associated with celebrities other than what dress they wore on the red carpet?"

Asked to what extent she felt Jolie's humanitarian activities were about enhancing her public image, the philanthopy consultant responded,

"I have no idea what her motivation is, but I can tell you about my own clients. They want to do something good, and they donate a lot of money to charities. Some of them even work very hard fundraising for their cause of the moment, but none of them gets their hands dirty like Jolie. I'd kill to have her as my client. Is she an altruist? Of course not, but hardly anybody in Hollywood is."

The advisor refused to identify her own clients but proceeded to name "a handful" of celebrities she believes to be altruists. She said that David Letterman has given "scads" of his own money to various charities over the years and to a lot of individuals in need. "I've heard that he won't allow any of the recipients to talk about it. I've had a few clients like that, who want no recognition. I still have some, but none of them is famous."

She explained that about thirty percent of her business is made up of celebrities who have been referred by agents, managers, and publicists to get some positive public exposure for their clients. "I like to say that when something tarnishes their image, it's my job to garnish their image." Still, she says most of her clients have their hearts in the right places and that the majority of celebrities in Hollywood are genuinely compassionate and want to use their money to do good. "There's a reason Fox News is always complaining about Hollywood liberals," she said, laughing.

She said that Barbra Streisand is another celebrity who gives very quietly and whose foundation is considered a model. She described Dolly Parton as a "genius" at using her money to achieve results. "Have you ever been to Dollywood?" she asked. "Dolly Parton practically rescued the entire Smoky Mountains region out of poverty. That's why she built it." Among the other celebrities she cited is Madonna, who has been raising money for AIDS and gay causes practically from the first time anybody heard of her. As for Jolie, "I'll cut the nuts off anyone who says that Angelina Jolie's humanitarian activities are phony," she warned. "She and Madonna do a lot of good."

Likewise, British entertainment journalist Annette Witheridge of the *Daily Mirror*, who has covered Jolie extensively, believes Jolie's efforts are sincere. "I want to believe her humanitarian work is for real," she said. "I don't think anyone could see such awful suffering without being affected. [The actor] Rupert Everett once went half-heartedly on an Oxfam mission to Africa. He hated it, couldn't wait to get home. And when he did, he realized that the sight of starving orphans had got to him. He couldn't get them out of his mind. Before he knew it, he was back on a plane working for Oxfam, still does stuff for them to this day. Maybe Angelina felt the same way. I can certainly understand her wanting the children to connect with their roots and from there taking on more and more commitments for UNICEF, etc. Pre-Maddox, I could not have imagined her popping up as a Mother Theresa character helping starving orphans. Motherhood clearly changed her."

Indeed, individually and together, Pitt and Jolie appeared to be everywhere lately, acting as professional do-gooders. Both the news section and the entertainment section of the newspaper seemed to report about their activities almost daily. One day she was testifying before a congressional committee, the next she was invited to sit in at the prestigious Council on Foreign Relations alongside such power hitters as Jimmy Carter, Bill Clinton, and Condoleezza Rice. She was giving millions of dollars of her own money to various causes and, with Neilson's help, had set up a foundation with Pitt, who was busy with various humanitarian enterprises of his own, including a widely hailed effort to build houses in Katrina-devastated New Orleans. They were indeed helping to change the world, whatever their motivations.

Meanwhile, it appeared that Jolie's humanitarian efforts had long since eclipsed her film career, which had suffered a bumpy road in the years since she had taken up with Pitt. *Mr. & Mrs. Smith*, perhaps capitalizing on the publicity surrounding their off-screen romance, was a major hit, taking in almost $200 million at the box office. But her subsequent performance in *Alexander*—playing Colin Farrell's mother even though he was only eleven months younger than her in real life— was savaged by critics and the film was a major box-office flop. Two other significant commercial disappointments followed: *The Good Shepherd*, starring Jolie and Robert DeNiro; and *A Mighty Heart*, in which Jolie played the role of Mariane Pearl, which had been originally designated for Jennifer Aniston.

"Is Angelina Jolie box office poison?" one newspaper wondered. It didn't seem to matter. One flop after another didn't seem to effect her earning power, as Jolie quickly became the top-paid actress in Hollywood, pulling in $15 million to $20 million a picture. Pitt earned even more. A clue to the couple's ability to continue bringing in this kind of money came from a survey conducted by AC Nielsen in forty-two markets across the globe, which found that Jolie and Pitt were now the world's "favorite celebrity endorsers."

The power of what the philanthropy advisor described as the Brangelina "brand" was made even clearer by the survey's finding that, while she and Pitt were number one as a couple, Jolie had actually been edged out by Jennifer Lopez as the favorite *individual* female endorser. It was becoming increasingly clear that as a couple, Pitt and Jolie were worth more than the sum of their parts.

In June, 2009, *Forbes* magazine named Jolie the most powerful celebrity on the planet, dethroning Oprah Winfrey, who had held the top spot for years. A *Forbes* editor explained that, although Oprah earns significantly more money, Jolie is by far the most famous woman on the planet. A Warner studio executive went further, saying that studios will pay a premium to have Jolie appear in their movies. "Other than her action films, where she's the only woman in that genre who can draw, her films have been something of a box-office disappointment, fair to middling at best. She can't necessarily open a film. But I think studios want to be associated with her because of the goodwill it brings. She now has that halo effect that helps immunize Hollywood from the usual shit they sling our way."

It was Trevor Neilson's job to build that brand and safeguard it from threats. For years, he did a masterful job, achieving the same impressive results as he had with Bill Gates. In June 2007, however, he may have crossed the line. That summer, as Jolie was readying a promotional blitz for her new film, *A Mighty Heart*, reporters wanting to interview the star were suddenly presented with a contract to sign. The contract started by stipulating that the interviewer will "not ask Ms. Jolie any questions about her personal relationships." More troubling still was the contract's third clause, which forbade the interview to be used "in a manner that is disparaging, demeaning or derogatory to Ms. Jolie." A palpable shock rippled through the media community at the terms of the bullying document.

Fox Online columnist Roger Friedman labeled Jolie a "mighty hypocrite," and a number of journalists threatened to boycott the film, prompting Jolie's handlers to withdraw the contract and blame the "mix-up" on an "overzealous lawyer." Few bought that explanation, though. It later emerged that Jolie's people had also insisted that journalists sign a contract restricting the use of interviews from the promotional tour for *Mr. & Mrs. Smith*, although the terms of that contract were not nearly as restrictive.

What made the blatant attempt to muzzle the media all the more paradoxical was that *A Mighty Heart* is about the importance of press freedom, and the premiere was scheduled as a benefit for Reporters Without Borders, an organization that campaigns against press censorship.

The brouhaha over the contract provided a revealing glimpse into a behind-the-scenes apparatus, orchestrated by Neilson, that attempted to control or manipulate virtually everything of significance written about the couple. And while the pesky tabloid press couldn't be so easily controlled, they could be kept at a distance.

When the couple announced that Jolie was pregnant with her first biological baby and was expecting to give birth in the spring of 2006, there was the same frenzy of media interest that accompanies most major celebrity births. But not every celebrity has the connections to bend a foreign government to their will. Jolie and Pitt announced she would give birth to their child in the southwest African nation of Namibia. The desire to get as far away from prying paparazzi was perhaps understandable. But when Namibia announced that it was refusing to grant foreign visas to foreign journalists without written permission from Pitt and Jolie, something more clearly was at play. Again, the tactic had the mark of Trevor Neilson all over it.

The image-controlling mastermind was at it again in the summer of 2008 when the couple was expecting twins, setting off a bidding war between celebrity magazines vying for the first photos. The money, they announced, would be donated to their foundation, which continued to do good work around the globe. Nobody could accuse them of exploiting their babies, knowing that the money was going to help end world hunger. But it was more than money that Neilson was looking for this time. According to the terms of the deal proposed by Jolie, the winning bidder was required to "offer coverage that would not reflect negatively on her or her family."

People magazine won the bidding war, and the resulting photo spread was a fawning portfolio. Notably, the hated term *Brangelina* appeared nowhere in the captions or accompanying article. At the same time, perhaps to deflect criticism, the magazine released a statement denying there were any terms placed on its coverage, and insisted that *People* magazine "does not determine editorial content based on the demands of outside parties." Yet two years earlier, *People* had also negotiated with Trevor Neilson on the sale of photos of Maddox, just after the couple adopted him in Cambodia. In that negotiation, Jolie explicitly made coverage of her charity work part of the sale and *People* appears to have acquiesced, though it must be said the restrictions actually benefited a good cause. In a December 2006 memo sent by Neilson to editors who wished to bid on the Maddox photos, they found, "While Angelina and Brad understand the interest in their family, they also expect that the publications who purchase these photos will use them in a way that also draws attention to the needs of the Cambodian people."

In November 2008, bristling at the continuing trickle of stories about how the couple were manipulating coverage of their activities, the *New York Times* ran an investigation headlined, "Angelina Jolie's Carefully Orchestrated Image." The paper describes a particularly revealing incident to illustrate how cleverly Jolie and her spin machine manipulate the public to enhance her image. According to the *Times* article, after Jolie divorced Billy Bob Thornton in 2003, *US Weekly* asked Jolie if she would agree to an interview and be photographed. According to two people involved, she declined, but then proceeded to offer the magazine a very different photo opportunity. Jolie informed the magazine what time and place she would be publicly playing with Maddox. "The resulting photo, the origin of which was not made public to *US* readers, presented Ms. Jolie in a new light: a young mother unsuccessfully trying to have a private moment with her son," the *Times* revealed.

Echoing what many publicists have said about Jolie's knack of changing the subject when she is under siege, America's "paper of record" describes her modus operandi. "Shifting the focus is one of Ms. Jolie's best maneuvers, magazine editors and publicity executives say. When she became romantically involved with Mr. Pitt, for instance, she faced a public relations crisis—being portrayed in the tabloid press as a predator who stole Mr. Pitt from his wife, Jennifer Aniston. This time, it was Ms. Jolie's charity work that helped turn the story. Long interested in international humanitarian work, Ms. Jolie appeared in Pakistan, where she visited camps housing Afghan refugees, and even met with President Pervez Musharraf. Ms. Jolie and Mr. Pitt made a subsequent trip to Kashmir to bring attention to earthquake victims."

The *New York Times* asked a respected publicist and media expert whether he believed the couple's humanitarian efforts were an attempt to shape their image. "Presto, they come out looking like serious people who have transformed a silly press obsession into a sincere attempt to help the needy," said Michael Levine, CEO of one of America's leading entertainment P.R. firms, LCO-Levine Communications, which has represented Michael Jackson, Bill Clinton, and Cameron Diaz, among other powerful celebrities.

But Neilson labeled this kind of criticism as "cynical nonsense" and retorted, "People don't realize the complexity of what Angie is doing. A lot of her charity work is done quietly and not in front of the media." Former *US Weekly* editor Bonnie Fuller agrees, but with a caveat. "She's scary smart," Fuller said. "But smart only takes you so far. She also has an amazing knack, perhaps more than any other star, for knowing how to shape a public image."

BRANGELINA

It's the summer of 2008, and I'm crouched in the dense forest outside Chateau Miraval, a lavish seventeenth-century vineyard estate in France's Provence region. Angelina Jolie has holed up here after having given birth to her twins, Vivienne Marcheline and Knox Leon, a week ago.

In the forest around me are some of the world's leading paparazzi, all vying for the first photos of the new twins. The photos could fetch millions. I am accompanied by a French photographer, named Thierry, who has been scouting the grounds since long before Jolie gave birth. He points out which areas were public property and which were the grounds of the estate, though it is difficult to determine where the boundary was.

"Be careful," Thierry warns. "The security that Monsieur Pitt and Mademoiselle Jolie have hired are like a tiny army. They will not be afraid of busting that camera over your head." A few days later, two photographers would, in fact, be accosted by the couple's security detail. A vicious brawl would ensue, during which one of the photographers would bite a guard hard enough to draw blood.

I cannot see any of the other paparazzi as I sit in the woods, peering at the magnificent grounds in the distance. As I sit waiting, I feel dirty, not because I am outside in the elements, but because there is something tawdry about lying in wait among what Jennifer Aniston calls the "ratsies" for the express purpose of invading someone's privacy. It's a reminder of what Pitt and Jolie, not to mention every other major celebrity, have to put up with on a daily basis.

I convince myself that my mission is a little different from that of these professional stalkers, even if not by much. For three years, there has been a constant stream of rumors about the state of the couple's relationship, with nearly daily reports that the couple is separating or that their relationship is little more than a facade. One thing strikes me, though: if one tries to track down these rumors, most of them turn out to be false. The stories are either contradictory, the timelines don't match, or they're logistically impossible. Yet the public laps up the reports without questioning them, so intent are they on believing the most salacious details about the so-called perfect couple.

It was around this time that I came to the realization that virtually everything that has been written about the couple's relationship is completely untrue. Worse still, it seems to have been almost entirely fabricated by the tabloids and by the less reputable entertainment weeklies preying on a gullible and gossip-hungry public.

I was also beginning to get the impression that, as saintly as Angelina Jolie's media image had become, a sizeable percentage of the population hates her. This seems to consist of an equal measure of women who still sympathize with Jennifer Aniston and consider Jolie a despicable home-wrecker and those who just can't stand the Saint Angelina image and aren't buying it for a minute. Many suspect that they are being manipulated by her—with good reason, as I have shown—but seem to revel in this hatred and accept at face value any news that casts her in a negative light. They hover over tabloids and gossip sheets, searching desperately for that critical piece of damning evidence that would finally "expose her hypocrisy."

Later in 2008, a New York City videographer who has worked with Michael Moore, among other documentary filmmakers, invited me to dinner to discuss an upcoming project. While we discussed things at his Chelsea apartment, I told him I was writing a book about Jolie and Pitt and mentioned how she was frequently compared to Princess Diana and Mother Teresa. At the mention of the late nun, he became quite animated and insisted that I watch a short documentary he had in his collection called *Hell's Angel*, which was filmed by the iconoclastic British journalist, Christopher Hitchens. I thought I knew where this was headed.

The film is a scathing indictment of the public deification of Mother Teresa, the Albanian nun who has become synonymous with virtue. Hitchens presents a well-documented investigation of her career and suggests that what we think we know about Mother Teresa does not reflect reality. He reveals that she cavorted with brutal dictators, traveled in luxury most of the year on private jets, and refused to account for the hundreds of millions of dollars she raised, purportedly to help the world's neediest citizens. He convincingly demonstrates that the so-called missions that she built around the world were appallingly shoddy and that her motives were almost entirely self-serving. Hitchens maintains that Mother Teresa's order spent very little of its significant income on its missions, preferring instead to use its funds for her political agenda, based upon her religious beliefs, which, among other things, included stopping abortion and birth control.

When we have finished watching the film, I expect my friend to use the frequent Mother Teresa-Angelina Jolie comparison to illustrate that Jolie too is a charlatan who has deceived the public by building a myth based on her good works. Instead, he surprises me.

"Did you see that? You can see for yourself that Mother Teresa was a phony who did more harm than good," he begins. "You think Angelina Jolie is in the same league as that pious old bitch? Have you ever seen the good she does in Africa? Go to Youtube and look at the videos of her working with those kids. Do you know how many people are being helped by her missions, or whatever she calls them? Probably millions, and that's real; that's not some P.R. bullshit like we just watched. I don't give a flying fuck why she does it, or if she thinks it helps her career. They should make her a saint instead of Mother Teresa. She does a hell of a lot more good."

* * * *

My challenge now, as I saw it, was to separate fact from fiction. I wanted to discern what might actually be going on with the couple, especially the state of their relationship, without being taken in by the never-ending stream of false stories, innuendo and gossip. I didn't want to fall into the same trap that others had fallen into.

The couple themselves don't make it easy to be sympathetic. After the *New York Times* reported the incident where Jolie alerted photographers to the exact time and place she could be seen playing with Maddox, I began paying attention to the amazing number of times Jolie or Pitt or both have been photographed taking their children to school or to McDonald's or some other heartwarming family occasion. The impression created is of two parents who spend significant quality time with their children, despite what must be grueling work and travel schedules. Even more surprising is that there is never a nanny in the photos.

Raising six children, including two infants, shooting several movies a year, and constant travel to international hotspots: who's looking after the kids? It didn't take long to discover that Jolie and Pitt employ a "multicultural" team of nannies to care for their young brood. In fact, the children often spend more time with those nannies than they do with their parents, who spend weeks at a time shooting films and traveling on goodwill trips, sometimes with a child or two in tow but never with all of them.

A hotel employee at the Dorchester Hotel in London, who sees many celebrities and their children, once overheard three-year-old Shiloh refer to one of her nannies as "Mommy." She also observed the efforts of celebrities to broadcast an image of a happy family. "There's sometimes as much of a production involved in avoiding the wrong shot as there is in making a movie," she confided. "Stars will never allow the nanny to be photographed with their kids. It sends the wrong message to their public. In fact, it ruins a perfect opportunity to show their warm human side. Sometimes you'll even have the nanny crouched down in the backseat of a car. It's quite comical."

Still, I haven't spoken to a single industry insider who suggests that either Pitt or Jolie are bad parents or that they are merely using their children as window dressing. "They love those kids," a contract employee of Pitt's company, Plan B Productions, said emphatically. "Anybody who tells you otherwise is an idiot or a liar. I can't tell you whether they love each other, but I can tell you that they'd kill for the children."

* * * *

In 2005, as the initial rumors started to swirl that Angelina Jolie and Brad Pitt were having an affair, she threatened to leave Hollywood for the first time. Her goal, she suddenly announced, was to "quit movies, be a great mom to Maddox and join the PTA." Her declaration conveniently served to emphasize that she was too devoted to her young son to even consider having an affair with a married man.

The next time the words came out of her mouth, she had just been criticized for exposing her newly adopted Vietnamese son, Pax Thien, to a media scrum, which had set the boy into a crying frenzy. "I will stay at home to help Pax adjust to his new life," she told a press conference in March 2007, shortly after cameras caught the boy crying. "I have four children, and caring for them is the most important thing for me at the moment. I'm very proud and happy to be their mother." She also made three movies in the next year and traveled all over the world on humanitarian missions.

In October 2008, shortly before signing on to make three more films, Jolie told *Vanity Fair*, "The kids are my priority, so it's possible that from now on I will make fewer movies. I may even stop altogether." And even more recently, she announced, "Brad and I are planning on doing one project a year so we can put all our time into the kids." Yet, according to her iMDB (internet movie database) page, she currently has four projects scheduled for release in 2011, all of which she will work on in 2010. Pitt has no fewer than six movies scheduled to be released in the next two years, with seventeen others currently "in development," though it's likely that several of those will never be made, and there is no timeline listed for the production of any of them.

Jolie has now publicly talked about quitting movies to look after her children at least fourteen times, yet she is committed to film projects for years to come. Perhaps, as she admitted in a 2000 interview, she really is "addicted to work." People involved in studio publicity say that this strategy of promising to quit to look after her children was designed by her manager, Geyer Kosinksi, to preempt any criticism or questions about how she can continue to keep up such a hectic schedule and still spend time with her children.

However, in the spring of 2009, Jolie's punishing schedule inadvertently raised another serious issue. In April, as Jolie was filming a new movie, *Salt*, about a rogue CIA agent, she was reported to have collapsed on the New York set. Sources told the *Chicago Sun Times* that Jolie suddenly complained that she couldn't catch her breath, felt dizzy, and buckled while shooting a scene. After seeking medical attention, she was back to work.

A little more than two weeks after Jolie was reported to have collapsed, I was able to hang out with three relatively high-level crew members for an extended period and quiz them about Jolie. Each of them had nothing but praise for her. One of them called her "very professional." A second crew member told me she "likes to get it done." I asked them if she was nice. "I wouldn't call her nice," one told me. "But she's not high maintenance." I asked whether it was true that she had collapsed on set. Only one of them was present at the time. "I wouldn't call it a collapse," he said. "There was an episode."

Photos had begun to emerge from the set weeks earlier showing Jolie looking unnaturally skinny. It was reported that she had been following a diet called "liquid detox" that was leaving her too weak to function. "She's way too thin, even by Angie's standards, and that's really skinny to begin with," the *Sun Times* quoted a source as saying—someone who was on the set when Jolie fainted. The next day, a Sony representative denied that there had been a collapse.

I received a tip from somebody I used to work with on films who claimed that the real reason behind Jolie's sudden weight loss was that she was taking "meth." Crystal meth is the drug of choice for Hollywood actors who want to lose weight rapidly. A self-professed "drug dealer to the stars" in Hollywood once put it in context: "You know all these actresses and singers who look like skeletons? It's meth. That's the secret. It kills your appetite for days at a time and lets you lose twenty pounds fast. You always read in the tabloids about how this actress or that one is anorexic because they look so skinny; the real truth is that they are on crystal meth. The funny thing is that the publicists encourage the anorexia rumors because it's not as damaging as the true story."

Was it possible that Jolie, who had once famously claimed to have done "every drug imaginable," had resorted to meth as a weight-loss shortcut? It seems like a dangerous thing for a former addict to do, and Jolie has stated that her drug days are long behind her.

* * * *

Brad Pitt's drug use is mild when compared to Jolie's, but it is not inconsequential. According to a well-known Hollywood journalist, "[Pitt and Jennifer Aniston] spent much of their married life stoned But where as he was chilled out, she could get pretty paranoid. Having said that, she was probably right to be paranoid bearing in mind what happened on the set of *Mr. & Mrs. Smith*."

Canadian entertainment journalist Christopher Heard, who has interviewed Pitt at least six times, reports that the subject of pot often comes up. "The last time I was with him to interview him in Beverly Hills he was a real pot head," Heard said. "In between every question about acting or his movie, he would ask me questions about the liberal pot laws in Canada and if we were actually going to decriminalize marijuana here. I thought he was just goofing around, but even after the interview ended, he asked me to keep him updated on how the pot laws were reforming here. He asked if Canada was going to become like Amsterdam. He seemed completely obsessed with pot."

* * * *

Given both Pitt's and Jolie's history with relationships, it's only natural to probe whether they've ever cheated on each other since their magical fairytale began. There was already some indication that Jolie may not have been entirely committed to monogamy since she took up with Pitt. Four years ago, after Jolie had already been with Brad Pitt for almost a year, her former lover, Jenny Shimizu—the woman whom Jolie said she would have married if she hadn't married Jonny Lee Miller—gave an interview to the *Sun* claiming that she and Jolie had never ended their relationship.

"She's always had lovers that she relies on," Shimizu told the newspaper. "If she can ring you and you can meet up, then she can take care of her sexual needs. Whenever she calls me up, I visit her. It's not always the case that we always have sex. Sometimes we go to her property in Cambodia and explore the jungle. It's definitely more of a deeper friendship. She's the person I'll always care about and always help and always be there for."

Jolie had in fact built an elaborate complex in the middle of the Cambodian jungle several years before, having promised at the time of Maddox's adoption that he would be brought up in both the United States and Cambodia. She has been known to escape there without Pitt, and it is the perfect getaway to escape the prying lenses of paparazzi. However, when Shimizu—who is currently a judge on the successful TV show *Make Me a Supermodel*—was asked by a reporter in 2009 whether she and Jolie were still involved, she responded, "No. This comes up every three years or so. Saying we're in Cambodia having an affair sells magazines."

The most persistent story that crops up time and again involves Pitt and a beautiful Sudanese model, Amma, whom Pitt met at a benefit for Darfur at the 2007 Cannes Film Festival. He was seen with her on at least one other occasion. Jolie has been alleged to accuse Pitt of cheating on her on more than one occasion, which is one of the reported sources of tension between the two.

If Pitt has cheated, it is certainly not with his ex, contrary to what the gossip sheets would like the world to think. A story has surfaced repeatedly in the tabloids that has Pitt secretly meeting up with Aniston, if only "to talk." I painstakingly traced each of these reports, including one that I initially fell for, which had the two meeting at a hotel during the 2008 Toronto Film Festival. I can say with a fair degree of certainty that Brad Pitt and Jennifer Aniston have not been together in any capacity since the first week of January 2005. However, I have confirmed that Aniston is still friendly with Pitt's parents, her former in-laws, and speaks to them regularly.

By most accounts, Aniston is still bitter about her breakup with Pitt and especially Jolie's subsequent comments about the start of her relationship with Pitt, which Aniston described as "uncool" to *Vogue* magazine in December 2008. Jolie had told a reporter that during the filming of *Mr. & Mrs. Smith*, she realized she "couldn't wait to get to work." In the same interview, Aniston said that she was still "in touch" with Pitt, setting off much speculation in the tabloid press. But there is no proof of this whatsoever.

Jolie-haters were encouraged by a report in April 2009 that the former head of Jolie's security detail, Mickey Brett, was planning to write an explosive tell-all book about his tenure working for Pitt and Jolie. Brett, who first started working for Jolie while she was still with Billy Bob Thornton, was allegedly fired by Pitt in 2008 for getting too rough with photographers and others who got too close to his clients. In April, Brett began shopping around a proposal for a book detailing his seven years working for Jolie, to be ghostwritten by British author Robin McGibbon. Among the sensational revelations reportedly promised in the proposal, Brett claims that he "walked in on Angelina being intimate with Brad in her trailer," three weeks into the filming of *Mr. & Mrs. Smith*.

He also reportedly claimed that Jolie cheated on Pitt several times during their relationship, including an affair with a famous female pop star. "Mickey set up at least twenty secret meetings for Angie with this woman at hotels when Brad was working," the proposal claimed.

The couple's attorney, Martin Singer, immediately moved to discredit Brett and claimed that he was an unreliable source and was bound by a confidentiality agreement. Singer also claimed that the stories in the proposal had been embellished by the ghostwriter, Robin McGibbon. But McGibbon insisted that he wrote down the stories exactly as Brett told them. A month later, facing threats of a lawsuit if he proceeded with the tell-all, Brett backed down and claimed that he had never considered writing a book.

* * * *

A woman who worked with Pitt while he was filming *Troy*, and who is in touch with other present-day employees who have witnessed some of what has gone on, offered to fill me in on the current status of Pitt and Jolie's relationship. "Well, first off, their relationship is not a fake," she begins:

> They were definitely in love but that's where it gets tricky. If you want to know if they're still together, the answer depends on when you ask the question. I've heard that they've broken up so many times it would make your head spin. No, really, like Linda Blair in *The Exorcist*, that's how often it's happened.
>
> Apparently it's always him that ends up moving out, after some big fight over who knows what. There are apparently screaming matches, usually with her doing the screaming. Nobody really witnesses that part of it; they just see him leaving in a huff. But then he ends up coming back again, and nobody knows what happened to bring him back. Partly I think he really does love her. Partly he considers them a family, and he loves that element of it. He's supposed to be a great dad with those kids. And partly there's the whole Brangelina thing.
>
> He's really committed to their work; it's like they're superheroes fighting evil together and saving the world. I'm not sure if he can give that up so easily. If you knew Brad, he's very earnest—no bullshit for him. But then again, I don't know how he can handle her crazy temper. I've never met her, and I've never seen them spend any time together; maybe I'd get a better sense if I could.

A woman who worked on the set of *Mr. & Mrs. Smith* when it was filming in Los Angeles recalled how they were on-set. "They were really into each other," the employee said, though she says she only heard rumors that they were having an affair at the time. She herself didn't witness anything physical between them. She says she knew somebody on the set who claimed to have seen them together. What she did see, however, makes her wonder how they've lasted so long. "She's very erratic," she told me in an interview. "Everybody who's seen her knows what I mean. She's not unpleasant. Just erratic."

An example of her volatility was related to me by a limousine driver. "I used to drive them both all the time," he replied. "I've driven everybody." He described the couple as "good kids" who were usually quite friendly. In the beginning of their public relationship, he recalled, they were very affectionate. Twice he said he saw them "going at it in the back seat." But in 2007, he saw what he described as a "U-turn" in their relationship when they got into an argument in the back of the car. "I was more worried about his safety than hers," the driver said. "She really flew off the handle, threatening him and lashing out at him. I'm not sure what it was all about, but after that I can't imagine how anyone would want to be with her every day, no matter how sexy she is. She has a temper like a cobra."

Other reports from people who have worked near the couple is that their relationship was shaky up until January 2007, when Jolie's mother, Marcheline Betrand, succumbed to ovarian cancer in Los Angeles after a long battle with the illness. "Angelina was absolutely devastated by her mother's death," said a crew member who had worked with her on the set of *Wanted* in the summer of 2007, a few months after Bertrand died. "I heard she sometimes burst into tears without any explanation while she was in the middle of a scene. She'd then explain that she couldn't stop thinking about her mom. Brad would fly in with the kids, and that would cheer her up. He was very attentive, and I think it really helped her mood."

In the months after Bertrand's death, media reports suddenly appeared with regularity claiming that her last wish was to have her daughter marry Pitt. No source was ever cited. "If you follow Jolie's familiar pattern, it means she was angling to be Mrs. Pitt and she may have even convinced Brad that this was her mother's deathbed request. I'm doubtful," says an L.A.-based journalist who covers the industry. "I met Marcheline three times, and I doubt if she cared one way or another about whether they made it official. I think Jon Voight is more old-fashioned than she was. If he does marry her, though, she won't be after his money, and they won't need a pre-nup. She's getting to be almost as rich as he is. Not quite, though; he had a head start. But she's no pauper."

Publicly, Pitt has always been coy about the prospect of marrying Jolie. At one point he said he would "consider" tying the knot with her when everybody else could legally marry, referring to the legalization of same-sex marriage in the United States.

* * * *

It's September 2009, and I'm drinking coffee at the Hollywood Farmer's Market with an experienced Jolie-Pitt watcher, who works for an industry publication and has covered the couple for almost three years. Like almost everybody in the entertainment media that I meet, she tells me that she can never keep all the rumors straight about the two of them. But she informs me she can already see the "signs." Then she makes a prediction.

"They'll be split within eighteen months, probably sooner," she assures me. "And here's how it's going to play out. They're going to split amicably, work out some kind of arrangement with the kids, and everything will be very civilized. Then you're going to see unidentified friends leak stories about how Angelina couldn't put up with Brad's partying and his drinking and his pot smoking. She's worried about the kids, and she's afraid it's not the right environment for them. Maybe he'll even take part of the blame and go along with that. You're already seeing him work his love of the herb into the occasional interview. For example, he recently claimed smoking pot was turning him into a 'doughnut.' Nothing that makes him out to be too much of a jerk, just enough to explain how the golden relationship slowly fizzled. That's exactly how it's going to happen. If they're still together in eighteen months, I'll buy you dinner at Morton's."

Still, given what I have learned about the nature of Pitt and Jolie while following the couple and their activities, I'm not sure I would venture a prediction with the same confidence as my journalist friend. On paper, all the signs point to exactly the scenario she laid out for me. But both players have a considerable investment in keeping the Brangelina brand alive, maybe more than either of them is willing to risk. It's possible that each of them might even feel they would be hurting their causes by breaking up the dynamic duo of social justice.

And yet, watching what they have become, I can't help but feel like I'm watching a fairy tale in reverse. It wouldn't surprise me in the least if the two have broken up by Christmas, 2010. Meanwhile, the world will continue to follow the couple with voyeuristic fascination, and the public will be kept in the dark about the real state of their relationship through a combination of misdirection and careful image management.

CONCLUSION

So who is "Brangelina"? It's not enough to say "Brad Pitt and Angelina Jolie." Not any more. While it may have begun as a cute phrase concocted by the tabloids to describe Hollywood's latest hot couple, Brangelina has moved beyond that. Despite the careful nurturing by sophisticated professionals to craft a flawless, fairytale image for an adoring public, there is yet something more behind the hype. Brangelina is not just a veneer, a shell composed of little but Hollywood superlatives. Brangelina actually has substance, thanks to its two component individuals.

The world fell hard for Pitt and Jolie when the couple went public more than four years ago. We can ask ourselves: Are these two really the ultra-glamorous superheroes of social justice that the world has come to admire and envy? Is Jolie really a supermother who can make three movies a year, travel around the globe saving the planet, and still change diapers while helping her kids with their homework? Are Jolie and Pitt really soul mates who have left behind their personal demons and found perfect fulfillment through their philanthropy and their children?

Maybe not. But all that means is that the two individuals who make up this couple are human.

Brad Pitt, the wholesome Midwesterner who charmed Hollywood— and quite a few of its women—is, by all accounts, a very nice guy. Easy to get along with. Likes his pals, dotes on his children. Drinks beer, and smokes a little pot, too, like plenty of average guys. No extreme vices. He left Jennifer Aniston for Jolie in a flight of passion, but, who knows, maybe if Aniston had gotten pregnant, he would have stayed and started a family with her.

Angelina Jolie is a more complicated person, to be sure. Intense, passionate, and very sexual, her life at times looks like an experiment in serial risk-taking. But she appears to have risen above her flamboyant and often troubled past and created stability for herself.

Both are acclaimed actors. Pitt has won a Golden Globe for best actor and has received two Academy Award nominations. Jolie has won an Oscar and three Golden Globe awards and has been nominated for two Emmys, two more Golden Globes, and another Oscar.

And both are humanitarians. Since 2001, Jolie's work for refugees has been unceasing, and she continues this work as a UN Goodwill Ambassador. She was an invited speaker at the World Economic Forum in Davos, Switzerland, and travels constantly around the world in support of the causes she believes in. Pitt has worked for AIDS prevention, has acted on behalf of the victims of Hurricane Katrina, and founded Not On Our Watch, an organization that combats genocide.

So Brangelina means something more than a pair of megastar lovebirds. It means a hard-working pair who have done extremely well in their admittedly glamorous, yet often fickle profession. It also means a couple that gives back to the world, a couple who uses their wealth and influence to do good, a lot of good.

And yes, they have used the smoke and mirrors of the Hollywood dream-making machine to their advantage: to distract public scrutiny from embarrassing situations, to promote pet causes, to convey the impression of a stable family life, in short to convince the public that everything in their lives is in balance, that they have succeeded in having and doing it all. But this is Hollywood. A public image that is anything less than perfection is failure to the myth-making machine.

But can Brangelina endure? Perhaps the better question is, can Angelina keep up the pace she has set for herself? Pitt seems to take things in stride, but Jolie seems driven, not just to achieve, but to convince the world that she can be everything to everyone: companion to her mate, mother both to her own and to her adopted children, advocate for the refugees she sees across the globe. Mother, star, activist . . . saint?

Jolie has always liked living on the edge. She reveled in knives when she was young, and that is almost a metaphor for her life. Knives cut; they make you bleed. This may make you feel more alive, but, as she found out, cutting too deep risks your life. Whether it was knives or sex or drugs, each consumed her until she had to pay a big price, coming all too close to self-destruction.

Jolie saved herself at a critical time by channelling her addictive impulses into other consuming drives. She now has three great passions: her films, her causes, and her children. And, despite her claims to the contrary, she shows no sign of giving any one of them up to concentrate on the others. She wants it all. But an addiction to work, to doing good, is still an addiction. At the moment, she seems to have mastered her impulses, but for how long?

Her own sharp edge is now fraying. She is "erratic." She has "episodes." Pitt is there, and has remained true. But how much can he take if she starts to fall apart? In many ways it would be a great shame if they broke up, not just for them personally or for the family they have created, but for the very public that so seeks their flaws. It would be a shame because Brangelina serves as an ideal for individual achievement and social commitment. It is a glittering standard for us all, even if a lot of it has been deliberately tailored for public consumption.

But looking at Brangelina now, the clock seems to be ticking louder. How long before there is another "episode," one from which Jolie doesn't recover fast, or at all? If she starts to self-destruct again, what and who will be affected? Will Pitt leave? Who will take on her causes? Who will take care of the kids?

But most of all, who will take care of Angelina?